Sympathetic Realism
in Nineteenth-Century
British Fiction

Sympathetic Realism in Nineteenth-Century British Fiction

RAE GREINER

The Johns Hopkins University Press

Baltimore

© 2012 The Johns Hopkins University Press
All rights reserved. Published 2012
Printed in the United States of America on acid-free paper
2 4 6 8 9 7 5 3 1

The Johns Hopkins University Press
2715 North Charles Street
Baltimore, Maryland 21218-4363
www.press.jhu.edu

Library of Congress Cataloging-in-Publication Data

Greiner, Rae.
Sympathetic realism in nineteenth-century British fiction / Rae Greiner.
p.   cm.
Includes bibliographical references and index.
ISBN 978-1-4214-0653-4 (hdbk. : alk. paper) — ISBN 978-1-4214-0745-6
(electronic) — ISBN 1-4214-0653-5 (hdbk. : alk. paper) —
ISBN 1-4214-0745-0 (electronic)
1. English fiction—19th century—History and criticism. 2. Realism in
literature. 3. Sympathy in literature. 4. Narration (Rhetoric)—History—
19th century. 5. Fiction—Technique. I. Title.
PR868.R4G74 2012
823'.80912—dc23   2012006337

A catalog record for this book is available from the British Library.

Special discounts are available for bulk purchases of this book.
For more information, please contact Special Sales at 410-516-6936 or
specialsales@press.jhu.edu.

The Johns Hopkins University Press uses environmentally friendly
book materials, including recycled text paper that is composed of at least
30 percent post-consumer waste, whenever possible.

Contents

Acknowledgments

My greatest debt is to Ian Duncan and Kent Puckett, my closest collaborators and mentors at the University of California, Berkeley, where I wrote the first drafts of this manuscript. This book is for them.

But a good deal of thanks is due to many others. For their inspiration and tireless support during my time in graduate school, I want to recognize Michael Mascuch, Kevis Goodman, Charles Altieri, Richard Halpern, Catherine Gallagher, Sharon Marcus, Kamilla Elliot, Kaja Silverman, and James Turner. In the Berkeley English Department, Mary Melinn and Lee Parsons made life run more smoothly on many occasions. Adrienne Williams-Boyarin, Leslie Walton-Monstavicius, Vlasta Vranjes, Connie You, Ryan McDermott, Padma Rangarajan, and Talissa Ford, I owe so much to your big brains and giant hearts.

At Indiana University, I have had the tremendous good fortune of finding many smart, tireless readers and interlocutors. Ivan Kreilkamp and Andrew H. Miller, especially, have read too many pages, and had too many conversations, to count. To Mary Favret, Patricia Ingham, Nick Williams, Jonathan Elmer, Lara Kriegel, Susan Gubar, Penelope Anderson, Judith Brown, Denise Cruz, Joss Marsh, Shannon Gayk, Jennifer Fleissner, Henry Glassie, Mary Gray, Catherine Guthrie, Scott Herring, Alyce Miller, Pravina Shukla, Shane Vogel, Ed Comentale, Jesse Molesworth, Christoph Irmscher, Richard Nash, Joshua Kates, Tarez Graban, and Alex Doty, your friendship and intelligence enrich my life and writing. Additional thanks are due to the English Department staff, the Nineteenth-Century Research Forum, the *Victorian Studies* staff, and my graduate and undergraduate students. The Poynter Center and the Institute for Advanced Study, joint sponsors of Indiana University's Empathy Workshop, provided valuable funding for this project.

Gracious interlocutors outside Indiana University include Jan Fergus, Monique Morgan, Rebecca Stern, Carolyn Williams, Rachel Ablow, Helen Hauser, David Kurnick, Jonathan Farina, Erika Wright, Alice Villaseñor, Adela Pinch,

Daniel Hack, Lucy Hartley, John Plotz, Nicholas Dames, and the members of the Dickens Project, especially John Jordan. I am deeply grateful to the Dickens Universe for many things, but most of all for the (weird, thrilling) intellectual environment it fosters. I thank the participants in the University of Michigan's Nineteenth-Century Forum for their invitation to share my work-in-progress and for their valuable feedback on it.

Earlier versions of parts of some chapters have been published as follows: from chapters 1 and 2, "The Art of Knowing Your Own Nothingness," *ELH* 77.4 (2010): 893–914, used with permission from the journal editor; from chapter 4, "Sympathy Time: Adam Smith, George Eliot, and the Realist Novel," *Narrative* 17.3 (2009): 291–311, used with permission from the Ohio State University Press; and from chapter 1 and the coda, "Thinking of Me Thinking of You: Sympathy v. Empathy in the Realist Novel," *Victorian Studies* 53.3 (2011): 417–26, used with permission from Indiana University Press.

It has been a tremendous pleasure working with the Johns Hopkins University Press, whose professionalism and efficiency were truly remarkable. I am grateful for the efforts of Matt McAdam, my editor, along with Juliana McCarthy, Glenn Perkins, Karen Wilmes, and the anonymous reader whose astute commentary improved the manuscript.

To my families, given and chosen: Peggy Greiner, Robert and Judy Greiner, all the Lutzes and Greiners, James and Kathleen Szymanski, as well as the BAPS, the COTAS, B-E (Meredith Fenton and Cara Dellaquila), the 5JANETS, and my SF crew, I love you all. Finally, without Zakary Szymanski's affection and patience this book would be much what it is now, but I would not. Therein a world of difference lies. Thank you.

Sympathetic Realism
in Nineteenth-Century
British Fiction

Thinking of Me Thinking of You

Sympathetic Realism

This book began in an effort to prove that one could write about sympathy in nineteenth-century fiction without writing about emotion. Emotions, I decided at the outset, are pesky and unruly creatures, hard to describe and still harder to define; it might be better just to avoid them. I had what I considered good reasons for doing so. For starters, the more I read and thought about sympathy, the more I came to recognize the significance of a well-known but often obscured fact, that sympathy and emotion are not the same.[1] Emotions can of course emerge from sympathy, but sympathy itself is something else, a form of thinking geared toward others, including the other that is myself as others see me. Thinking of me thinking of you, thinking of you thinking of me—in these formulations, sympathy emerged as a cognitive exercise with strong affinities to intentionality and will. Frequently said to *be* a feeling—a "higher emotion," "a kind of tenderheartedness linked to, but distinct from love"—sympathy came to look instead like an imaginative undertaking in which feeling played no absolutely necessary part (Lanzoni 273, 266). Moreover, I saw that this type of sympathetic imagining follows from aesthetic principles. Sympathy is formal. Its formal properties could thus be analyzed irrespective of whatever emotions were (or were not) produced or shared. On the basis of these findings, sympathy began to seem an especially valuable conceptual tool for understanding the nineteenth-century realist novels that were my principal object of study. Jane Austen, Charles Dickens, George Eliot: these were among those authors eager to render sympathy in art. But they were also, as I saw it, suspicious of the notion that knowing or feeling what others feel inspires ethical behavior in us.

The book I wrote still holds that "thinking of me thinking of you," and vice versa, is what sympathy is all about. But severing thinking from feeling turned out to be trickier than I had imagined, particularly when I began looking into what contemporary philosophers and literary critics had to say on the subject. In the past twenty years or so, studies of emotion have proliferated, including Antonio Damasio's *The Feeling of What Happens: Body and Emotion in the Making of Consciousness* (1999), Eve Kosofsky Sedgwick's *Touching Feeling: Affect, Pedagogy, Performativity* (2002), Rei Terada's *Feeling in Theory: Emotion after the "Death of the Subject"* (2004), Charles Altieri's *The Particulars of Rapture: An Aesthetics of the Affects* (2004), and Martha Nussbaum's *Upheavals of Thought: The Intelligence of Emotions* (2003), to name only a fraction of the works I found perspicuous. In none of these is the role of cognition a minor issue. The scholarly field known as "the philosophy of emotion," as Robert C. Solomon writes, is "by one measure quite recent," emotion having been dismissed by philosophers around the time of the Second World War as "mere subjectivity" at best, at worst "nothing but physiology plus dumb sensation" (3). Such views, if they are still tenable, are no longer typical, with the result that there are now many smart, complicated theories of the affects to which one might turn in the effort to distinguish, say, (bodily) feeling from (cognitive) emotion, or primitive (animal) emotions from advanced (human) thought—or theories to inform you of the many reasons why such distinctions inevitably fall apart.

Dating to the Stoics, the belief that emotions entail judgment has received much recent scrutiny by cognitivists and others for whom it is no longer possible to deny emotions to animals and infants on the basis that emotions require language, because implying propositional content: that emotions, in other words, involve evaluative assessments of existing states of affairs. As Nussbaum suggests, not all cognitive appraisals need involve self-consciousness; to understand emotions as providing "acknowledgments of our goals and their status" is to affirm their general usefulness for basic cognitive skills like "intending an object and marking it as salient" (135, 129). My argument emphasizes the intentional and evaluative aspects of sympathy but makes no attempt to answer some of the most urgent questions inspiring Nussbaum and others: how feelings and emotions differ, how emotions can involve unthinking and cognitive elements at once, whether animals emote or empathize and, if they do, if that ability can be biochemically explained (in them and in us).[2] It does, however, respond to claims that the linguistic properties of emotion take a specific, novelistic shape. According to Nussbaum, emotions have "a complicated cognitive structure that is in part narrative in form, involving a story of our relation to cherished objects that extends over time" (2). Emotions work like stories do. Embedded in "narrative history," they make sense in relation to what might happen and to what came before (236). Moreover, emotions elicited by art, responsive *to* representations, are no less authentic than those inspired by experienced events. The cognitive content of an emotion felt in relation to fictional characters can be the same as that felt in life. In judging that a specific fictional representation is "held to life . . . by threads of plausibility," one deems it true or possible in a general way for living people in the world and reacts accordingly (245). These ideas suggest why it is important to isolate certain properties of narrative (especially where realist "plausibility" is concerned) and consider their relation to the emotions and conceptions they represent or elicit. But Nussbaum's nuanced account of how emotion and judgment intertwine highlights the difficulty of telling them apart. The present study attempts at times to pry apart thinking and feeling so we might better appreciate sympathy's cognitive demands, and tease out parallel sympathetic and narrative effects taking place even when no feeling is present. But it also records the failure of forcing that separation. Arguing that sympathy without feeling is entirely possible, this book also testifies to the difficulty in pinpointing where feelings and thoughts begin and end.

The argument for the intelligence of emotions would not have surprised Adam Smith, nor would the history Nussbaum tells of emotions viewed as "unthinking energies that simply push [people] around" and subsequent attempts to confirm or revise that belief (24). Smith famously advocated emotional self-control, conceiving sympathy as a means not only of sharing others' feeling but also of restricting that feeling's access. He held that quality in common with the Victorians, for whom understanding what and how much to feel and developing protocols for emotional maintenance were as important as they were for the quasi-Stoical Smith. The subject of several issues of the British philosophical journal *Mind,* first published in 1876, the value of emotion and emotional sharing was a disputed topic at the end of the nineteenth century and had long been a concern for moral philosophy, especially during the Scottish Enlightenment. By 1882 Leslie Stephen may have considered sympathy "the condition for the possibility of thinking about others in any fashion at all," but in 1759 Smith had made a related claim in *The Theory of Moral Sentiments* (*TMS*): that sympathy is a way of thinking about others, not an embodiment of their emotions, and not reserved for sorrow.[3] "In every passion of which the mind of man is susceptible, the emotions of the by-stander always correspond to what, by bringing the case home to himself, he imagines should be the sentiments of the sufferer," Smith writes; neither "is it those circumstances only, which create pain or sorrow, that call forth our fellow-feeling. Whatever is the passion which arises from any object in the person principally concerned, an analogous emotion springs up, at the thought of his situation, in the breast of every attentive spectator."[4] The conditions of sympathy are overwhelmingly imaginative: one "bring[s] the case home" by imagining the other's feelings, reconstructed in "the thought of his situation." And though Smith refers to a "sufferer," sympathy pertains to the full range of human sentiments, experienced in "analogous" ways (10). Predating Stephen's theory of sympathy by some 120 years, Smith's theory is in some ways consistent with it, but Smith also emphasizes the reverse formulation: thinking is the condition for the possibility of sympathizing with others. Only when certain mental activities take place can sympathy flower and thus "be made use of to denote our fellow-feeling with any passion whatever" (10).

As these comments suggest, I believe there is a long and underappreciated history of connection between Smith's cognitive model and sympathy's nineteenth-century literary incarnations. These writings form a tradition that portrays sympathy as a mental action involving the creation and exchange of imagined feeling, a way of sharing attitudes and modes of thought independent of the need to verify another's feeling and resistant to a conception of feeling as "ineluctable animal force" (Nussbaum 370). Recalling those features unique to Smith's account allows us better insight into how sympathy operates in the realist novels published in the wake of his influential theory and the critiques arising in response to it. This book aims to show that, insofar as sympathetic processes of thought were central to the narrative forms they crafted, the realists shared certain affinities with the skeptical Smith. They were, for instance, far from convinced that we sympathize best with those whose feelings we share absolutely, or even with those we most intimately know. Against the standard claim that knowing more and seeing further into the hidden hearts and minds of characters heightens our sympathy with them, novels of the period are dubious of the tie that binds sympathy to knowledge. What's more, sympathy resists identification.[5] Time and again, characters inhabiting the fiction find the mirror a pathological emblem of the need to see oneself in others; the identity of emotions is presented as a threat to, not an achievement of, sympathetic connection. In those moments when sympathy succeeds in inspiring us to feel with others, it does so because we have undertaken the difficult task of thinking in particular ways about them first. In this way, sympathetic thinking leads to fellow-feeling, an affective, social mode of understanding central to reality as the nineteenth-century novelists sought to depict it. They fashioned realism to equip the mind to comprehend a reality that was itself sympathetic, a reality whose realism found sanction in the imaginative fellowship we have with others. To cultivate that shared mentality was to insist that the world is produced by sympathetic mental practices, by what the late-Victorian philosopher James Sully called "the reciprocal action of many minds."[6]

Critics such as James Chandler and Ian Duncan have shown that, in the early years of the nineteenth century, Scottish philosophy and literature found an international reading public strongly influenced by Smith and his contemporaries (Duncan, introduction xiii). Yet while Duncan calls *TMS* "the most famous of the Scottish Enlightenment treatises on socialization" (xxxii), and Chandler considers it "the most energetic and influential account of imaginative sympathy," David Hume's influence dominates in the criticism of the English realist novel ("Languages" 26). The critics' key distinction between Smith and Hume—that Smith's sympathizer abstracts feeling, routing it through cognition, while Hume allows for sensation to be transmitted both directly and unconsciously from one person to the next—has elicited a kind of continental drift in a criticism understandably enamored with Humean tropes of vibration, contagion, and "force" (Hume, *Treatise* 1.1.6:16). For Chandler, the long history of "materialist affectivity" that culminates in the mid-eighteenth-century coinage of the term "sentimental" engages with a central problem: how to account for the role of the affections at a time when "the vital principle of human beings begins to be explained in terms of matter and motion," terms that more strongly suggest sympathetic emotional travel than (private) emotion alone ("Languages" 22). Following from David Hartley's associationism through to Charles Darwin's vibratory body—pervaded, in *The Expression of the Emotions in Man and Animals* (1872), by an "involuntary transmission of nerve-force" that "may or may not be accompanied by consciousness"—literary critics today often favor theories privileging unthinking embodiment: at the beginning of the century, those emphasizing the physiological responses (tears, horror) associated with sentimental and Gothic fiction; and at the end, those emerging from scientific discourses concerned with instincts and drives.[7] More recently, cognitive approaches to the novel, borrowing from neuroscience, stress the biological components of emotions and the chemical brain activities to which they can be traced, while some theories exploring "the feeling of reading" wed physiology and biochemistry to the development of ethical and aesthetic values.[8]

Darwin mentioned Smith directly in *The Descent of Man* (1871), comparing *TMS* (especially "the first and striking chapter") to *Mental and Moral Science,* an 1868 book by another Scot, the journal *Mind* founder Alexander Bain, whose pioneering work in empiricist psychology did much to renew scholarly interest in Hume (78 n.17). Nevertheless, as Thomas Dixon notes, although "the Darwinian account of morality had a distinct pedigree from other influential scientific approaches to ethics" by virtue of its bearing "the indelible stamp of its eighteenth-century British [moral philosophical] origins"—including the ideas of Hume and Smith—"Das Adam Smith Problem" continues to be a critical impediment, despite attempts in Darwin's own time to put the by then decades-old issue to rest (133). In 1897, the German economist August Oncken tried to explain once and for all how to accommodate the capitalist of *Wealth of Nations* to the altruist of *TMS*.[9] According to Keith Tribe, however, the 1850s–1890s saw among Germans a revival of interest in Smith's economic and social theories that failed to carry over into Britain until years later.[10] A century earlier, initial sales of *TMS* "were brisk" when the book was first published in London in April 1759, with a print run of 1,000 copies; the sixth edition (1790), expanded to two volumes and the last to appear during Smith's lifetime, had the same print run, indicating that "the publishers sensed a renewal of interest in the book" (Sher 1, 17). "A steady seller from the outset," *TMS* was, by the time of Smith's death, "a more imposing book and a more popular one as well" (Sher 19). Though it remained in print throughout the nineteenth century, *TMS*'s popularity fluctuated, hitting a low point in the 1830s. More importantly, in Tribe's view, is that while English editions of *Wealth of Nations* were published almost annually from the 1860s onward, and *TMS* "at regular intervals (1861, 1871, 1880, 1887, and 1892)," these were books "bought, perhaps read through, but not studied" by scholars ("Das Adam Smith" 515). The one serious treatment of Smith's oeuvre, appearing in volume 2 of Henry Thomas Buckle's *History of Civilization in England* in 1861, seems to have had little impact on political economic thought, though Tribe adds that the book "did of course have a wider, and more general, reception."[11] By the late 1800s, convincing political economists of the viability of Smith's theory was an uphill battle. When the Edinburgh political economy professor Joseph Nicholson addressed the British Association for the Advancement of Science in 1894, he may have done so as "an orthodox follower" of Smith, but he spent much of his time dispelling the doctrines of a popular Smith detractor, one Karl Marx (Dixon 237).

Marx alone is not to blame for Smith's image problems, but it is fair to say that literary critics have not yet fully accounted for the wider and more general reception of Smith's writings by those who were not trained philosophers or professional economists. Tribe suggests that, "in the last third of the nineteenth century," *Wealth* was printed often and sold well because interest had shifted away from its "doctrinal principles" onto "its method," a shift that brought *TMS* "back into consideration" ("Adam Smith" 42). Yet literary evidence shows Smith's name, book titles, formulations, and chosen metaphors regularly alluded to

throughout the period. In Maria Edgeworth's *Belinda* (1801), *TMS* sits alongside La Bruyere and John Moore on a reading table, and *Wealth*—along with a
slew of invisible hands—is referenced openly in such texts as Harriet Martin-
eau's *Illustrations of Political Economy* (1832–34) and George Eliot's *Middlemarch*
(1871–72).[12] Such references were usually mixed, except where Smith's literari-
ness was concerned. In "Adam Smith as a Person," published in the *Fortnightly
Review* in July 1876, Walter Bagehot describes an "awkward Scotch professor,
apparently choked with books and absorbed in abstractions," who had once been
mistaken in an Edinburgh fishmarket for an idiot. Yet he praises *TMS* as the
"greatest" of Smith's books, calling Smith "a literary marvel."[13] Contemporary
Britons, Bagehot suggests, could not appreciate the immensity of Smith's intellectual accomplishments, for having been "bred upon" Smith's tenets, they were
more inclined to wonder "how any one could help seeing them" (25). This result
proved Smith's unparalleled effectiveness at cultivating the "borderland between
theory and practice" (26). Nevertheless, Bagehot concluded, Smithian theory had
run its course. Similarly, in 1892 the Oxford fellow L. L. Price declared, "To say
anything new on Adam Smith is not easy; but to say anything of importance or
profit, which has not been said before, is well-nigh impossible" (239). Still, Price
attests to Smith's "wide popularity" and the "air of unmistakable reality in his
writing," adding that Smith "always seems to be in touch with actual present fact"
(243–44).

Reviews like these were not uncommon. The same voices criticizing Smith's
unsystematic, overly abstract economic theory praised *Wealth* and, especially,
TMS as highly readable, enjoyable books displaying a descriptive knack and full
of "illustrations . . . at once abundant and apt" (Price 244). Clearly awed that
Smith appealed equally to the "plain practical man" and the trained economist,
Price concluded that "[f]ew, if any, writers on a subject, which has to deal with
the changing phenomena of human society, could stand so well the test of a hundred years of study and criticism, or, after the lapse of so long a time, appear so
fresh and apposite" (244). Even otherwise negative assessments of Smith's ideas
acknowledged what Bagehot called his "power of expressing and illustrating arguments in a way likely to influence [the] minds" of ordinary merchants and
scholars alike (26). Smith looked to many later Victorians like a powerful thinker
whose specific recommendations had grown outdated, not the dangerous conservative he can seem today. His skill at storytelling was to them undeniable.

Modern critics may thus be casting a blind eye to key aspects of his nineteenth-
century afterlife when asserting, to take one example, that Smith "put the radical
genie of sympathy back into the bottle out of which . . . Hume had released it."[14]

This characterization—with Hume on the side of "spontaneous and passionate subjective dispersal" and Smith as the humorless disciplinarian—is not new, and it is accurate, to a point (Lowe 9). Smith does tamp down Hume's wilder energies in favor of an "impartial spectator" who guides and limits our emotional display. It is through this figure that Smith stresses the importance of social environment to the sympathetic protocols he developed. Yet disciplinary oversight isn't the most pressing cause for Smith's restraint. As Duncan points out, Smith attenuates those elements of Humean sympathy that most threaten "identity theft" by turning them into so many figures of speech (*Shadow* 268). As Smith has it, we "enter *as it were* into" the body of the other, becoming "*in some measure* the same person as him" (*TMS* 9, emphasis added). Quite cheery in his riposte to Hume, Smith proposes a theory of emotional engagement in which the inability to spontaneously share others' feelings is a blessing, not reactionary paranoia and not a curse. After all, how close do we really want to get? Smith suggests that sympathetic identification can prove disastrous when one loses the capacity to distinguish self from other. What's more, forbidding direct emotional transfer could do more than protect against bodily invasion. For rather than enabling us to share *one* feeling, sympathy, in Smith's conception of it, is a highly creative process. Analogies and figures of speech, surplus affects, imagined communities of feeling—these are the fruits of a sympathy freed from the rather more brainless task of duplicating whatever single emotion already exists.

Furthermore, to claim for Humean sympathetic theory a radical intersubjectivity starkly contrastive to the spectatorial regime of Smith is to repeat the questionable practice of characterizing Smithian sympathy as a predominantly visual affair. The high level of abstraction enabling Smith to disarm the threat of Humean emotional contagion also underwrites a complexly intersubjective model of human understanding where, because seeing others does not guarantee our sympathy (and instead frequently prevents it), reflection becomes an indispensible activity in which potential sympathizers engage. The mere sight of violent feelings, happy or sad, is inimical to sympathy as Smith understands it; time and again, he calls on the abstracting powers of figuration to mitigate the deleterious effects brought on by strong visual and emotional display. Even impartial spectatorship, the most often pointed-to evidence in the argument for spectatorial sympathy, might be properly said to involve speculation rather than vision. Thinking, not simply seeing, enables the imagined exchange of places and circumstance facilitated by impartial spectatorship. This emphasis on imaginative reflection is central to understanding the attraction Smith's model may have held for the realist novelists. With a narrativizing impulse written into its core, Smithian sympathy describes a way of thinking and feeling with others who are, like fictional characters, nowhere in sight.

Among these and other reasons explored in this book for revisiting Smith's nineteenth-century afterlife, sympathy's role in producing a social understanding of reality proves to be the most impressive and profound. Michael McKeon has described the society Smithian sympathy imagines as a "virtual reality" transforming the "actual particularity" of others "into the concrete particularity of others-as-ourselves, who thereby become susceptible to collective generalization"; as a "virtual reality" that sympathy enables us to experience, society can be "achieved well or badly" depending on a given community's sympathetic powers (377). To a rich body of scholarship on moral philosophy, narrative theory, novel history, and theories of mind and emotion, this book adds an account of Smith's theory of sympathy in relation to the nineteenth-century realists, who produced what I call "sympathetic realism": a realism (in a variety of incarnations) for which virtual, Smithian forms of sympathy prove central to our understanding, and which are perceptible in some of realism's most familiar techniques. Free indirect discourse, realist metonymy and characterization, the representation of sentimentalized acts of casuistry—each is designed to cultivate in readers distinctly sympathetic modes of thought. In novels crafted with sympathetic purposes in mind, "fellow-feeling"—sympathy's hoped-for result—names a dynamic relation between readers and represented mental states. Describing the nineteenth-century novel, "particularly in its psychological-realist mode," as "a kind of machine for thinking about other people," Adela Pinch notes that a common way of explaining how this happens, through omniscient access to "transparent minds," obscures how hard novels actually work to portray the ordinary, often erroneous thinking we do of others whose minds remain (thankfully) opaque (*Thinking* 144). The ideal of the "total mind-read," Pinch points out, is regularly refuted in nineteenth-century novels, where thinking and knowing are frequently disaggregated, the former taking place, happily, without the latter (147). Pinch thus begins to disentangle some of the same knots as I do in the following pages. In her book and in this one, thinking about others is revealed to be, at least some of the time, "most social when it is least omniscient, and most wrong" (150).

Perhaps this book's most important claim is that sympathy produces realism; the protocols of sympathy are most fully realized there. Often thematized in the realist novel, sympathy is not merely a matter of content but a defining feature of novelistic form. This is, I would venture to say, something most students of the period know (at least intuitively) already. But we are far from having exhausted the subject. Thus, while feeling is a crucial aspect of sympathetic realism, "fellow-feeling" is the conceptual category that matters most. It is an attitude toward and a relation with others not tied to exact emotional reproduction or to any definitive emotional content. Fellow-feeling generates forms of intellectual and affective engagement without demanding that particular feelings become manifest, for it too is fictive, a social fantasy in which (as Smith put it) we "go along with" others in kind of contentless companionship (*TMS* 83). Long designated a genre littered with things and stuff that, simply by being there, produce a reality effect, the nineteenth-century realist novel differs most from novels of the previous century in granting to fellow-feeling—not objects—the task of maintaining reality. By depicting social reality as a product of fellow-feeling, the realist novel portrays the real as both fictive and sympathetic. Fellow-feeling, sympathy's most sustained and important fiction, underwrites reality, deciding what gains significance, and what does not. More so than "It"-narratives, which track the adventures of things, or even sentimental novels, in which elaborately staged emotional displays force readers to emote on the other's behalf, the realist novel lays claim to the imaginative social affectivity through which human communities generate the meanings they hold dear. In so doing, it depicts the sympathetic consciousness as the basis for reality itself.

This book engages with some recent and compelling claims made on behalf of nineteenth-century literary realism. Harry E. Shaw's treatment of realism's historicizing capacities provides the most extensively treated case in point. Like the historicism Shaw describes, sympathy works in a world of provisionality, in full awareness that we do not have access to transparent minds, and that even the imperfect approximations sympathy allows occur fitfully, often with strenuous imaginative labor. Historicism and sympathy go hand-in-hand in a realism that reflects the legacy of Enlightenment skepticism and the resultant moral urgency of making-do. Smithian sympathy is particularly well suited for comprehending the realists' historicizing purpose: the fallen temporality characterizing our uncertainty in encountering others, for instance, is recast as the temporal unfolding of events in historical time; confronting fictional characters is seen to resemble confrontations with the past, where both characters and the past revive in the sympathetic thought processes of attentive readers. In a variety of ways, the sympathetic fellow-feeling this book describes binds the reading of fiction to the task of endowing others, and the historical past, with virtual life. Moreover, though it may strike us now as decidedly novelistic, *TMS* was intended to describe how we experience mundane reality, the realist novel's definitive focus.

Whereas sympathetic connection with others in Smith occurs only after their feelings are abstracted into the domain of representation, the realists—with sympathetic purpose in mind—abstract feeling into narrative form in order to make ordinary life feel freshly vibrant and alive to us.

Unlike theories of the novel that align realist fiction with the rise of subjective individualism, and in marked contrast to approaches that claim to reveal the false promise of realist mimesis, this project emphasizes the sentimental and rhetorical dimensions of a social realism not content to mirror reality and all that is typically encountered in it.[15] The result is historical without being deterministic. Mine is not, with some exceptions, an argument for Smith's direct influence on the novelists. The approach I take rather resembles that adopted by Marshall Brown when he argued for Hegel's impact on the realists. By his own admission, Brown had a heavier burden of proof; Hegel's *Science of Logic* was a "seldom read masterpiece" with which "few realists and theorists of realism have been acquainted" (225). Barred from arguing for direct lines of influence, Brown instead makes a case for "mutual reflection" and "tacit knowing," a not fully conscious intuition or mediated comprehension that "prestructures" realist forms of practice (224). Smith's writings, unlike Hegel's *Science,* were widely available and known, yet one need not have owned or even read *TMS* to have been familiar with the ideas that book made famous; as we've seen, Bagehot thought Britons "bred upon" Smithian precepts (25). Given Smith's well-documented influence on novelists like Sir Walter Scott, whose popularity (with other novelists especially) lasted well into the nineteenth century, we can surmise that some of Smith's major insights percolated through to the later realists by way of fiction itself. Brown may be correct in stating that the meaning of realism "will be found in a system that was lost to the realists themselves," but I make a modified case for "prestructuring," arguing that writers Smith directly influenced, including Scott and James Hogg, recorded Smith's ideas in their fiction and that subsequent writers experimented with the full range of sympathetic protocols discoverable in the works of their literary forebears (224). Moreover, Smith provides a lens through which to examine the novels of the nineteenth-century realists irrespective of their attempts (conscious or otherwise) to enact Smithian sympathy in their novels' pages. Whether the novelists in question recognized Smith's sympathetic formulas in, say, Scott's *Waverley* (1814) or saw Hogg's *Confessions of a Justified Sinner* (1824) as staging a battle between the Humean and Smithian accounts, Smith's theory serves as a critical tool with which to examine the realist project and so better comprehend those methods for cultivating sympathy the novelists tried on, rejected, or embraced.[16]

Chapter 1 lays the conceptual groundwork for the chapters that follow by defining "sympathetic realism" and offering an account of its development. Starting with the premise that nineteenth-century realist fiction is devoted to representing the exertions of sympathetic labor so as to hone readers' sympathetic powers, this chapter details the most striking formal and conceptual affinities between Smithian sympathy and realist form and technique. Part 1 situates novel theories that characterize realism in terms of historically particular "states of mind" alongside Smith's rich description of sympathy as the ability to "go along with" the mentalities of others. This section underscores those narrative elements of Smith's theory that are later adapted to a realism that builds on and reinvents them for a number of different purposes, most pointedly a special brand of imaginative historicism. From Walter Scott to George Eliot, "sympathizing" and "historicizing" are related, co-implicating activities, involving similar imaginative efforts. Part 2 discusses a selection of representational techniques that reflect Smithian incentives. Realist metonymy, for instance, brings fellow-feeling to bear on the imaginative reconstruction of the historical past, while free indirect discourse weds the individual and the public mind so as to define subjectivity as one of narrative's most important sympathetic effects.

The ensuing chapters are organized around individual features of Smith's model, which I treat as conceptual starting points for the readings that follow. Chapter 2 begins by briefly charting the development of the case form, inherited from casuistry and "sentimentalized" by Smith. Building on work by James Chandler, this chapter demonstrates how Smith's "case," his chosen vehicle for the narratives sympathetic thinking creates, facilitates an increase in the value of fiction for a wide range of imaginative purposes—specifically, in Jeremy Bentham's theories of grammar and fiction and in Jane Austen's historicizing fiction, both developed concomitantly in the post-Waterloo years, and in the philosophical historicism of R. G. Collingwood in the twentieth century. The so-called enemy of fictions, Bentham produces a theory of language in which the sympathetic imagination is utterly central. His writings consistently rehearse the persuasive and affective qualities of word phrases in their expressive contexts and the social-sympathetic processes out of which linguistic meaning derives. In Austen's *Persuasion* (1818), sympathetic case-thinking becomes a way to reopen and rewrite the closed cases of the past. Anne Elliot's repeated efforts to revitalize her own case dovetail with Bentham's and Collingwood's efforts to describe the recomposition of the past, foreclosed possibilities, and other apparently dead forms of life.

Chapter 3 links several unique features of Dickensian form to the demand for sympathetic "harmony," achieved when emotional expressions are lowered or raised in accordance with what Smith calls "proper" (*not* perfect) "pitch" (*TMS* 39, 27). Pitch, another Smithian abstraction, functions as a measure of a listener's psychoacoustical perception, doing so in the service of formal compromise, making-do between tonal and emotional highs and lows. Similarly, Charles Dickens's version of "proper pitch" links sympathy to issues of representational and tonal balance, as well as to ethical modes of listening. Part 1 reads through several novels to show that Dickens's fascination with botched words and other forms of inarticulacy posits "sympathetic translation" as a major feature of his fiction. The frequency with which tongue-tied characters appear is matched only by their remarkable feats of communication, as when (in *Our Mutual Friend*) Eugene Wrayburn, pulverized into mute paralysis, marries his beloved through the help of a translator, Jenny Wren. Cracking words open, Dickens elicits sympathy's power to regenerate sentences—and people—violently damaged, lost, or broken apart. In part 2, *Little Dorrit*'s linguistic landscape breeds strange mnemonic formulas open to sympathetic resignification. Finding the proper pitch of expression becomes a way of sounding the difference between words that fail to transmit meaning and the emotional translations that can give them new voice.

What it might mean to disentangle sympathy from omniscience, identification, and knowledge is the main concern of the book's final chapter. The "impartial spectator" emerges as a figure for omniscient narration, and for the multiple refractions taking place in the social mirror, whose reflections Smith trusted to reveal us to ourselves. George Eliot is so central to accounts of nineteenth-century sympathy that no book on the subject is complete without her, but part 1 is devoted to those moments in her fiction when sympathy does not work. In *Impressions of Theophrastus Such* (1879), Eliot continues to dwell on problems explored in what is considered her most oddball (because least realist) novel, *The Lifted Veil* (1859), a book that levels a strong critique against the assumption that omniscience and sympathy go hand in hand. Latimer cannot give or receive sympathy because, an omniscient, he knows too much. Comparing Latimer's mental omnipotence with that of both Theophrastus and *Middlemarch*'s (1871–72) Rosamond Vincy, this chapter casts doubt on the persistent truism that we sympathize best with those whose minds most closely mirror our own. Part 2 focuses on two late-century novels in which omniscience, no longer isolated in sick individuals, enlists whole masses of people into nightmarish forms of groupthink. Joseph Conrad's *The Nigger of the 'Narcissus'* (1897) portrays consciousness as beset on all sides by the prying minds of others. Fellow-feeling takes a diabolical turn as the ship's crew, with a mutinous single-mindedness, heap moral responsibility onto one of their members, dehumanizing him in the process. In Henry James's *The Sacred Fount* (1901), a similarly conspiratorial desire leads to a crisis when the attempt to know other minds all but guarantees for the narrator that he cannot prevent others from stealing into his. He falls prey to a mental and emotional cannibalism that his fantasy of omniscience has unleashed.

The book's coda considers the modernist turn away from nineteenth-century realism toward the fusional and symbolic, and toward empathy. Newly coined at the turn of the century, "empathy"—with its poetic, metaphoric structure—contrasts sympathy's narrative, metonymic form. Rather than collapsing the terms together, the concluding pages sharpen their differences so as to better appreciate the distinctive features of both.

CHAPTER I

Going Along with Others

Adam Smith and the Realists

PART I. SMITH'S SYMPATHETIC PROTOCOLS

If [a man] would act so as that the impartial spectator may enter into the principles of his conduct, which is what of all things he has the greatest desire to
do, he must, upon this, as upon all other occasions, humble the arrogance of
his self-love, and bring it down to something which other men can go along
with.

—Adam Smith, *The Theory of Moral Sentiments*

Contrasting three approaches to literary realism—that of medieval typology, Ian
Watt's "formal realism," and the causal realism of novelists like George Eliot—
Marshall Brown concludes that realism is "an attribute, a quality, an impression
created by the novel."[1] Not "something 'in' the novel but the novel's impact on
readers," realism names a way of responding *to* literary texts: it designates "a
structure of consciousness" (233, 226). Harry E. Shaw makes a comparable claim
on behalf of nineteenth-century realism in particular. Charting patterns and relations, it cultivates a "habit"—or habits—"of mind."[2] Following this line of thinking, I argue that the realism of the nineteenth-century British novel—the "period
and genre that gave [realism] currency"—is best understood as a "sympathetic realism," not simply because these novels promote or are about sympathy (though
they often do, and are), but because they employ forms designed to enact sympathetic habits of mind in readers: structures of consciousness shaped according to
sympathetic protocols (Brown 224). And because his conception of sympathy is
instrumental for our understanding of the realism developed in this period, I fo-

cus on Adam Smith, about whose theory of sympathy I will be putting forth three main claims. First, Smith's 1759 *The Theory of Moral Sentiments* (*TMS*) offers not merely a sentimental moral theory, in which moral value derives in conjunction with human sentiments, but a social theory in which narrative plays a major role. Second, Smith's model of sympathy—a highly abstract operation for producing fellow-feeling—helps to clarify the sympathetic dimensions of some of the realists' signature formal and technical innovations. And, third, the most significant of these innovations, realist historicism, is best explained relative to sympathetic premises devised by Smith.

This argument hinges on the easily forgotten fact that sympathy and feeling are not the same. A mechanism by way of which we imagine and (sometimes) produce feelings, sympathy is an operation of mind, fundamentally a cognitive process. Sympathy usually results in feeling but is not equivalent to it. Understanding it in this way allows us to see that sympathy, like the realism Brown describes, designates a way for minds to conceive other people and situations and make judgments about their conditions. When sympathy works, people typically respond feelingly, to be sure, but not with any necessary feeling more precise than that which Smith calls the feeling of "going along with" others.[3] That last phrase will prove crucial. "Something which other men can go along with" signifies an attitude, a state of mind, common to both sympathy and realist verisimilitude in the historicist mode (*TMS* 83). In sympathetically "going along with" another, one shares with her an imagined mental companionship rather than a one-dimensional emotional identity. Nineteenth-century realism engenders and refines such states of mind, thus giving shape to a double impression: that these novels feel real is an effect of the imaginative experiences of mental sharing they generate, and of the fellow-feeling to which those experiences give rise.

And—a further step—it is in this complex rhetorical and imaginative process that the nineteenth-century realist novel makes it claims on history. For in responding to the situations in which others find themselves, in "going along with" their imagined states of mind, we enter into what Shaw describes as "a mode of grasping life in history," an appreciation of the narrative unfolding of historical events (131). Sympathy with others (including other selves) is at the very heart of the realist novel's historical enterprise. Building on Shaw's contention that nineteenth-century realist plots are "primarily involved in the mobilization of will," and that they are "in this sense 'rhetorical,' for they call upon the reader to respond," I show that the responses demanded by realism are often sympathetic, since sympathy alone guarantees the reader's fullest contact with realism's most sought-after cognitive and emotional effects.[4] Sympathetic realism mobilizes the imagination in encouraging readers to "go along with" the virtual perspectives of others situated in time and space. The historicizing impulse meets the sympathetic in nineteenth-century realism, which depends for both on the power to imagine what it's like to be somebody else, somewhere else entirely.

Feeling in the Abstract

> Sympathy . . . does not arise so much from the view of the passion, as from that of the situation which excites it. We sometimes feel for another, a passion of which he himself seems to be altogether incapable; because, when we put ourselves in his case, that passion arises in our breast from the imagination, though it does not in his from the reality.
>
> —Adam Smith, *The Theory of Moral Sentiments*

Adam Smith and his friend David Hume were members of the sentimental school. Both placed sympathy at the heart of the moral question and argued that human action is motivated by a multiplicity of causes, emotion first among them.[5] Engaging sympathetically with others meant formulating thoughts and judgments about their emotional behavior. But Smith felt that sympathy facilitated special modes of thinking about feeling even when feeling itself did not develop. Those who describe Humean sympathy as "contagious" do so to emphasize his belief that feeling can transfer directly from one person to another "so perfectly as to lose nothing of it in the transition."[6] By contrast, and as a corrective to Hume, Smith insists that such transfer is neither possible nor desirable; it is "the impressions of our own senses only, not those of [the other], which our imaginations copy" (*TMS* 9). No original feeling need even be present. When we "put ourselves in his case," we can conjure feelings "from the imagination" that do not derive from the sufferer's "reality" (12). The burden of proof falls away. I need not worry whether I feel what the other feels.

Such a sympathy is grounded in the pursuit of narrative effects rather than epistemological certainty. It rests entirely on our ability to reconstruct imaginatively another's "situation," to simulate his point of view—so thoroughly that we can sometimes find ourselves experiencing emotions he is "altogether incapable" of feeling (12). Smith presses on this point. Others needn't feel anything for us to sympathize with them. According to Smith, this is why we can sympathize with many kinds of people who cannot respond in kind, or feel anything at all: illiterates and children, idiots and madmen, or—in his most stunning example—the dead. As corpses are "no longer capable of feeling . . . any sentiment," whatever "imaginary" feelings we "in fancy . . . lend to the dead" are entirely of our own making (71).

Smith's most deliberate departure from Hume lies in this methodical abstraction of feeling. He consistently dematerializes those bodily sensations that in Hume had the power to invade another's skin, abstracting particular joys and pains away from their physical causes. Again and again, Smith insists that another's feeling must be imagined and reflected upon, but it need not be felt.[7] Sympathy begins *before* feeling, which must become fully ideational before would-be sympathizers can return any emotional response of their own. "All the passions which take their origin from the body," Smith maintains, "excite either no sympathy at all, or such a degree of it, as is altogether disproportioned to the violence of what is felt by the sufferer" (*TMS* 29). Smith considers the example of extreme hunger abstracted into language, as when "we read the description of it in the journal of a siege, or a sea voyage." As "we do not grow hungry," he explains, we cannot be said to sympathize with the participants' hunger, but we may—thanks in part to the mediation of print—"feel, ourselves, some degree of those passions" that "the distress [of] excessive hunger occasions" (28). Even as he hopes for a more complete correspondence between our sentiments and those of the people with whom we sympathize, Smith insists that it is all but impossible to achieve. Where in Hume "the distinction between spectator and fearful incident" is "de-emphasized," Smith broadens the gap between self and other (Flesch 117). And while both Hume and Smith thought vast physical distances prohibitive of sympathy, bodies that are too close are in Smith a frequent cause for concern.[8] Sufferers who keep a measured distance have better odds at earning our sympathy; their chances increase if they can be but dimly heard. Throughout *TMS* other people's too loud, overly near expressions of feeling "disgust," "provoke," and "aggravate" us (11). Even those who are "too happy" give us "the spleen" (16). We cannot "go along with" anyone whose emotional expression seems excessive or who acts cavalierly toward the dictates of propriety.[9] We refuse to grant our "approbation" (*TMS* 17).

Approbation marks our judgment that an emotional expression fits the occasion of its utterance. The processes of sympathy thus make context extremely important. Critics continue to debate how much it mattered to Smith and Hume that a sympathizer be able to verify an emotion's originating cause.[10] Yet while Smith agrees that to "approve of the passions of another" is to judge those passions "suitable to their objects," he insists that the "propriety of every passion excited by objects" depends on the expressive context (*TMS* 16). Some passions "are indecent to express very strongly, even upon those occasions, in which it is acknowledged that we cannot avoid feeling them in the highest degree"; at other times, strong emotions are "extremely graceful" even if "the passions themselves do not . . . arise so necessarily." Passions "are regarded as decent, or indecent, just in proportion as mankind are more or less disposed to sympathize with them" (27). Their propriety depends less on determinations of origin than on their reception by us. Though we often try to ascertain the events prompting other people's emotions, and sometimes succeed, what must always be available for contemplation are the conditions in which those emotions are given vent.

For this reason, sympathy regularly fails to develop even when, on the basis of causes, it should, simply because we do not invest enough energy into a full consideration of the situation in all its elements. On occasion, we can have what Smith tantalizingly calls "conditional sympathy," an acknowledgment that *if* we "took time to consider [the other's] situation" we *would* sympathize—and yet, we do not. It is "upon the consciousness of this conditional sympathy," Smith writes, "that our approbation of [the other's] sorrow is founded, even in those cases in which that sympathy does not actually take place." Guided by "our preceding experience of what our sentiments would commonly correspond with," we can "correct" "the impropriety of our present emotions" by thinking of other contexts—in the past and in possible futures—in which we might feel differently, and more (*TMS* 18). Conditional sympathy is like sympathy with the dead in reverse: now it is we who feel nothing of the other's sorrow. Yet our approbation can be granted even in the absence of adequate—or any—emotional response. A form of sympathy, but not experienced feeling, results.

It might seem, then, that sympathy is an easy thing to accomplish, given that the absence of living people and felt emotions does little to discourage it. And in practice, as we shall see, it often is. Yet if *TMS* leaves a single, unassailable impression on readers, it is that sympathy is really hard. Most of the time, it just shouldn't work, for there are too many impediments standing in its way. Couple other people's acute emotional experiences, and their often frustrated attempts at expression, with our unwillingness to add to our personal share of painful feeling—much less to shoulder that burden for others—and you'd have to be a betting man to hold out for sympathy's flowering. The following passage helps nail down some of the difficulty:

> [W]hen we condole with our friends in their afflictions, how little do we feel, in com
> parison of what they feel? We sit down by them, we look at them, and while they
> relate to us the circumstances of their misfortune, we listen to them with gravity
> and attention. But while their narration is every moment interrupted by those natu-

ral bursts of passion which often seem to choak them in the midst of it; how far are the languid emotions of our hearts from keeping time to the transports of theirs? . . . We may even inwardly reproach ourselves with our own want of sensibility, and perhaps, on that account, work ourselves up into an artificial sympathy, which, however, when it is raised, is always the slightest and most transitory imaginable; and generally, as soon as we have left the room, vanishes, and is gone for ever. Nature, it seems, when she loaded us with our own sorrows, thought that they were enough, and therefore did not command us to take any further share of those of others, than what was necessary to prompt us to relieve them (*TMS* 47).

Despite the added effort we put forth in condoling our friends, it is a challenge to "go along" even with them. We feel nothing, or nothing approaching what they do. The "gravity" and "attention" with which we listen is unmatched by an equivalent emotional response. Even if we manage to "work ourselves up into an artificial sympathy," that work is hard and the payoff slight, the "most transitory imaginable." Our "languid emotions" morphing into embarrassed "self-reproach," we flee those friends choked by despair; just as quickly, our ersatz sympathy for them "vanishes."

This appreciation of the burdens of sympathy helps to account for Smith's insistence on the importance of keeping our feelings to ourselves. "[B]ursts of passion," however natural, are repeatedly rebuked as the kind of bad form that even good-hearted people rarely go along with. Far from developing an account of sympathy in which it is necessary for spectators to witness scenes nakedly present to the eye and then share a perfectly transferred emotion, Smith insists that it is frequently what we do *not* see, do *not* feel, that fuels the sympathetic endeavor.[11] An example is Cato, that rare "mortal who can support . . . the most dreadful calamities" with hardly any outward show: we "feel what an immense effort is requisite to silence those violent emotions which naturally agitate and distract those in his situation." Our sympathy turns on Cato's self-silencing efforts, the fact that he "command[s] himself so entirely"; we are gladdened by his refusal to entreat us for "those miserable sympathetic tears which we are always so unwilling to give" (*TMS* 48). It may seem that the effort is all on one side, but Smith describes a crucial reciprocity, for Cato's muffling of his feeling, minimizing its volume, makes our responsiveness newly desirable. Our straining to feel in Cato's place evens the affective field, filling in the gap between his violently suppressed feeling on the one hand, its bare expression on the other. Cato's self-mastery, what Smith calls his "strength of mind," prompts a countervailing mindfulness in us.[12] Tears, should they come, can confirm our sympathy, but they do not produce it. Shared understanding and analogous perspectives must be cultivated first.

Smith's rule of thumb couldn't be clearer; we "are more apt to weep and shed tears" for those who "seem to feel nothing for themselves" (*TMS* 48). This is unfortunate for the man "sunk in sorrow and dejection" and others like him; we "cannot bring ourselves to feel for him what he feels for himself," and so, Smith sniffs, we "despise him" (49). Such masculine stoicism can be galling. After all, the only error committed by "our friends in their afflictions" was to show what they really felt in an unfiltered way (47). Yet we should also register the extent to which this process ushers in something less punitive and more profound, a rich affective productivity. When the hard work of sympathy pays off, it vitalizes a host of potential responses: we can supply a wider ranging sensibility, more and more varied sentiments, once sympathy requires neither certain knowledge nor that a single feeling pass identically from one person to the next. Sympathy is productive, not simply mimetic. Smith describes the "admiration" we feel for Cato as the "sentiment of complete sympathy and approbation, mixed and animated with wonder and surprise." Cato thrills by rousing our "wonder and surprise" (a more potent version of what Smith usually terms "interest"); his blank expression "animate[s]" us in multiple ways (48). Though Cato is not a typical case, sympathy in Smith generally works this way, as feeling, dematerialized, is transformed into new, at times entirely virtual forms of embodiment. In a striking passage, Smith explains that what sparks our sympathy with Cato is his seeming to feel for himself what we feel for him, which is, at least initially, "nothing" at all: his "firmness . . . coincides with our *insensibility*" to what he feels (48, emphasis added). Here too, Smith's admiration for feats of emotional reserve, a "distant, but affective, coldness" of behavior, accomplishes more than a championing of Stoical self-control, for a generative open-endedness adheres in that insensible, empty "nothing" (24). Our job in sympathy is to turn nothing into something, often into something *else*—for though our feelings might match perfectly, we can never know for sure. Smith presents this mismatch as an opportunity rather than a problem. When other people's situations rouse our interest, when we contemplate how the conditions of experience shape the attitudes that can be expressed within them, fellow-feeling forges imaginative, but no less powerfully affective, bonds.

Sympathy, at base a descriptive enterprise, in this way strenuously exercises our capacity for invention. As Lynn Festa observes, by dividing the self "into spectator, actor, and third person, Smith forces the self to sympathize (or not) with sentiments of its own making" (28). Yet these projections cannot be dismissed as egotistical, the product of private subjectivity run amok. For both the would-be sympathizer *and* the object of his sympathy must inhabit alternative, virtual realities not available to sight (or any of the senses) alone. Feeling is not enough. One's passions matter—indeed, can be said to exist—only insofar as others credit them; others confirm us to ourselves by returning (some version of) our sentiments to us. Yet in making a potentially dangerous argument for the social sanctioning of human feeling, Smith aims to do more than console us with the fact that the imagination can ably substitute for feelings that can be real to us in no other way. For he sees great value in this uncertainty. The insistence that sympathy deals in representations alone turns private emotion into public currency. The result is a conception of feeling as profoundly social, and a flexible sympathy in which thinking of others thinking of us, and the reverse, is the psychological mechanism enabling the sense of self.[13]

Smith didn't much care for novels, but one can see why his conception of sympathy proves useful for understanding the nineteenth-century novel.[14] The preference for emotional reserve hints at a connection; satirizing those persons incapable of stemming their emotional tides was one way the realists distanced themselves from Gothic and sentimental excess. But there are still more pervasive parallels to be made. For Smith's account helps us appreciate the degree to which sympathetic protocols inform the realists' desire to balance the real feelings of others, which (as "nothing") we cannot know firsthand, and our strategies for crediting, sharing, or denying them. As we shall see, by emphasizing abstraction, directing our attention to expressive contexts, and encouraging moderation, the realist novel, like the sympathy just described, sought ways to manifest feeling and limit its production. Fostering a kind of contentless fellow-feeling, the imaginative condition sympathy enables, sympathetic realism attempted to negotiate the individual's affective needs and communicative demands in relation to those of others.

In certain features of nineteenth-century realist form we can detect a commitment to those sympathetic protocols best able to serve that fiction's representational and moral purposes. In asking that we do more than feel, realist sympathy strains to meet the demands of what Christine Korsgaard calls "reflective endorsement," a method arising from the philosophical position, shared in the eighteenth century by Hume and Smith, and by Jeremy Bentham and John Stuart Mill in the nineteenth, that "the moral value of actions and objects is a projection of human sentiments" (50). Attempting to discover what compels moral behavior, reflective endorsement also seeks to understand what goes wrong when knowing our moral obligations to others is not enough to compel moral action.[15] For the sentimentalists, feeling was part of the answer; morality depended on the other's ability "to intrude on [our] reflections," to "get under [our] skin" (Korsgaard 50). From this view, the "normative demands of meaning and reason are not demands that are made on us by objects," for values and meanings reside instead in "the relations we have with ourselves and one another"—an idea resonant, for example, in George Eliot's contention that "the soul of art lies in its treatment and not in its subject."[16] Smith sought a way to manage these relations, to control which sentiments made it skin deep, and that same desire shapes the sympathetic realist novel. There sympathy offers a way to live in a world evacuated of the authority of external norms, harnessing psychology to the social processes that take its place. Sympathy provides a means for casting judgment on our own and the conduct of others. But it is also more than that. By denoting "our fellow-feeling with any passion whatever," sympathy is the faculty through which the full range of human expression enters into our reflections, in "every passion of which the mind of man is susceptible" (*TMS* 10). It is how we go along with the hearts and minds of others. In this way, sympathy comes to serve as the basis for reality itself.

Going Along with Others: Sympathetic Historicism

For the argument I make, one of the most influential recent accounts of realism is Harry E. Shaw's *Narrating Reality,* and it is worthwhile briefly to recall his argument.[17] Although "sympathy" and "sentiment" appear infrequently in that book, Shaw makes two large claims that are consequential for what follows. The first and most important is that nineteenth-century realism is pervasively historicist. Realism stands in a "determinate, positive relationship with historicism," responding to "similar problems" with "similar tactics."[18] The signal feature of these tactics is that they do not rely on claims about mimesis. It is not that realistic texts pick out the features of the world and represent them accurately. Instead, Shaw's historicist realism emerges through the involvement of the reader; the processes involved in the reader's coming to terms with the realities represented are where realism plants its stakes as a historical enterprise. This leads to the second claim, that nineteenth-century realism should be understood "as an attempt to balance procedure and substance, in the concrete modes by which it invites the reader to come to terms with realities, imagined and real" (xi). Realist fiction motivates particular mental habits, those engagements of mind with text that allow us to experience meaning as it emerges temporally in particular contexts, both our own and those of fictional characters. The production of this experience, Shaw concludes, makes a text both realistic and historicist at once.

In emphasizing the first point, Shaw is responding to critical assessments of realism that have focused on various forms of substance, from the things and stuff littering the novel's pages to a noumenal real beyond stuff, and beyond language. George Levine, for instance, argues that the nineteenth-century realists "used language to get beyond language, to discover some non-verbal truth out there."[19] This raises obvious epistemological problems which for Levine emerge especially in difficulties of perspective: how can a language issued from a single subjective position find suitable proof of the "non-verbal" realities it seeks out and wants desperately to defend? Shaw, charting a way "beyond this impasse," sees language as "already past any one incarnation of itself, and already past single-observer epistemology," realizing its full potential "not in single words striving to attach themselves to single things, but in sentences and in narratives" (71). Capitalizing on the very thing that poses a problem for Levine—that novels are made of words, not things—realist form anchors the mimetic impulse not in a fantasy of correspondence between language and the world but in the temporal unfolding of meaning in grammar and story. Its realism is not the product of concrete detail but is primarily rhetorical and affective. As the mind comes into contact with the "texture" of narrative, we experience "a sense of movement, involving both the movement of our own minds as we confront the story and the narrator's movement between scenes dispersed in time and space."[20] Meaning in realist narrative exists in the "going along with"—what Shaw calls the "sense of movement"—of mind as it engages form. Jane Thrailkill makes a similar point on behalf of the American realists. "[F]irst and foremost committed to elaborating what William James . . . described as 'feelings of reality,'" they downplayed "mimesis, referentiality, and fixity" in favor of contingency and mobility: "mediation, relationality, and above all *motion*" organize realism's design (9–10, original emphasis).

Shaw sounds remarkably Smithian in his description of a realism that works cumulatively to balance local and global registers, encouraging readers to weigh their own ways of being and thinking against those of others or belonging to the past. The "acts of attention evoked by Austen and Scott and Eliot can create, *if we enter into them,* a readiness to encounter subsequent unpredictable but cognizable movements of reality," Shaw writes (262, emphasis added). In a chapter on George Eliot, he demonstrates how this works in a passage from *Middlemarch* wherein Dorothea watches old Featherstone's funeral procession pass beneath her window:

> But for her visitors Dorothea too might have been shut up in the library, and would not have witnessed this scene of old Featherstone's funeral, which, aloof as it seemed to be from the tenor of her life, always afterwards came back to her at the touch of certain sensitive points in memory . . . Scenes which make vital changes in our neighbours' lot are but the background of our own, yet, like a particular aspect of the fields and trees, they become associated for us with the epochs of our own history, and make a part of that unity which lies in the selection of our keenest consciousness.
>
> The dream-like association of something alien and ill-understood with the deepest secrets of her experience seemed to mirror that sense of loneliness which was due to the very ardor of Dorothea's nature. The country gentry of old time lived in a rarefied social air: dotted apart on their stations up the mountain they looked down with imperfect discrimination on the belts of thicker life below. And Dorothea was not at ease in the perspective and chillness of that height (306).

Shaw first points out the extended metaphor through which Dorothea, trapped in "the stillborn world of Mr. Casaubon," compares the scene beyond the window to her own life (232). At times, the narrator suggests, we all do the same, bringing our neighbors' lives, ordinarily in "the background," into close coincidence with our own. Having long desired immersion in the world at large, Dorothea's attempts at connection grow increasingly poignant; the funeral scene, "mak[ing] a part of that unity" with her "own history," seems the epitome of her melancholy "consciousness." The same metaphor fusing Dorothea's mind with the world emblematizes her isolation from it.

But fusion isn't the only effect produced, nor is it enough that readers "respond to Dorothea's feelings": in "some forms of romance, this is all we would be called upon to do," Shaw writes, "[b]ut not in *Middlemarch*."[21] Certain additional formal elements make it difficult for metaphor to complete its unification once it has begun, for "a great deal occurs in the scene that keeps our own minds working along nonmetaphorical lines" (232). The same is true for Dorothea; situated within and against several backgrounds, she cannot entirely fuse with just one. The goings-on inside the house prevent her from merging entirely with the funereal mood outside, for Dorothea witnesses the procession in the company of visitors who have come, under Mrs. Cadwallader's direction, to watch it. Dorothea may "transmut[e] the external environment into a subjective symbol," but she does so in the midst of a social call. Alongside the metaphorical and symbolic impulses, metonymic meaning begins building chains of resonances, discoverable by readers even as they remain obscure to the characters involved. Sir James Chettam only vaguely "senses the web of meanings gathering around the mention of Will Ladislaw," whose appearance in the procession causes some confusion (232–33). Dorothea suspects what the others are thinking: they assume Will has come because she has asked her uncle Brooke to invite him. This is not so, but she cannot say it out loud. If the funeral provides Dorothea with the perfect metaphor for her emotions, she has "local, immediate, and personal reasons for keeping the exact bearings of that metaphor from emerging." More importantly, Shaw argues, she "has a stake in feelings that remain inchoate, that fail to reach clarity of expression" (235). For these in turn serve as "a marker for a large faithfulness to the promise of history." Embracing feelings "for which she has no precise names, instead of defining them into the tameness of the known," Dorothea "keeps alive a demand that history have utopian possibilities" (236).

In this passage, a sense of reality emerges in the interplay of what can and cannot be expressed, in what one might say aloud or what one must keep to oneself. Social pressures of this sort had been central to realism at least since Austen, where, as Blakey Vermeule suggests, characters are always being made to choose, even while knowing that their decisions are "conditioned by the hydraulic pressure of other people's choices" (183). As Shaw notes, the *Middlemarch* passage "filiates with its context" to such an extent that even its metaphors are localized.[22] Living aloof atop the mountain are "the country gentry of old time," not gods, and "rarefied" though it may be, theirs too is a "social air" (*Middlemarch* 306).When the metaphorical impulse does take over, its effects remain partial. Dorothea's "dream-like association of something alien and ill-understood with the deepest secrets of her experience *seemed to mirror* [her] sense of loneliness"; the "mirror" incompletely aligns its reflected parts (ibid., emphasis added). Dorothea's thoughts are vaguely comparable to her secrets, which are like "but not identical with" her loneliness (Shaw 235). Exactly how isn't clear, to her or to us. And it is in the not-quite-knowing, in the partial fitting-together, that the novel encourages readers to participate in Dorothea's cognitive strivings, her working through how to feel, think, and behave. Dorothea "is involved in the difficult attempt to elicit meaning which the sentence suggests the narrator is engaged in," and we, "as we read the sentence," are involved in the same (236). For Shaw, this dynamic use of form to foster an experience of mental sharing—between reader, character, and narrator—makes Eliot's prose historicist. We might recall Walter Houghton's provocative claim that by the mid-nineteenth century one no longer asked of the past, "What do I think of this? is it good? is it true?" but rather, "How shall I account for it? Why did men believe that it was good or true?" (15). Here, history is a mindset adopted in relation to a world of conditions; to study the past is to study the sentiments motivating human behaviors, the situations in and through which they thought. This attitude of historical open-endedness in turn enables history's utopian dimension. In it lies the possibility that new conditions might replace those in which one is living now.

Throughout his analysis, Shaw describes the effects of sympathy without quite naming it, even suggesting that readers "merge affectively with the subjectivity of Dorothea-in-history" (236). Both Dorothea's subjectivity and the reader's developing affective responsiveness to it derive from the narrative unfolding of her mental state. Dorothea cannot identify her feelings and, even if she could, they cannot (being fictive) transfer to us in any direct, material way. Yet the novel's refusal to name those feelings does as much to keep readers' sympathies alive as it does for history's utopian possibilities; their lack of precise definition widens the array of responses that readers might be inclined to experience. It may thus be better to say that we "go along" rather than "merge . . . with" the novelistic subjectivities whose reality unfolds in this way (236). *Middlemarch* pushes against our ability to fuse with Dorothea by keeping her feelings only dimly identified and, likewise, by keeping us at a distance. As Shaw puts it, we "feel her wanting to know" (235). Seeking to convey Dorothea's uncertain state of mind, and inviting us to experience how she processes that uncertainty, the novel elicits the sympathetic imagination. It, not Dorothea's feeling, fuels the novel's realism, which is itself fueled by our continuing, wondering, sympathetic interest in its characters' minds and plots.

In addition, as Shaw later suggests, although Eliot's third-person narrators are often said to be "securely removed" from the fictional worlds they describe, their perspectives frequently shift *between* modes of detachment and desire. An important effect of this is the blurring of the boundary between narration's extradiegetic distance, on the one hand, and on the other a level of affective engagement (and historical embeddedness) ordinarily the provenance of characters only (249). "There may be worse ways of attempting to describe this remarkable bifurcation and coalescence," Shaw writes, than to suggest that Eliot's narrators "evince a strong impulse" to enter the "story space" their characters inhabit (249–50). For Shaw, that impulse signals "a form of narration in the historical grain" (252). But this "bifurcation and coalescence," this impulse to cross into the other's fictional world, also closely resembles the sympathetic process. The attempt to enter into the "story space," what Smith calls the "case" of the other, and to become "in some measure the same person" as him, can succeed only partially for narrators and living persons alike, and only in relation to the abstract discourses of an imagined social mean (*TMS* 9). To become "in some measure the same person" as another requires this mismatch between first- and third-person orientations, for it requires our oscillation between embedded personhood and distanced, impersonal narration alike. We might say, then, that narration in the sympathetic grain describes Eliot's historical project.

That possibility begins to confirm a second Smithian insight, that the other's feeling sparks our interest "not as a passion, but as a situation that gives occasion to other passions which interest us" (*TMS* 32). As Smith saw it, the objects of our senses quickly fade, but an "idea of the imagination" persists in fascinating: it is "by no means over with the word" (29). The passage from *Middlemarch* helps us see how imaginative historicism and imaginative sympathy converge: following Dorothea's mental movements as she puzzles out the fit between her feelings and her world, we think along with her about "what are, or to what, under a certain condition, would be, or to what, we imagine, ought to be" her feelings, given the limitations ("a certain condition") of time and place (*TMS* 110). When Shaw tells us, then, that the realist novel historicizes by calling on readers to experience how historical forces shape ways of thinking (then and now), or when Gillian Beer describes Eliot's method as a striving "persistently *to set alongside*" so that "lateral and well as causal relations are emphasized," we can conclude that our imaginative powers of sympathy enable these narrative effects (*Darwin's Plots* 152, original emphasis). Affiliating Dorothea's psychology with her social situation, and enjoining us to share in the mental movements undertaken (by both character and narrator) in the effort to make sense of her world, Eliot puts sympathy to use for purposes that are realist and historicist at once.

One of Shaw's most perceptive claims is that literary realism, in whatever period it arises, "always carries with it an ontological claim" (94). Minimal though they are in number, these lines from *Middlemarch* begin to show how nineteenth-century realism satisfies that claim in the experience of sympathetically "going along with" the historically embedded mentalities of others. Fellow-feeling is the broad ontological condition to which that realism aspires. As such, Smith's reasons for being glad that we cannot fuse with others are ones that realist historicism exploits. To ensure that their aesthetic effects would endure, the realists sought to enjoin sympathy to elicit and sustain their readers' attention, knowing full well that feeling alone would not suffice for long. Sympathy with the workings of represented minds, and not simply an accurate accounting of the concrete details of life as it really is (or was), was a surer guarantee that a novel's realism would endure for decades to come. When we "go along with others" in the manner Shaw describes, we rely on the sympathetic habits of mind elicited by the narrative processes in which their subjectivities grow real; likewise, we can inhabit a novel's other times and places by imaginatively taking on and fleshing out the mentalities they shape, enable, or disavow. By pressing beyond a simple alignment of sympathy and feeling, as if the two were analogous, the nineteenth-century realist novel mobilizes the sympathetic mind for ends beyond emoting alone. Dorothea feels real to us, even now, not because we feel what she does or know what she knows, but because we can experience what it feels like to think along with her—to consider her situation in light of the attitudes she can (and cannot) hold or express within it, the emotions she can (and cannot) feel or even name.

Thus far I have attempted to demonstrate the minute, sentence-level embed-dedness of sympathetic protocols in realist narrative, a feature of novels appearing at a moment when "the pleasures of the imagination and the pleasures of social calculation" were seen as "mutually enhancing" (Lynch, *Economy* 219). We have noted some of the ways sympathetic realism capitalized on those pleasures for aesthetic and historicist ends. Yet if widely shareable social feeling was the affective experience the realist novel most assiduously pursued, we might turn again to Smith to consider how thinking "along with" fictional characters manifests the large-scale sympathy for which realism is known. I have suggested that the sympathy Smith outlines is difficult in theory but easy in practice. Hard as it is to achieve a harmonious balance of affection equally satisfying to all, particu-larly where specific individuals are involved, the sympathy underwriting ordinary life manages to occur without much effort, simply by making do. "Fellow-feel-ing" thus names the more or less constant state of mind in which we carry on life's mundane routines; it settles for a vaguer confidence, assuming that indi-viduals will move, think, and behave generally as we expect them to do. As Smith explains, unlike the "love, esteem, and affection" with which we "distinguish our particular friends and acquaintance," fellow-feeling is reserved for those for whom such "exquisite sentiments" are impossible to feel—which is everyone else (*TMS* 90). In this way, it resembles the "nothing" we felt for Cato more so than the "exquisite" something we feel for those closest to us. Our "regard for the mul-titude," Smith explains, is "compounded and made up of the particular regards which we feel for the different individuals of which it is so composed"; "general fellow-feeling" consists of feeling departicularized, extrapolated into a kind of contentless care.[23] Such abstraction on a grand scale gives us the confidence to feel that we are all more or less living in the same, shareable world. Sympathy in this way designates mundane reality as the greatest fiction of all.[24]

Understanding sympathetic departicularization as one of realist fiction's ultimate goals helps us appreciate how fellow-feeling governs its design, registering as an elaboration of shared activities and shareable modes of thought so engrained in our patterns of behavior that it becomes the very texture and condition of habit. Ian Duncan describes Smithian social life in just this way, as "a white noise of affective gratification through which common life keeps going." The real is, for Smith, "customary and continuous, reproduced by microscopic transactions of exchange" operating so smoothly "as to go unremarked." And fellow-feeling is the medium in which those transactions take place. Enabling the mind to make sense of the world, it forges the "illusions of spatial and temporal continuity, and of subjective as well as objective identity" (*Scott's Shadow* 120). Duncan considers Hume responsible for "establish[ing] the philosophical matrix for the ascendancy of fictional realism in modern British literature" (124). But Smith offers literary realism something Hume does not. By insisting that sympathy trades exclusively in represented feeling, by requiring feeling's dematerialization in *every* case, Smith puts sympathetic abstraction at the center of the real, making it the perfect vehicle for representing fictional reality. If not just any fiction but the fiction *of fellow-feeling* underwrites reality, then the realist novelists might turn to sympathy to secure the reality of their representations. And if the sympathetic departicularization of feeling—not the copying of actual, existing ones—is the effect fictional realism most energetically seeks out, Smith's narrative-dependent sympathy is especially well suited for that purpose. Realist fiction's commitment to the project of representing an ordinary, shareable world might be seen as relying on a sympathetic premise, that fellow-feeling is the only guarantor of objectivity in a world depleted of metaphysical norms.[25] Directed at nobody in particular, fellow-feeling serves as a model for understanding realism's backdrop of featureless mediocrity, the "white noise" of a social reality it was continually at pains to represent.

The next part of this chapter considers three representational techniques important to the form of nineteenth-century realist narrative. Insisting on the sympathetic design of each, realism attempts to move beyond the simple promotion of feeling as such. Indeed, sympathy infiltrates realist form more completely than we have acknowledged because we have tended to look for it on only those pages in which the word "sympathy" (or its cognates) actually appears. The following examples show the deep-rootedness of sympathy in some of realism's most recognizable techniques. For while in many nineteenth-century novels, from *Pride and Prejudice* to *Great Expectations,* a radical reversal of opinion or awakening to error constitutes the novel's moral epicenter, those pivotal moments are dramatic manifestations of the pervasive, yet far subtler, sympathy that has implicitly underwritten the novels' ethical systems all along. Changes of mind may be among the commonest crises represented in the era's fiction, but they are also at the core of the realist novel's more routine ways of enabling sympathy, by changing one mind with, and for, another.

PART 2. SYMPATHETIC FORM
Sympathetic Metonymy

> Were it possible that a human creature could grow up to manhood in some solitary place, without any communication with his own species, he could no more think of his own character, of the propriety or demerit of his own sentiments and conduct, of the beauty or deformity of his own mind, than of the beauty or deformity of his own face. All these are objects which he cannot easily see, which naturally he does not look at, and with regard to which he is provided with no mirror which can present them to his view. Bring him into society, and he is immediately provided with the mirror which he wanted before.
>
> —Adam Smith, *The Theory of Moral Sentiments*

Roman Jakobson famously identified the centrality of metonymy to realism, and we have begun to glimpse the importance of that claim for subsequent critics. Jakobson's thesis, which distinguishes metaphor from metonymy, has held up remarkably well despite various attempts to revise it: metaphor, organized on the basis of similarity, is the master trope of poetry; metonymy, organized by contiguity, is the master trope of prose, especially realist narrative.[26] This formulation led Jakobson to judge metonymy the less inventive of the two. The figure in which nongiven meanings are forged, metaphor licenses a creative power denied to metonymy, and also, therefore, to realist narrative, which according to Jakobson simply reproduces the contingent actualities of time and space. Metaphor could make new worlds; metonymy was restricted to documenting what already existed. Worse, metonymy remained partial despite efforts to cover up its own lack. It seemed destined to fake what metaphor authentically achieved. As Paul Atkinson observes, metaphor "implies a more holistic perspective," while metonymy "select[s] from multiple elements," operating by "deletion" and so necessitating a "'filling in' [of] the deletions in order to recover the whole which is implied or referred to."[27] Though this notion of "filling in" gaps suggests a kind of historicism, discussions of metonymy tend to emphasize existential reality over syntax, following from a basic conclusion that metaphor parades its artifice, whereas metonymy naturalizes itself. While critics like Brian McHale distinguish between synecdoche and metonymy—synecdoche becoming the trope of "selection," metonymy "ordering" selected details in space and time—it remains commonplace to say that metonymy substitutes parts for wholes, that in so doing it infers absent or invisible things, and that in the realist fiction with which it has been associated at least since Jakobson, it misleadingly purports to having close connections with the reality for which its substitutions stand.[28]

In response, Shaw points out that cause and effect, a relationship traditionally identified with metonymy, was missing from Jakobson's formulation. This omission left metonymic processes too random to explain the realist enterprise adequately. Realist metonymy, Shaw argues, need not be confined to "'mere' contiguity and contingency," the "just-happening-to-be-there associations sure to crop up if we are operating under the assumption that our experience is really flux" (102). It is neither hostage to the actual nor a record of sheer randomness. If realist metonymy is to be understood as contingent at all, Shaw argues, it should be seen as eliciting a sense of the contingency of historical life. As he says, "life in history is contingent (as opposed to logically or conceptually necessary) just because it is historical"; cause and effect, not randomness, is realist metonymy's "typifying instance" (102–3). Realist metonymy patterns meaning in the same way the human experience of history does. Most germane to nineteenth-century realism, historical meaning designates potential meaning, as in the possible connections arising as readers mentally reconstruct lived experiences in relation to an absent past. Accidents of life thus become explicable *because* they occur in particular places and times. For this reason, metonymic conjunctions need not impute a hidden depth but can instead keep things "very much on the surface" (105). To fully appreciate the "complex and proliferating surface network[s]" enacted by metonymy in a given text, one must read through a range of passages in order to determine how it asks to be read, with this as one possible result: that it "teaches us to attend to the importance, oddness, unpredictability, and yet ultimate rationality of chains of cause and effect" (105, 107).

We have seen that causality, after Hume and Smith, was among those "illusions of spatial and temporal continuity" made possible by the sympathetic understanding (Duncan, *Shadow* 120). Feeling oneself to be of the same mind as others enabled continuous, mundane reality to take shape. Yet Shaw's conception of metonymy is particularly resonant with sympathy as described by Smith. First, it appeals to expressive contexts for whatever meanings it acquires. This is the usual reason given for metonymy's suitability to realist fiction. Metonymy is said to index reality by reading its visible signs, thereby imputing a close, even deterministic relation to it.[29] For Shaw, though, realist metonymy doesn't so much impute direct ties to the actual as engender historicizing modes of thought. Jane Austen's method of "immers[ing] her characters and readers in remarkably fine and nuanced processes of distinction-making" is seen as an exercise in mapping the "mental movements that will be needed to make sense of history" (Shaw 166). In her novels, where world-historical events have seemed mostly absent, the historical is embedded in a form in which "distinguishing . . . helps to carve out a place to be oneself in the interstices of a seemingly all-encompassing social network" (162). Thus, an important second feature of realist metonymy is that it mediates individual and group psychology in ways Smith identified as sympathetic. Metonymy facilitates such comparisons because it studies parts in relation to wholes; *historicist* metonymy, even better equipped for realism's sympathetic project, privileges the relation between part and whole that exists between individuals and their milieux. Historicist metonymy sharpens our focus on only some aspects of a given whole, excluding others. Prompting us to consider the causes of events, who or what authorizes how events are explained, it invites speculation about how and why certain parts of any whole are selected for or excluded from consideration. It asks that we imagine (and this is Shaw's major point) that "there is a web of causality informing our situations in history." Thus, "at its most ambitious," realist fiction "offers us the possibility of participating in the workings of a mind capable of following the unfolding of that most real of modern phenomena, the workings of history itself" (107).

In order to recognize how causal webs shape historical experience, individuals must perceive themselves as both in and outside a reality characterized in terms of mental life. Here, too, the affinities between Smithian sympathy and realist historicism grow clear: in both, individual subjectivity depends on the ability to imaginatively adopt the viewpoints of others; in both, one integrates into society by imagining worlds one does not inhabit. (It is worth noting that Mark Salber Phillips characterizes Scottish intellectual life in the time of Smith and Hume as a looking from the outside in: the Scots "lived in watchful intimacy with the dominant society," he writes; *Sentiment* 155.) Shaw argues that our sense of self increases in thinking of our own perspective from a view outside it; this is historicism's trademark. Thus, the "historicist moment par excellence" involves the recognition "that a social milieu has its own customs and its own consciousness, a recognition that can only come from feeling oneself separate from that milieu" (Shaw 107). Two conclusions follow: first, that one cannot develop "a historicist vision of other societies" unless one maintains a certain distance from one's own; second, that this same self-distancing enables a historicist vision of one's own moment (108). Recognizing how cultures shape their members has the desirable effect of "distanc[ing] the recognizer from the shaping." This leads to a crucial insight, that "the moments of identity-making and difference-making are the *same* moments; they are mutually reinforcing" (107, original emphasis).

Now consider Smith's claim that in sympathy one is "constantly led to imagine in what manner he would be affected if he was only one of the spectators of his own situation" (*TMS* 22). Shaw's "historicist moment par excellence" involves the very kind of thought project that in Smith's account of sympathy is critical for developing a sense of self. No man can even "think of his own character," much less the propriety of "his sentiments and conduct," without imagining how he appears to the minds of others; without that mental "mirror," even the self is an "object which he cannot easily see, [and] which naturally he does not look at." He lacks all comprehension "of his own mind" (*TMS* 110). By way of illustration, Smith imagines a man living in total isolation. On a good day, he might "view his own temper and character with that sort of satisfaction with which we consider a well-contrived machine," and on a bad, as "a very awkward and clumsy contrivance" (192–93). Selfhood is so unthinkable on the social margin that only a minimal subjectivity is possible outside it. A man who cannot "suppose the idea of some other being, who is the natural judge of the person who feels," is also incapable of having a self, for only through sympathy "can [he] conceive, either the triumph of self-applause, or the shame of self-condemnation" (193). Bereft of an "idea of some other being"—an awareness of others, and therefore of perspectives other than his own—Smith's marooned man is deprived of more than human company. Unable to picture the minds of others, he cannot picture his own. Lacking that representational ability, incapable of forming an *idea* of self, he ranks himself little more than "machine."

Smith's insistence that subjectivity cannot develop beyond a kind of bare life without an "idea of some other being" correlates with Shaw's description of historical consciousness as self-consciousness. By imaginatively reliving past conditions and the mentalities those conditions enabled, we begin to view "our own societies and our own historical selves as 'other,' as products of history, not nature" (Shaw 123). And if the realists relied on metonymic forms to highlight the mental labors involved in cultivating such perspectives, they may have done so believing them sympathetic: believing, in other words, that to conceive the self sympathetically, through others, facilitates the self-othering required in the making of historical selves. Shaw comes close to suggesting that realist metonymy serves a sympathetic purpose when he writes that its "logic of connection-making" works, analogously, to create "affective bond[s]" between readers and texts (108). We might add that the particular kinds of connections associated with metonymy are especially well suited to a sympathy that proscribes any absolute correspondence between its compared parts. Metonymy's nonintrinsic, nontranscendent similarities are tailor-made to meet the needs of a sympathy that involves the adjacency, but not the exact identity, of its participants' emotions and states of mind.

And this metonymy is sympathetic, not just historicist, in its reliance on narrative extension, the building-up of partial connections and the accumulative gathering together of temporally unfolding meanings, to vivify what is absent or unknowable in the present. Turning a final time to *Narrating Reality*, we see evidence of this sympathetic metonymy in the way that Shaw contrasts Sir Walter Scott with the narrator of Scott's "The Two Drovers." Like Scott, Chrystal Croftangry is a genteel Scots lawyer, but unlike him, Croftangry alienates himself from the Highlanders whose story he relates. Croftangry's narrative method is to pack his tale with Gaelic nouns but then translate them without comment into standard English. The result is a deadening effect on language: groupings like "*leadbhar-dhu* (black pocket-book)," or "*sporran* (pouch of goatskin)," lead to a "heaping up of Gaelic vocabulary," a "dead metonymy" that does nothing to "promote a sense that certain Gaelic words encapsulate a mode of cultural perception or practice unavailable to us in our own language" (Shaw 199). Shaw doesn't describe "dead metonymy" as an unsympathetic form, but he might have. In Croftangry's hands, Gaelic words "become labels"; they "sound exotic," lending little sense of reality to their represented worlds (199). Dead metonymy fails not because the terms in which it deals are incomprehensible—assigning meaning is all too easy—but because their meanings seem utterly fixed, in settings alien and irrelevant. The assumption that one set of words simply substitutes for another, regardless of the contexts in which they developed (and make sense), all but guarantees that a sympathetic reading experience cannot occur. Swapping (modern) English phrases for (primitive) Scottish terms cements the archaism of the latter; it does nothing to persuade readers to imaginatively re-create the living syntax of which they were once a part.

By contrast, Scott explains in his notes to *The Minstrelsy of the Scottish Border* that the "single word *haugh* conveys to a Scotsman almost all that I have endeavored to explain in the text, by circumlocutory description" (208). Acknowledging that single words cannot be translated without loss into modern English equivalents, Scott offers an alternative method for delineating their full cultural significance while increasing their affective and imaginative power. Meanings impossible to transmit spontaneously to readers, as might ("almost") be done for a Scotsman by a single word, are conveyed instead by way of metonymic surplus, "circumlocutory description"—aspects of narrative that argue against an understanding of realism as substituting words for worldly things. Historicist metonymy thus looks to be another departicularizing technique with sympathetic promise. With meanings that accrue during the reading process, its effects are "by no means over with the word" (*TMS* 29).

The example of Scott clarifies Shaw's insight that while the "defining trope of *all* realisms is metonymy . . . it is metonymy *as defined in the light of the ontology to which a given realism appeals*" (103, original emphasis). We can now see sympathetic fellow-feeling as the ontology to which the historicist metonymy of nineteenth-century realism makes its most sustained appeal. That metonymy portrays historical reality as the project of "going along with" others: imaginatively following the mental tracks embedded in syntax, mentally feeling out the lines of their thinking in relation to the contexts in which their attitudes formed. If metonymic historicism relies on sympathetic interpretive processes that are themselves designed to provide imaginative access to other minds, the resulting form brings history and sympathy together to re-create, even to change (not merely copy), the real.[30] For the reality of these texts must now be said to rely on nonspontaneous forms of sympathy. Rather than affirming our effortless susceptibility to the feelings of others, such a sympathy enlists the mind to will them, whenever possible, into life.

"A Certain Mediocrity": Free Indirect Discourse

When sympathy is not understood as a merely solipsistic enterprise in which we congratulate ourselves for our good sentiments toward others, it is typically seen as a matter solely between two figures, the sufferer and the sympathizer. And yet within Smith's account, and in the uses to which the realist novelists put it, sympathy is a much more broadly social force. The novelists seem to have recognized in sympathy's narrative dimensions a means for promoting a harmonious social vision without didactically doling out the mandates of moral law or even a single, domineering omniscience. And they did this through their insistence on representing the middling, the mediocre—not just thematically but formally as well. As we shall see, it was through the formal representation of social mediocrity that the novelists demonstrated the sympathetic constitution of reality. Though we can explain this preference along generic lines—realism's steering clear of Gothic highs and melodramatic lows—sympathy suggests another motive for jockeying for the middle. The constant ratcheting toward what Smith called "a certain mediocrity" attenuates perspectival and emotional extremes so as to forge a comfortable average (*TMS* 27). It is toward this desideratum that realist fiction wends its way: when artists are urged in Anne Brontë's *The Professor* to create "fewer pictures chequered with vivid contrasts of light and shade" (140), or when George Eliot ridicules the "unexceptionable opinions" of those who "act unexceptionably" in novels where the "most faulty characters" are always "on the wrong side," the "virtuous ones on the right" (*Adam Bede* 160). Eliot's complaint, like that leveled in *The Mill on the Floss* against "men of maxims" who are "guided in their judgment solely by general rules" (628), strongly echoes Smith's critique of the casuists. Failing to take "internal feeling" into account, the latter err in laying down "many precise rules that are to hold good unexceptionably in all particular cases" (*TMS* 328).

Mediocrity is a means of disciplining affective excess, to be sure, but in doing so by way of reference to an ideal average, Smith makes the mediocre exemplary. And we can see the effects of a similar effort in free indirect discourse (FID), another submechanism of sympathetic understanding. Shuttling between a generalizing, impersonal standard of judgment and individual perspectives that revise and refute it, FID reproduces the sympathetic circuit between collective and particular stances. Moreover, distance is requisite to the sympathy opera-tive in FID: it isn't merely a feature of the "ironic" stance often counterpoised to sympathy and framed as its opposite (ironic detachment versus sympathetic identification). For by rendering a character's thought "in his own idiom" while routing it through a fictive third-person (im)persona, FID offers an experience of fellow-feeling as we have thus far defined it (Cohn 100). Impersonal yet richly affective, it involves multiple minds "going along" together while remaining cru-cially mismatched and distinct.

Smith's description of mediocrity links Stoical philosophy and Aristotelian virtue under the heading of "Systems which make Virtue consist in Propriety" (*TMS* 267). "Virtue, according to Aristotle, consists in the habit of mediocrity according to right reason," Smith writes, locating virtue "in a kind of middle be-tween two opposite vices, of which the one offends from being too much, and the other from being too little affected by a particular species of objects" (270). Simply having "moderate and right affections" is not enough to achieve virtue, nor is the performance of a virtuous action proof of virtuous character (it might have been a fluke). One needs to be "in the habit of this moderation," choosing to behave in such a way that mediates in "a kind of middle" between the dictates of propriety and the realities of experiential life (271). To locate that middle ground—say, that of "fortitude" between the extremes of "cowardice" and "rashness," or of "magnanimity" between "arrogance" and "pusillanimity"—one needs to account for the circumstances in which a given action takes place (270–71). One mean will not be identical to another, nor is any sentiment invariably good in every context.

Fortitude does not seem like an especially middling quality, but that is part of the point: our better selves are realized in the mediocre. Smith stresses the difficulty of achieving mediocrity when magnanimity (in the *Oxford English Dictionary*, 2nd ed., "greatness of thought or purpose") is considered a middling accomplishment. Likely as we are to fall sway to selfish feelings, it is simply easier to be extreme, much harder getting to the middle. Thus, the "propriety of every passion excited by objects peculiarly related to ourselves, the pitch which the spectator can go along with, must lie, it is evident, in a certain mediocrity": passions too high and low are those we "cannot enter into" and cannot, therefore, "go along with" (*TMS* 27). Moderation of pitch leads to "harmony," the "happy commerce" of different sentiments tempered to a comfortable, mediocre average (39). This demand for emotional propriety is not prescriptive against some passions, endorsing others. No single rule can tell you if your pitch is off. Since "every affection is useful when it is confined to a certain degree of moderation," virtue is not intrinsic to certain feelings but exists "in the proper degree of all the affections" (306). "A certain mediocrity" makes sociability the cornerstone of moral life (27).

To find our way to the middle, we call upon a figure Smith calls the "impartial spectator," a "proper remedy and correction" for taming our self-interest (*TMS* 292). The "real or even the imaginary presence of the impartial spectator, the authority of the man within the breast, is always at hand to overawe [our selfish passions] into the proper tone and temper of moderation," Smith writes. "To direct the judgments of this inmate [of the breast] is the great purpose of all systems of morality" (292–93). Calling this internal monitor an "impartial spectator," Smith seems to privilege its objectivity along with its capacity for surveillance, and this is how it has generally been understood. Most famous is John Bender's account, in *Imagining the Penitentiary*, of *TMS* as "strenuously normative," the impartial spectator an internalization of an external authority that is rational, consistent, and omniscient (224). For Bender, the effect of Smithian self-consciousness is isolation in a modern form. Unlike that of the dungeon cell, this is "isolation under inspection," a "structure of observation crystallized in the idea of the impartial spectator" and implanted "in the subjectivity that attends the ideal citizen in the society Smith delineates" (226). "Governmental punishment follows spontaneously, for Smith, from public resentment generated by sympathy," Bender writes; the "breath of sympathy animates the whole system, which always remains, fundamentally, a matter of self-judgment and self-inflicted punishment" (222–23). Insofar as the realist novel is concerned, Bender's has proven a persistent account: Smith bequeaths to realism a view from which everything made to seem self-evident is in fact carefully monitored by an uncompromising omniscience. The realist novel's "regime of narrative discipline" reveals itself in third-person narrators who, nowhere and everywhere at once, surveil an entirely visible world (Bender 44).

Impartial spectatorship *is* normative but hardly as sinister as Bender makes it seem. Seeking compromise, its goal is to make do, so as to make human imperfection more bearable. Because we fashion ourselves after (and hold others to) impossibly high standards, ones "no human conduct ever did, or ever can come up to," comparison to that standard alone makes "the actions of all men . . . for ever appear blamable and imperfect" (*TMS* 26). And so impartial spectatorship takes a second standard into consideration, the "idea of that degree of proximity or distance from this complete perfection, which the actions of the greater part of men commonly arrive at." "Whatsoever goes beyond this degree, how far soever it may be removed from absolute perfection, seems to deserve applause," Smith maintains, "and whatever falls short of it, to deserve blame." Though Smith regularly identifies the impartial spectator with the standard of reason, its function cannot be aligned solely with the "complete propriety and perfection" side of the equation. For in preventing us from finding "nothing but faults and imperfections" in human actions that never measure up, impartial spectatorship grants enormous value to the "common degree" (26). The Victorian critic John Abercrombie understood it to work in just this way, as concerned above all with daily practice: it neither supplied "the place of a fundamental rule of right and wrong" nor sought the "origin of it," pertaining "only to the application of a principle."[31] Less a bodiless avatar of perfect authority than a crowded field of oscillating viewpoints, impartial spectatorship puts our perspectives "into . . . balance," engineering a view "from the place and with the eyes of a third person," a middle ground between the ideal and actuality.[32] As Charles Griswold notes, Smith's repeated use of the first person plural "replicates what he takes to be a fact of moral psychology, namely that one's moral judgments are mediated by community."[33] More "we" than "I," impartial spectatorship is the mechanism through which a social average is imaginatively taken on.

A similarly impersonal "third person" inhabits nineteenth-century realist narration, the omniscient or semi-omniscient narrator. Linked to impartial spectatorship, third-person narration secures the tie between impartial spectatorship, novels, and free indirect discourse, a technique Frances Ferguson considers the novel's "one and only formal contribution to literature."[34] Yet standard understandings of FID would make it seem problematic for the sympathy I have described. We have seen that knowledge of others has a funny way of preventing sympathy rather than promoting it. In Smith's account, sympathy sours the dream of total access. And FID is commonly thought to pull us more closely into characters so that we can see ourselves reflected in them and thus better understand what makes them tick.[35] Often this intimacy is presented loosely as a matter of sympathetic identification, the assumption being that we are predisposed to sympathize with those we perceive as most like ourselves. FID on this reading furthers identification through experiments in omniscience: plumbing the depths of a character's unspoken thoughts and feelings, it grants a sympathy-promoting access that is impossible in real life. Expressions narrated in FID have been characterized in different ways—as belonging to no one because technically they are unspeakable; as hypothetical, close to what a character would say, even though she does not; or as registering the process by which language, for reasons of necessity, records thought as speech.[36] Still, Alan Palmer isn't alone in describing FID as solipsistic or "centripetal" in nature, "direct[ing] the reader's attention inward into scenes of thoughtful self-communion" rather than "outward into the context of social situation and action" (86). According to a standard claim, FID collapses narrator and character into a single consciousness, producing a simultaneity effect. Dorrit Cohn refers to the narrator's "identification" with a "character's mentality" as one so complete that "narrated *monologue*" replaces "FID" as her preferred term of analysis (112, original emphasis).

Yet if we consider FID to be, like metonymy, a technique developed with sympathetic protocols in mind, we might focus on how it, like sympathy, inhibits the full collapse of self into other. Differing accounts of how FID functions—and many exist—can accommodate this feature of its design. FID is sometimes called an "intermediate form" between direct and indirect speech, or between two voices or subjectivities (Bal 49). Even critics who do not see FID as a "dual voice" form describe in terms of some kind of shift or incongruity the very phenomena that make FID identifiable in the first place. The shift might be verbal, so that the past tense "She loved him" could be a "free indirect rendition of a projected direct statement"; or it might be contextual and so "constituted in the perceived difference of voice in the FID utterance from the voice of the broader utterance in which it is embedded."[37] Narrators in FID frequently adopt a character's speech patterns while at the same time casting judgment on her thoughts, criticizing her in her own voice. In such cases as these, FID registers moments in which narrator and character "go along" together idiomatically while their discourse situations remain distinct.

This sounds a lot like Smithian sympathy as Bender understands it, as the impersonal, self-criticizing mechanism through which we surveil and correct ourselves. But that's not all there is to it. For starters, readers frequently need to rely on their sympathetic powers to register a narrative effect that might otherwise go unnoticed. As Monika Fludernik suggests, FID "materializes in the reading process," arising in the same way realism does, as sentences are read, remembered, and reflected on (*Fictions* 441). Richard Aczel, Manfred Jahn, and many others agree: to recognize FID often involves comparing certain sentences to others, listening for familiar verbal tics so as to infer which voice or voices they contain. Not uncommonly, FID registers the changing voices that belong to the same character, but at different times. Dramatizing the gap between who a character was and who she is now (often after a change of mind or heart), FID can remain invisible until sentences are reread, appearing only after the fact.

FID thus requires deftness on the part of readers, who must make a "cognitive leap" from linguistic signal to discursive meaning or be willing to "reinterpret" material to which prior meanings have been assigned.[38] Readers of Dickens's *Great Expectations* who come across the sentence, "Miss Havisham was going to make my fortune on a grand scale," might at first take Pip's claim as just one more retrospective detail, only to realize later that the sentiment it contains is the product of hope, not fact (125). Fludernik characterizes this sentence as "a classic passage of free indirect discourse in the first person," a reminder that FID splits first-person subjectivities into the units of sympathy (actor, spectator, and judge) ("Linguistic" 102). FID is for such reasons less a narrative "device" than an experience of how discursive meaning evolves. To the extent that readers recognize it when it happens, keeping track of and assessing its effects, FID works like metonymic meaning does, cumulatively and over time, in the processes of narrative unfolding. The multiple mindsets associated with FID, and the "anticipatory and reinterpretive processes" it demands, seem more aligned with the processes of sympathy and metonymy than empathy or metaphor.[39] FID produces not so much the fused identity of narrator and character, character and reader, but the partial, merely approximate cohabitation of individualized persons and an impersonal, virtual voice.

These qualities help to explain why FID is considered "quotational," a "composite configuration of voices, whose identity lies in the rhetorical organization of their constituent elements" (Aczel 495). The rhetorical situation of a given expression is one of FID's principal objects. Conveying the common view, not simply private thoughts, is one of FID's noted specialties. And while some critics have aligned that view with the disembodied, totalizing authority of omniscience, others have found in FID more nuanced portrayals of collective life.[40] Ferguson, for instance, brings FID's sympathetic orientation sharply into focus in arguing that Austenian FID underscores the "communal contribution" to individual subjectivity ("Jane Austen" 164). Consciousness in Austen, she writes, is not "merely an individual project." "Like any external or logical representation," FID provides no "basis for any individual or individualized point of view for author or character" (180). In a similar vein, Daniel Gunn sees Austenian FID as producing a "pervasive atmosphere" of mimicry in sentences saturated with multiple idioms.[41] Even *Emma*'s distant, ironic narrator "echo[es] a collective subjectivity other than" her own.[42] Gunn upsets the conventional wisdom which sees FID as an autonomous, impersonal mode of representation in which narrators disappear into speakerless objectivity.[43] But because the unimpeachable authority of the Austen narrator is, for Gunn, never in question, the figural subjectivity of Austenian FID is, as it were, never alone: there is always "a second subjectivity, outside of the character's," filtering and inflecting her thoughts. Gunn finds the essential feature of Austenian FID to be "the *imitation of figural subjectivity* within a context of narrative report" (37, original emphasis). The result is the "*incorporation* of figural speech and thought into the complex artifice of narrative voice" (43, original emphasis).

For our purposes, the central thing to notice is that both of these critics consider FID a technique of "incorporation" in which represented feeling and thought leads to a plural conception of self, abstractly embodied in *figural* subjectivity, *narrative* voice. For Ferguson, that embodiment is uniquely realist in contrast to the theater and the epistolary novel. Theater relies on direct quotation, insisting on the public "speakability" of feelings and thoughts; epistolary novels rely on indirect quotation, with isolated, private characters summarizing in their own words what others have said ("Jane Austen" 169). Through FID, the realist novel compromises between the two, insisting that one's private sentiments be speakable by others. In Austen's hands, where "an individual can be seen as an individual only through a chorus," the result is that subjectivity emerges only in relation to the "communal stance" (165). Explaining FID in this way, Ferguson identifies its sympathetic design; a middle ground between direct and indirect quotation, FID presumes the social basis of private subjectivity. But Ferguson also shows FID to build from an even more specific Smithian insight. For, as she argues, if through the use of FID novels could portray "characters and society speaking the same language," that portrayal depended on a sympathetic premise—that the feelings of others "are not so much to be experienced as deduced" (170, 166). The point is significant. Public sentiment is speakable without being available for emotional sharing; one adduces but cannot feel it, because there is no "it" to speak of: public feeling is entirely fictive and abstract. It is also unstable, tied to no enduring body and capable of changing on a dime. Thus in *Emma,* public opinion doesn't dictate all that individuals will do or can become, and it can be wrong—not a bad thing in a world featuring a Mrs. Elton, who is "never mistaken," alongside an Emma, who frequently is (Ferguson, "Jane Austen" 174). The contentlessness of public feeling means that it cannot supply a fixed standard of judgment. Its integrity and authority are fictions that must continually be reproduced.

Though Ferguson aligns FID with the concept of "transparent minds," the idea that characters are "highly legible to their narrator even when they are not directly speaking or acting," transparency fails to capture the processes just described, how much they involve not seeing into other heads but guessing what is in them, getting things wrong and making things up ("Jane Austen" 170). To be sure, the protocols of sympathy seem readily apparent when sentences in FID seem to speak as if from a middle ground in which narrators, by inhabiting their minds, see into others without having to share their feelings and thoughts. Yet even more striking is how FID's impersonal, yet crowded, third-person subjectivity is made to seem the ordinary mindset we ordinarily adopt in shaping our relation to the social world. To "speak the same language" as one's milieu, to harmonize with it, is to view the self as a medium for transmitting the sentiments of others and vice versa. "Figural subjectivity" describes the third-person attitude of fellow-feeling through which mundane reality takes shape. FID thus not only "marks the advent of fictionality in the most ordinary exchanges of daily life" but also identifies that fictionality with sympathy writ large, as the process through which public sentiment, social reality, is (as much as it can be) incarnated in us (167). William Flesch makes a similar claim in describing our predisposition to third-person kinds of enjoyment: "constituted to take an intense emotional interest in the nonactual," human beings delight in watching those figures (like narrators) "who involve themselves in adjusting the outcomes of nonactual events."[44] Human cooperation is inextricable from the pleasures of fiction, but it doesn't require our identification with others. Our responses can be "affectively saturated without our emotions in any way implying our identification with the signaler or our putting ourselves in his or her place" (Flesch 122).

Just as its benefits are significantly widened if sympathy names not the transfer of a single, embodied feeling but a generalized propensity to feel and think collectively with others, so too can we better comprehend the sympathetic dimensions of FID when it is not restricted to portrayals of the "inside view." For we can then appreciate the extent to which FID makes isolated, private feeling seem impossible, insofar as subjectivity depends for its development on our imaginative projections of social life—for Smith, the only kind of life that mattered and the life the realist novel most wanted to represent. Blakey Vermeule has called FID "a vehicle for bearing an emotional tone" (78). Henry Louis Gates describes it as "mood come alive" (209). In each of these characterizations, FID generates not feeling per se but what I have been calling "fellow-feeling," a departicularized affectivity, fictive and shared. As Charles Altieri suggests, "moods" are subjective and impersonal at once; they occur when "the sense of subjectivity becomes diffuse and sensation merges into something close to atmosphere, something that seems to pervade an entire scene or situation."[45] "Tone," likewise, designates an implied author's attitudinal stance; it names a textual sentiment tied to a projected, impersonal identity, materialized nowhere else but in the reading process. Concepts like "living mood" and "emotional tone" thus usefully pinpoint the unique affectivity of FID. In granting the experience of social life a virtual, figural embodiment, FID fulfills a sympathetic purpose.

Shared Separateness, Group Particularity: Sympathetic Character

In Anthony Trollope's *The Way We Live Now,* Roger Carbury describes his friend Paul Montague as being like and unlike his good-for-nothing scamp of a cousin, Sir Felix. This characterization occurs in conversation with Felix's mother, Lady Carbury, on two highly charged emotional subjects. Felix, having nearly bankrupted his mother, threatens permanently to damage the Carbury name; moreover, Roger loves Henrietta, Felix's sister, but she (preferring Paul) does not reciprocate. The first speaker is Roger, the second Lady Carbury:

"I will wait till to-morrow [to visit Henrietta],—when I call to see Felix. I should like her to know that I am coming. Paul Montague was in town the other day. He was here, I suppose?"

"Yes; he called."

"Was that all you saw of him?"

"He was at the Melmotte's ball. Felix got a card for him;—and we were there. Has he gone down to Carbury?"

"No;—not to Carbury. I think he had some business about his partners at Liver-pool. There is another case of a young man without anything to do. Not that Paul is at all like Sir Felix" (1:63).

This conversation, routine in its way, is dense with emotional and metonymic complexity. Thinking of Henrietta leads to thinking of Paul, for some time Roger's bosom friend but now a romantic rival. In describing his comings and goings, Lady Carbury unwittingly relays what must seem to Roger evidence of Paul's accumulated crimes. Paul has called on Hetta at home and attended Melmotte's Ball; it is hard to say which offense Roger considers worse. If Lady Carbury has quieted her suspicions about the formidable Melmotte, Roger has not. To Roger and the reader, if not (or not quite willingly) to Lady Carbury, Melmotte seems another, more successful version of Sir Felix. Further connecting the two is a scheme by Felix and his mother to marry Felix into the Melmotte clan. Worse, in these few lines Paul's association with Felix, and so with Melmotte, grows more dangerous and deep. A notorious, swindling financier, Melmotte is, like Felix, a heartless liar and a sham, but he is also head of the managerial board on which both Sir Felix and Paul hold seats. Roger's comment, "I think [Paul] had some business about his partners at Liverpool," is studded with these associations and more. Paul's business partners, too, are practicing a sham, the Vera Cruz railway project into which Melmotte has been ensconced as symbolic figurehead. These convergences meet head-on in Roger's pointed, unstable comparison: "There is another case of a young man without anything to do. Not that Paul is at all like Sir Felix."

That "case" is not easily settled despite Roger's attempt, on opening it, to snap it shut. It may be that Roger is right in aligning Paul with Felix. Or it may be that he isn't, quite. Roger has good reasons, tinged with jealousy though they are, for taking an uncharitable view of Paul. Yet his haste to undo the comparison also makes plain the working of a guilty conscience. Both sides of the case have their truths: Paul does resemble Felix (both are involved in questionable affairs, romantic and economic), yet he is utterly unlike him in many respects. Through-out the novel, Trollope invites us to consider what makes one person like or un-like another, as well as the relationship between individuals and the classes or types to which they belong. Such questions are ongoing and rarely resolved. As Deidre Lynch observes of the form generally, the novel "did not so much resolve

as exploit . . . the tensions arising from one's sense that the relation between individual and society is at once a relation of mismatching and, because individuals
may be understood to be thoroughly determined by their social context, a relation of redundancy" (*Economy* 251). That same tension is laid bare in Austenian
FID, where "individuals can be described as having temporal extension and a
traceable history only from the standpoint of the constant comparison of their
current situations to a projected communal stance, but individuals would cease
to be individuals (would become indistinguishable from one another) if they ever
actually coincided with the communal stance" (Ferguson, "Jane Austen" 465).

For Catherine Gallagher, that problematic is central to how the realist novel
billed itself as true to life. Its characters needed to be two contradictory things at
once—individually specific, therefore realistic, and generically common, therefore realistic. The novel's "founding claim," what distinguished it from personal
satire, was "the insistence that the referent of the text was a generalization about,
and not an extratextual, embodied instance of, a 'species.' "[46] Novels proved their
fictionality by not depicting actual (individual) people, as satires had done; they
proved their *reality* by depicting fictional (general) types. In so doing, they effectively reversed ordinary empirical assumptions. The general category—a
nonempirical abstraction deduced from real particulars in the world—became
the privileged "middle category," sandwiched between actual living persons and
highly particularized, fictional ones ("George Eliot" 61). Gallagher's "middle category," like Ferguson's "projected communal stance," is equivalent to Smith's
contentless "mediocrity"; all posit a social abstraction, a nonempirical generality,
as the organizing fiction on which fictional realism is grounded. But for this very
reason, fictional characters destined to become the most real, distinctive, or individual could not reside there for long. Gallagher represents character formation
as a triptych, with the general category bounded on either side by two ontologi-
cally distinct sets of particulars, real individuals and fictional individuals. Realist
characterization emerges out of the tension generated between these two poles.

Our passage from Trollope bears this out. Just as Paul seems "another case"
of the type—young men, like Sir Felix, with nothing to do—he is "not at all
like" the man who exemplifies the type.[47] The novel veers toward and away from
general classification, hurtling even apparent opposites into close proximity and
resemblance before driving a wedge between them. In a second example, Paul's
declaration that "[n]obody was like Roger Carbury," the "best man that ever lived
in the world," follows on the heels of the opposite assertion, which sees Roger
and his tenant, John Crumb, as "alike": both "pant[ing] for the companionship
of a fellow-creature whom each had chosen," both "thwarted" in his romantic

pursuits (Trollope 1:479, 439). Roger, like nobody else in the world, is like a relative nobody, a flour-dusted bumpkin. For Gallagher, this move is the hallmark
of realist characterization, which pits referential fidelity against realist ontology,
straining the effort for meaning against the effort to be. In *Middlemarch* (her example), the more distinctive Dorothea becomes, the more she edges away from
the real person on whom she is based—Saint Theresa of Avila—and the type to
which she initially belongs, Saint Theresas born since. At the novel's conclusion,
new instances of type appear (new Theresas), but so does an entirely new category, "Dorotheas," a general class made possible by Dorothea's having become
thoroughly particular—as real as she will ever be.

From this oscillation between generality and particularity, Gallagher draws
an important conclusion: fiction is the only place where Dorothea can gain particular embodiment, for fiction alone grants "nobodies" like her the specificity
that distinguishes them from the (fictional) generality out of which they emerge.
Fiction is where generalities can be realized, where abstractions gain human
dimension, shape. According to Gallagher, Eliot constructs character in this way
for a unique purpose, to provide readers something they might otherwise never
experience, "a *desire* to be real" ("George Eliot" 61, original emphasis). In so doing, Eliot participates in a larger nineteenth-century trend, a "massive redirec-
tion of longing away from disembodied transcendence and toward embodied
immanence," a yearning of spirit to become flesh (72). That momentum, shifting
away from generality toward being, shifts character toward what Gallagher calls
"the *fictionally* specific" and makes "compassionate particularization" the task of
novelist, reader, and character alike (68, 70, original emphasis). In *Middlemarch*,
Gallagher concludes, Eliot's "incarnation myth" presents a supple reworking of
the Feuerbachian insight that humans endow their gods with life. Now it is "a
disembodied spirit, the novel character," who "only craves to be" (73).

Realist characterization emerges as distinctly sympathetic. Rewriting "compassionate" as "sympathetic particularization" only increases our awareness that
a character's reality depends not only on the reader's animating sympathy but on
a sympathy born of form, by narrative arrangement rather than feeling as such.
But what Gallagher construes as an erotic desire for particular embodiment can
look, from the perspective of sympathy, like an incarnation story of a different
kind. We have already seen that the animation of conjectured selves is as much
the task of sympathy as it is of the realist novel; our sympathy grants Dorothea
human feeling that she, like Smith's corpse, can have in no other way. More
important still is what Eliot's, and Trollope's, and countless other realist novels
reveal to be the stakes involved in structuring character in this way. In designat-

ing *fictionally specific* embodiment as that which grants literary characters a reality they otherwise wouldn't possess—and in defining nonempirical categories (Dorotheas, young men with nothing to do) as the *fictionally general* basis for novelistic realism as a whole—these novels depend on a sympathetic understanding of character for whatever realism they acquire. Sympathy operates on both sides of the general/particular equation, for particularization is but one part of the imaginative work needed. Sympathetic *departicularization* anchors reality in the fictionally general, nonempirical field; "fellow-feeling" names the imaginative attitude that makes general categories, human types, feel real in the first place. An empty, fictive "nothing," it is where, as Smith saw it, the "particular regards which we feel for . . . individuals" are extrapolated into general care (*TMS* 89). It is through fellow-feeling, then, that sympathy *generates* the real rather than simply mirroring or describing it; sympathy forges those fictions of shared humanity ("Dorotheas") by way of which the world is made flesh. Eliot echoes this Smithian insight when she writes, "Through my union and fellowship with men I *have* seen, I feel a like, though a fainter, sympathy with those I have *not* seen; and I am able to live in imagination with the generations to come, that their good is not alien to me, and is a stimulus to me to labor for ends which will not benefit myself, but will benefit them."[48] Eliot's desire to live imaginatively with "generations to come" is undoubtedly an expression of her sympathy. But it is also a statement about mundane reality as she sought to depict it, as the fictive medium through which shared human experience—not just the realist novel—carries on.

Audrey Jaffe suggests that the nineteenth-century novel is "often concerned with the need to attend to, contend with, and even occasionally embrace the average within."[49] That desire makes the most sense once we see averages, mediocrities, and middles as exemplary in the ways just described. Embracing the average and gestures akin to it seem closely related to a phenomenon described by recent critics in terms of the counterfactual, "optative" tendencies of the realist novel. For some, this looks like a continual imagining of alternative, merely possible lives, visible at the margins of whatever particular life the novel captures in focused detail; for others, it involves a sense that what I share with others is my singularity, that what we hold in common is an attachment to just one body, just one life.[50] The realist novel's desire to cultivate alternatives to its own central plots, its habit of fantasizing about all the people its protagonists never turned out to be, should remind us that seeking after averages need not always be taken as proof of conservative difference-reduction. Shared separateness, group particularity: experiences of these, invoked as they are in the possible lives one has not lived or is not living (but might have, might yet), seem one more manifestation of a sympathetic reality in which even my sense of self is "oddly vicarious," my sentiments not merely my own but "called forth by other people" (A. Miller, "Lives" 59; *Burdens* 105). Gallagher gets at something similar when she writes that by making us imagine "not an independently living and breathing Dorothea, but instead an idea called Dorothea requiring that we conceive her bodily sensations to make her real," Eliot makes our own reality "newly desirable" ("George Eliot" 73). It is an accomplishment of realist characterization which reflects a sympathetic insight—that imagining the sensations of others enables us to feel real to ourselves.

CHAPTER 2

The Art of Knowing Your Own Nothingness

Bentham, Austen, and the Realist Case

PART I. SYMPATHY AND THE CASE FOR REALISM

The previous chapter characterized the reality represented in nineteenth-century fiction as irreducible to objects that may be said to exist outside human language and thought. Devoted instead to portraying the texture of experienced life—the grain of historical reality, in the past and in the present—the realist novel highlighted sympathy's role in maintaining social reality, from the seamless routines of ordinary living to the imaginative ability to inhabit other minds and distant places and times. By illuminating the sympathetic side of its historical project, we began to trace realism's attempt at making absent worlds come alive by enabling readers to "go along with" the mentalities of others, an ability that in turn made readers' own worlds the object of historical scrutiny (Smith, *TMS* 83). And we saw that the closer we regard all that conditions our experience of the real, the more the usefulness of affect, and fiction, increases: these become the privileged modes through which we communicate reality. As Wolfgang Iser has shown, the early nineteenth century saw a shift in empirical thought, wherein fiction was "upgraded" after a long association with mere lies (117). Depicting a world inaccessible to direct cognition, Humean skepticism ushered in a depreciation of knowledge that in turn granted imaginative processes increased significance. In such a world, reality requires fictive forms for its expression because conditions, not realities, are all that can be expressed. Softening the blow leveled by Hume's insight, Adam Smith emphasized the social character of meaning by turning sentiment into social currency. Feeling, he saw, tells us what is, insofar as others can be said to share it. For the realist novelists writing in the aftermath of such conclusions, reality would depend on the practice, and the central proposition, of sympathy—that what is true in a given moment is that which is collectively thinkable and can be felt as such.

This democratic imperative runs throughout the nineteenth-century realist novel, in part because its attention is focused on common people living ordinary lives, but also because the reality it represents relies for its existence on imaginative agreements of mind born of sympathetic thought. Thus, it is through sympathetic practices that these novels demand to be read. This chapter considers the relevance of Smithian sympathy to three authors connected by the innovations they brought to bear on "sympathetic realism" in several forms: in Jeremy Bentham's linguistic philosophy, Jane Austen's social realist fiction, and, in the twentieth century, in R. G. Collingwood's historical method. All three describe historical reality as a phenomenon for whose understanding sympathy was paramount. It is sometimes said that the realist novel educates its readers, and that realism, as "an instrument of moral education," enhanced understanding "by nurturing sympathy," "confirmed above all in the power to feel a common humanity at work in humble modes of life, petty aspirations, thwarted desire" (Adams, *History* 189). Populated with naive protagonists with hard lessons in store, there can be little doubt that providing a moral education is key to the realist novel's tutorial aims. But to argue that nineteenth-century realist form generates a sympathetic representational economy is to suggest that the education it provides is, like that of Bentham's Chrestomathic School, less focused on the objects of knowledge than on evaluative and reflective processes, sympathy first among them.[1] Training readers to hone their interpretive powers in an effort to decide what to think, how and how much to feel, the realists conceptualized "the real" relative to social feeling. Once reality is designated as that which humans have a hand in deciding, the real begins increasingly to consist of whatever ideas, sentiments, and attitudes can be (and are) held in common at a given moment.

The "case," a rhetorical form central to Smith's sympathetic operation, facilitates the realist project of imaginatively feeling out other places and times, other selves, and the alternative realities they imply. What Smith called putting yourself "in the case" of the other becomes vital to the experience of social reality as the realist novelists sought to depict it (*TMS* 12). As James Chandler suggests, the "case" in the eighteenth and nineteenth centuries functions as "a discourse, a genre, and a way of thinking" ("On the Face" 837). For the realists, a sentimentalized conception of the case form proved a key heuristic for achieving sympathetic aims. In the previous chapter, we began to see that considering a person's case makes her interesting, that her case—not her passion alone—causes us to care. The case is for that reason vital to cultivating what I call "sympathetic realism," that fiction of shared purpose and understanding underwriting the realist novel's appreciation of all that threatens to remain undervalued and unnoticed: "all those frivolous nothings" and mundane "little occurrences" that make up everyday life (*TMS* 41). As Ian Duncan suggests, there are two reasons why fiction, "tradition-ally stigmatized as inauthentic for its divergence from truth or fact," so success-fully becomes by the late eighteenth century "the mode of representation best fitted to render the 'nothing' that is the empirical domain of common life"—first, "because that 'nothing' had gone unremarked by the historical record," and sec-ond, "because that domain is itself already fictive, an intersubjective represen-tation sanctioned by custom" (*Shadow* 125). Combining these representational goals under the auspices of sympathetic realism (in Collingwood's case, "sympa-thetic historicism"), the writings explored in this chapter rely on cases to render the "nothingness" of others' feelings as well as our capacity to make them real to us.

Moreover, the Smithian case is instrumental for realizing a second, crucial feature of sympathy, the contribution it makes to human subjectivity. For Smith insists that our full experience of reality requires us to make cases of—to sympa-thize with—ourselves. Austen's *Persuasion* provides us with a striking instance of the benefits gained in sympathy with the self. More broadly, by examining their modifications of the case form, this chapter seeks to better gauge Smith's impact on the nineteenth-century realists who were, in different ways, making a case for the sympathetic organization of the real. Given that so few modern discourses have managed to get by without recourse to the language of the case, it is worth considering the extent to which a given realism's evaluative economy is shaped by the cases it makes available or denies.

Decomposed and Recomposed: Smith, Collingwood, and the Historical Case

> The historian's thought . . . neither contains nor involves any copy of its ob-ject. The historian's thought is, or rather contains as one of its elements, that object itself, namely the act of thought which the historian is trying to understand, re-thought in the present by himself.
>
> —R. G. Collingwood, *The Idea of History*

In *England in 1819,* James Chandler details an important moment in the history of the case form. Moving away from the moral cases of casuistry, the case in the Romantic period begins to be historicized. A unique species of example "organized as a historical state of affairs," the Romantic case situates events in particular places and times.[2] Adapted to portrayals of historical contingency, cases can thus be put to new purpose, including political reform. Chandler argues that writers like Jeremy Bentham outlined "a casuistry of the *general* will," a method for transforming the current state of affairs by conceiving England's political order as a case and, therefore, subject to alteration and improvement (239, original emphasis). He uses as an example Bentham's *Plan of Parliamentary Reform,* which suggests that a "historically determinate political system that structures situations for a given individual to inhabit can also be said to constitute a macrosituation for the will of the people itself" (238). Romantic historicism developed an understanding of the public will as an abstraction capable of being gauged but also shaped, given direction. For once history was seen as an arena of shifting norms, reality—now *social* reality—became subject to alteration. The Romantic case facilitated that goal by pressing beyond what mere examples could do. Rather than instantiating existing norms, it imaginatively projected times and places in which existing norms had been renovated or made obsolete. As Chandler explains, the case "is the place where what is realized is the process of judgment but not its result" (223).

Pivotal to this refashioning, Adam Smith had in the eighteenth century begun altering the case form inherited from casuistry. Having insisted that our sympathy with others arises not from direct contact with their feelings but from the imagination, and in particular from thoughtful consideration of the expressive situations in which those feelings arise, Smith shifted the focus away from what persons should be doing to what they *might* do, where they *are.* In so doing, Smith made what Chandler calls "a sentimental case against casuistry" (309). In a move that would guarantee the form's attractiveness to the pragmatic Bentham, Smith gave the case a practical focus: the conditions people actually inhabit. Smith's case in this way acts as a barometer of social feeling. Contemplating another's case involves thinking about audience, taking stock of how situations will generally be perceived; it is also conjectural, a way of imagining possible outcomes. As Frances Ferguson has shown, Bentham was one among many writers of his time seeking to explain the role of social feeling, necessarily expressed through means other than direct personal testimony. Collective will, she argues, was the only genuine political authority for Bentham because, as a "general repository of social regard," it governed by way of impersonal feeling, available (theoretically) to all ("Beliefs" 250). As we began to see in the last chapter, it was through sympathy that individuals contributed to and drew from that general fund. And Smith's sympathetic case was designed to negotiate between the real, experienced conditions in which people lived and an abstract social feeling governing the rules of behavior. In Chandler's view, however, Smith's transformation of the case readies it for a historicism not fully realized until the Romantic period. Smith's cases, still more moral than historical, would not be fully adapted to historicism until writers like Percy Shelley and Sir Walter Scott came along to finish the job.

This idea is worth revisiting. For Smith develops his new conception of the case at a time when history was being aggressively sentimentalized. Before turning our full attention to Bentham, then, we will first consider the historicizing elements of Smith's case by comparing it to a twentieth-century historiography with which it shares common features. As we now know, Smith makes narrative essential to the workings of sympathy. "Case" is his preferred term for the situations inspiring sympathy, as these are reconstructed in the stories we tell in representing others' feelings to ourselves. As Robert Mitchell notes, sympathy in Smith's hands becomes a high-powered descriptive machine, propagating itself "by accommodating ever more examples of its central claims" (89). Unlike Hume, who attempted in *A Treatise of Human Nature* to refine his readers' proficiency for systematic thought, Smith encouraged "perpetually mobile attentiveness to the ways in which sympathy ordered particular situations."[3] As a result, *TMS* reads like a series of narrative vignettes. Its cases illuminate the workings of sympathy in descriptions of ordinary life.

Trained on experiential reality, not moral norms, Smith's sympathetic case becomes instrumental for the task of historicizing the everyday. Turning other people's (real) sentiments into the stuff of story, the sympathetic case optimizes our moral capacities by cultivating a kind of historical awareness that might be considered novelistic. Hume thought history an "invention" useful for "extend[ing] our experience" beyond ourselves, "to all past ages" and to minds unlike our own.[4] But in refashioning the case for the imaginative projection of other times and alternative selves, Smith intended equally to make us care about ordinary reality in ways that moral norms, the cases of casuistry, never could. Moreover, because Smithian sympathy abstracts feeling into narrative, the case could easily be adopted to other, more explicitly historical projects—say, tracking how feeling travels from one era to the next or gauging the conditions in which societies (including our own) form, uphold, or dispense with certain attitudes and beliefs.[5]

In his historical writing, Smith's cases emphasize the congruity of the mental processes involved in sympathetic and historicizing thought. As Mark Salber Phillips says of Smith's *Lectures in Rhetoric and Belles Lettres*, Smith "assimilates history . . . to narrative" as part of "a serious attempt to produce a theory of history in which narrative effects rather than moral examples would be key" ("Belletrist"

71–72). Though Phillips bristles at the suggestion that Smith had novels in mind, he agrees that history and narration were "more or less interchangeable terms for Smith" and that Smithian history, though oriented toward fact, is also "in some measure the narrative of things unseen."[6] Those unseen forces were human sentiments. As Smith explains, historians are concerned with "two different Sorts of facts," the first "externall, [and] consisting of the transactions that pass without us, and the other internall, to wit the thoughts sentiments or designs of men, which pass in their minds." The "Design of History," he concludes, is "compounded of both" (*Lectures*, Glasgow ed. 84). Smith writes admiringly of how Tacitus, ostensibly a most unsentimental historian, relates events "rather by the internall effects" they produce: he "leads us so far into the sentiments and mind of the actors" that even in describing "the more important actions he does not give us an account of their externall causes, but only of the internall ones." Though he worries that this strategy "perhaps will not tend so much to instruct us in the knowledge of the causes of events," Smith decides that "it will be more interesting," perhaps inaugurating a "usefull" "science" equipped to deal with "the motives by which men act" (121). In this sympathetic "science," the historian seeks to reconstruct, and so comprehend, the sentiments giving rise to historical events. To do so, he makes past mentalities come alive by setting them in motion in the minds of the present.

Throughout this process, feeling remains imaginary. The history of "internall" causes is "interesting" even when (as is likely) the feelings animating the past remain largely if not entirely unfelt in the present. Historians must think about the sentiments underlying historical action; the goal is to inhabit the conditions of mind out of which human actions arise. And the more history comes to be associated with the production of such narrative effects, the more important sympathy becomes for reconceiving the role of feeling in historical life. Smith's sentimentalized case weds narrative effects to affect in such a way that he begins to historicize feeling itself: the effort to situate others into cases flows in the reverse direction; bringing the sentiments of others to bear on one's own, a historicist conception of feeling results. Claiming that history involves sympathetic understanding—in revivifying the "designs" ordering past attitudes and the "motives" underlying past behavior—compels us to acts of mental reconstruction that turn our own patterns of thought and feeling into historical evidence. As Chandler maintains, "[t]o be able to make a case of one's own time is to imagine it otherwise constituted. But it is also in some important way to cease to be able to imagine the cases of one's own time as the cases of another time" (*England* 240).

The example of R. G. Collingwood suggests that modern historiography owes a debt to this conception of sympathy, as revealed in the reconstructive, case-based practices he recommends. Collingwood's theory of history is itself a reconstruction, gleaned from a selection of his writings (many now lost) and published posthumously in 1946 as *The Idea of History*. The historian as Collingwood describes him attends to traditional sources of evidence (facts, events, and so on) in all the ways one would expect, but what matters is what historians do with that evidence. Successful historicism in Collingwood's view requires mental "*re-enactment*" of the past.[7] Because the past is always "ideal," being "wholly and utterly non-existent" except to the mind, the only "actuality" exists in the manner of thinking historians craft. The historian's thought "neither contains nor involves any copy of its object" but "is, or rather contains as one of its elements, that object itself, namely the act of thought which the historian is trying to understand, re-thought in the present by himself." "We understand what Newton thought by thinking—not *copies* of his thoughts," Collingwood insists, "but his thoughts themselves over again" (450). "Re-enactment" cannot return the dead to life, but it can, "without any necromancy," revive a past event, so long as "that event is itself a thought" (Collingwood 444).

Most significant for our purposes is the proposal that historical thinking re-creates without copying its object, the "act of thought" motivating historical actors, through what we have identified as a sympathetic form of imagining. One thinks not merely *of what* others thought but *as* they thought. Moreover, their ways of thinking are the object pursued because, unlike events (which are dead and gone), these are already representational and for that reason can be renewed in living minds. Collingwood repeatedly states that the mere exposition of historical fact deadens history, whereas reviving the perspectives of historical actors—beliefs and opinions held, ways of justifying them and acting on their behalf—could make history a vibrant and perpetual project. In "all cases where the history in question is the history of thought," Collingwood concludes, "a literal re-enactment of the past is possible and is an essential element in all history" (444).

Implicit in this claim is that it is *as* a case—indeed as a sympathetic case—that one reenacts the past. Facts alone do not suffice; historical reenactment makes the sympathetic case an indispensable imaginative tool. And though Collingwood understands that some historical undertakings do not revive the sentiments of historical actors, his method poses an argument against them. For in failing to attend to the sentimental contexts in which the events of history take place—the attitudes shaping their development, giving rise to their occurrence and reception—the historian fails to achieve the kind of understanding that counts, an awareness of "what principles guided the persons whose actions he is studying." The historian should not assume that these principles "have always been the same." Putting himself into the cases of others frees the historian from the error of materialist history. Furthermore, because every event, "so far as that event is an expression of human thought," implies "a conscious reaction to a situation, not the effect of a cause," Collingwood's method represents historical actors as actively conditioning historical reality (475). That point bears repeating. Recovering the mentalities of past actors in situ presupposes their deliberate involvement in shaping the worlds in which they lived.

Collingwood's call for historical reenactment situates sympathy squarely at the heart of historiographical method. Because "the past as past has no existence whatever, consisting as it does of occurrences no longer occurring, events that have finished happening," it is, like the feelings of others, an idea existing nowhere except in the mind (475). It might seem wrong to compare living people's feelings to those of the dead, as though each were equally nonexistent, but Smith saw that insofar as they could gain social reality, by becoming alive to others, both were reenacted in identical ways. Collingwood's premises are in some ways radically unlike Smith's, yet both solved a skeptical problem using similar tactics, describing the sympathetic imagination as key to making otherwise inaccessible realities present to the mind. To be clear, Collingwood was (from the standpoint of philosophy) an antirealist; he believed unmediated access to reality impossible. Yet for this very reason his goals are consistent with those of nineteenth-century fictional realism as we have so far described it. Indeed, Collingwood, an admirer of Sir Walter Scott, thought of the past in ways not unlike those discussed in the previous chapter. Insisting that it "cannot be a single self-contained body of fact awaiting discovery," Collingwood characterizes the past as "a growing and changing body of thoughts, decomposed and recomposed by every new generation of historical workers." The "exhaustibility of historical fact," he declared, "is an illusion" (456).

Convinced that this "body of thoughts" is an inexhaustible resource, Collingwood articulates a theory of history that had already been understood, in the early decades of the nineteenth century, to involve a sympathetic enterprise. Then, the sympathetic case, equally inexhaustible, proved a useful vehicle for "decomposing and recomposing" the real in the ways Collingwood describes. Putting Collingwood in the company of the realists thus clarifies the role of sympathy in their similar portrayals of historical reality. Like him, the novelists considered in this book objected to a realism without predicates, to a belief that the real exists independently of how it is known.[8] The basic fact of existence is, in Collingwood's view, not "a real predicate," for it "fails to describe an object in any way"; objects without predicates other than existence cannot be understood "since we cannot say anything about them other than that they are" ("Robin George Collingwood"). For Collingwood, as for the writers to whom I turn next, the real remained inexplicable without recourse to predicates, the conditions through which reality is conceived.

In examining Bentham's grammatical case, we will see that his theory of language is informed by a similarly sympathetic logic, expressed at the level of syntax. A committed positivist, Bentham never embraced the extreme skepticism of Smith and Hume. And yet, as Iser explains, he felt that there could be "no reality that is not based on modality"; instead, the imagination "spins out of itself those fictions that make real entities into facts of life" (125). Bentham was one of several early-nineteenth-century thinkers for whom fiction was paramount for conceiving the "facts of life," the shared assumptions and routine ways of thinking organizing ordinary human experience. Further securing the link between sympathy and reality, Bentham's grammatical writings call attention to the contentlessness of language and the sympathetic processes that fill it up. Emptying words of any direct connection to the things they describe, Bentham continued working through the perceived gap between reality and our experiences of it.[9] He sought better to understand those fictions of language that made it possible to share our sentiments with others—with the result that, as Iser puts it, "reality is gradually replaced by the world" (126).

Subjects and Predicates: Bentham and the Grammatical Case

> Does a predicate transform the subject into an object? . . . Is *being* a predicate? Is *being* something a subject can *have* and remain a subject?
> —Barbara Johnson, *Persons and Things*

"I think, therefore I know the rules of grammar." Barbara Johnson rewrites the Cartesian formula this way so as to call attention to that formula's missing predicate, the fact that for Descartes, thinking is enough: *what* one thinks is, apparently, irrelevant (50). By the time we get to Bentham, predication has taken on new significance and the definition of consciousness has changed. As Iser suggests, once philosophy had decided that real bodies "never present themselves as raw data but are always in a state of conditionality," predication alone could communicate the real because the real was communicable only in the modes of its presentation (120). To put it another way, once presence "means being enveloped in something else, because real bodies evidently cannot specify themselves or give themselves presence," realities are "just as dependent upon connections as predicates are, for without this interdependence the former would remain sealed off and the latter would be a phantasm" (121). The result, impossible for Descartes, is that consciousness legitimizes fiction; no longer reality's opposite, fiction offers a means for accessing it.[10] This explains why fiction, *as* fiction, gained new value in the period. In describing the qualities of the real, fiction alone made it coherent. But fiction could do so only insofar as its fictiveness was an openly acknowledged fact.

Throughout his life Bentham held that there was a difference between extra-linguistic realities and their discursive classifications, but he saw the two merging in real-world practice. Reality without recourse to the fictions of language was impossible to access. As Iser puts it, the only reality one could "talk about" was that of "discourse-related real entities."[11] Carefully studying the behavior of language, Bentham believed, helped us to better understand reality, as particular modes of thinking were "embalmed" in it (Yntema 1082). It is unsurprising then that Bentham's interest in parts of speech led him to the grammatical case, to its unfolding of subjects from predicates, the circumstantiality of its operation. As Chandler observes, the grammatical case reveals "the 'fallenness' of our words," their declension from "upright," nominative positions into partiality, conditions, contexts (*England* 348). We "can think of 'the case' as involving a fall," he says, one "precipitated . . . by predication itself": "By a kind of Hegelian logic, in which the subject establishes itself only in falling from itself into objectivity, one might say that the rectitude of the nominative case, though in one sense the starting point of a predication, is itself equally a result of predication. In producing the accusative case, predication also produces the case from which it marks a lapse. We call this a lapse into circumstance, into occasionality, into 'caseness' as such" ("Theory" n.p.). Falling from "erect" into "oblique" positions, subjects slip into direct objects, predicates, situations. But falling into predication is also how they *become* subjects. The fallenness of a subject—into conditions, into caseness—produces the fiction of its integrity, the "rectitude" it ostensibly lost.[12]

As we saw in chapter 1, Smith put the sympathetic case to identical use in producing two important fictions of integrity, human subjectivity and the social reality that makes it possible. There, too, what seemed the starting point of predication was its result. The human subject's "fall" into representation—his making a case of, an *idea* of himself, by projecting other minds—enabled his having a self at all. With this in mind, we turn to Bentham, a man who spent his life thinking of cases, grammatical and legal. He found cases especially useful for revealing the semantic relationships by way of which reality is constructed. In "Fragments on Universal Grammar," Bentham describes a noun substantive as an entity "susceptible of a multitude of relations as towards other entities." "When it is viewed in the character of the subject, or the predicate of a proposition, there is continual occasion for giving expression to those relations," he says. In the oblique case, nouns act as predicates; in the nominative case the noun acts as subject, expressing "the subject of the proposition, the minor terminus, the subject in which motion commences." The grammatical case form is labile, equipped with "starting-points" and termini, signifying "situation, either quiescent, or the result of motion." Cases are "goal-expressing," indicating human intent (n.p.). This idea of substantives as positioned in relation to beginnings and (desired) ends is crucial for understanding the special qualities of Bentham's grammatical case: it is sentiment-laden, expressive of attitudes and will; it situates subjects into the contexts out of which their meanings, their very rectitude, derive. Chandler exemplifies this point in describing the formal symmetry of cases grammatical and historical: the first "situates nouns in predication" while the second situates "agents in events" (*England* 348).

Case-thinking filters throughout Bentham's most striking grammatical innovations. Long fascinated by the expository function of language, Bentham wanted to know how real phenomena correlated to the metaphors and other figures of speech commonly used to describe them. It was for this purpose that Bentham invented the expository device of "paraphrasis," developed from his conviction that "substantives gain their meaning, even when they have no real reference, by the context of the whole sentence in which they appear" (Bender 214). Though they were nouns or parts of speech acting like nouns, substantives, Bentham came to discover, contained nothing in themselves. Some had "no real reference" at all, for they designated fictional entities rather than real ones. Such substantives could not be sufficiently explained by a word-for-word replacement that swapped a single term for another.[13] One needed paraphrasis, which first positioned a word into "some whole *sentence* of which it forms a part," then translated the whole into "another *sentence*" (Bentham, "Government" n.p.). Paraphrasis facilitated meaning in two ways, by placing words into expressive contexts (sentences) and by fashioning new sentences as alternatives to the first. What Bentham's case demonstrated at the grammatical level, paraphrasis highlighted about exposition generally—that word values are mobile "occurrences," arising not from substances but syntax; that "sentences, not individual words, are primary integers in the analysis of meaning" (Bender 214). Dependent for their meanings on discursive environments, words gathered substance incrementally, as they were repurposed in a limitless arena of language production. To a project Locke had begun in separating words from things, Bentham added the insight that linguistic meaning depended on use, on cases and expressive contexts.[14]

Grammar was, for this reason, a conduit of human desire. Underwriting the assertion that words aggregated their meanings through use was the supposition that grammar bore the imprints of human intention, that sentences charted the comings and goings of affect. As Emmanuelle de Champs writes, paraphrasis "must make the source and recipient of pleasure or pain obvious."[15] Bentham's theory embedded sentiment into grammar so that actions in the world and the meanings of words in sentences are seen to be mutually informing concerns.[16] But if we are not surprised to find in Bentham's grammar a version of the felicific calculus—the happiness formula for which he is famous—the pleasures and pains of paraphrasis are surprisingly unrealized and unfelt. As Bentham explains, paraphrasis concerns "the idea of eventual sensation": *anticipated* feeling rather than feeling as such ("Logic" n.p.). Catherine Gallagher lists Smith and Bentham together as philosophers for whom happiness and enjoyment are "the ultimate values," but it is the tacit, simulated feeling of sympathy, more than experienced sensation, that guides the paraphrastic process.[17] Calculated "to raise *images* either of *substances* perceived, or of *emotions*," the two "sources" from which "every idea must be drawn," paraphrasis could elucidate the path of pain and pleasure, but it did not have to make anyone feel anything (Bentham, "Government" n.p., original emphasis). It needed to accomplish a sympathetic realism, raising "images" of emotions internal to language so that the ideas they prompted could be passed on.

This demand in turn had several important implications. For feeling to be anticipated or recovered, it could not be conceived of as personal property; nor could extant feeling sufficiently explain (or lead to) sympathetic engagement. Like Smith before him, Bentham defined sympathy not first in terms of feeling but of "interest": "in the case of *sympathy, conjugates* of the word *interest* are employed, and even the word itself," he writes, offering this as an example: "*There stands a man, in whose behalf I feel myself strongly interested*" (*Springs* 16). And if language was the vehicle through which feelings *as* ideas were communicated, paraphrasis communicated that ideational feeling in a unique way. According to the *Oxford English Dictionary* (2nd ed.), "paraphrasis" involves a "rewording of something written or spoken by someone else," but Bentham gave its social and productive qualities added emphasis: it "present[s] exactly the same import, but without containing in it a word belonging to the part of speech thus undertaken to be expounded," he explained ("Grammar" n.p.). As Ross Harrison writes, statements like this one suggest that paraphrasis is the source of linguistic meaning, not a further clarification of it: "the analysis gives meaning or import to the original." A kind of sympathetic case, paraphrasis is the means through which human feeling and intention become meaningful by, in Bentham's words, being "illustrated" and thus "rendered intelligible" (in Harrison 72). Paraphrastic reconstruction allows the "import" of words, the senses intended by their users, to grow palpable to the understanding. Only by paraphrastic "rewording" could original sentiments be revived and communicated. Moreover, because it did not simply copy an original, but required new users and parts of speech, paraphrasis could "be termed . . . development" (Bentham, "Grammar" n.p.).

Consider "phraseoplerosis," the expository activity by which paraphrasis is completed, and involving what Bentham calls the "filling up" of one phrase by another.[18] Once again, meaning occurs both cumulatively and retroactively. A fictional concept like "obligation," having taken on "the character of the subject of a proposition," gains the predicate that gives it definition: "[t]aking the name of the subject for the *basis*, by the addition of this predicate, *incumbent on a man*, and the copula *is*, the phrase is completed" ("Logic" n.p., original emphasis). But phraseoplerosis also anticipates affective futures. An "obligation" is binding "in so far as, in the event of [a man's] failing to conduct himself in that manner, pain, or loss of pleasure, is considered as *about to be experienced* by him" ("Exposition" 55, emphasis added). Here too, fictional subjects gain a kind of virtual reality through acts of predication, as do—with important real-life effects—the injunctions they make on human behavior. Here too, one understands the meaning and import of words by anticipating their potential emotional effects. Even questions of fact involved such work. One had to consider "the strength of a man's *persuasion* in relation to this or that fact" in ascertaining the certainty of it; for when "a man is himself persuaded . . . of the existence of a fact, it is a matter of pain and vexation to him to suppose that this same persuasion fails of being entertained" by others (*Theory* 56–58, original emphasis). Facts are subject to a sentimental calculus in which sympathy plays a crucial part, and not only because "pain and vexation" may result when fellow-feeling (a "same persuasion") fails to develop. For filling up one phrase with another involves acts of figuration closely aligned with the sympathetic process and derived from the same fundamental premise: that to understand how people think, what they mean, one must anticipate, project, or imagine their feelings—but need not feel them. Communicating the complete thoughts, the propositions of speakers, meant reconstructing the feelings that underwrote their meanings, but one needed sentences, not feelings, to do it. Nor could single words effectively convey emotion or illustrate states of human affairs. Words devoid of the projected, imagined feeling embedded in grammar conveyed nothing at all. "[T]ake away *pleasures* and *pains*," Bentham explains, and even words such as "happiness" devolved into "so many empty sounds" (*Springs* 3).

As Bender sees it, it is "a short step" from Bentham's theory of paraphrasis to a theory of fictional realism in which the goal of total visibility was paramount. The monitorial system of Bentham's Chrestomathic Day School, he says, conceives realism as the "ultimate representational system."[19] True, Bentham saw as the purpose of exposition "the exclusion or expulsion of unclearness in any shape" (*Theory* 76). But if there is transparency of any kind, it is emotional transparency: "pain and pleasure," Bentham quips, "are words which a man has no need, we may hope, to go to a lawyer to know the meaning of" ("Government" n.p.). Yet not even feeling is so self-evident. If it were, there would be no need for the sympathetic protocols that make reconstituting the sentences and the sentiments of others seem like variations of the same imaginative process. Indeed, a reenactment similar to that taking place in Collingwood's historical case occurs whenever language communicates the only thing that, according to Bentham, it can, the propositions of mind of which our words are merely the remnants. For language, consisting of "decomposed" thoughts, was the corpselike remainder of living ideas; words were "formed by the decomposition of propositions," and letters by "the decomposition of words" (*Theory* 74). Meaning thus involved ceaseless acts of linguistic reanimation. Mental fragments required new sentences; letters demanded regrouping and arrangement to reconstitute the human feeling buried beneath. As the next section demonstrates more fully, it is in this recognition that Bentham's linguistic theory most clearly extends the narrativizing work of sympathy later recast, in similar ways, by Collingwood. In the writings of both, an otherwise inaccessible reality gains new life and renewed significance through an imaginative sympathy through which we revive the sentiments of others by rewriting their sentences in our own minds.

Beardmore's Blues: Bentham's Theory of Fictions

O that I could decompose myself like a polypus. Could I make half a dozen selfs, I have work for all.

—Jeremy Bentham, *Memoirs*

Bentham's most lasting legacy, his "theory of fictions," was pieced together from his collected writings on legal, linguistic, and philosophical subjects, and published in 1932 by the philosopher C. K. Ogden, who was credited with rescuing Bentham from obscurity.[20] Ranking him "sixth in line" after Bacon, Hobbes, Locke, Berkeley, and Hume (and before Mill), Ogden describes Bentham as both an underrated philosopher and a kind of exorcist, writing in the section entitled "Spectres and Bogeys" that even Bentham's servants knew the man to be haunted by "the subject of ghosts" (introduction xi). In Ogden's biographical account, that subject recurs in Bentham's later life where, as a legal scholar, he devoted himself to ridding the courts of the bogeys of legal fictions. Ogden treats his fear of ghosts as the "grim foundation" out of which sprang Bentham's long campaign against fiction: the unreality, fraud, and chicanery embedded into language and law (xv).[21]

The man who asked that his corpse be publicly dissected and turned into an "auto-icon"—a self-representation—so that the dead might benefit the living had a long interest in that which pointed only to itself, existing as it did in language alone. The ghostly forms that in the last section didn't seem so terrible posed serious threats when they infected a body of laws, where "an improper word would be a national calamity," with civil war as one possible consequence. As Ogden points out, much of Bentham's "best work on language" was done in the year of Waterloo, and all of it was composed during the Napoleonic wars and "the distressful years which followed" (introduction cxlviii). According to John Bowring, Bentham's original editor, no one paid much attention at the time to "the small still voice of one weighing the meaning of words used," a voice that was "even less heeded when the storm had died down" (introduction 41). Yet Bentham's belief that "[out] of one foolish word may start a thousand daggers" reflects these conditions, which in turn explain his urgent sense of the damage words could do (quoted in Ogden, introduction cxlviii).

Ogden's introduction to *Bentham's Theory of Fictions* concludes with an epitaph, a ghost story of sorts appearing first in *Chrestomathia* under the heading "the Effects of Ennui."[22] The story derives from the obituary of one John Beardmore, who died in 1814 (the year *Persuasion's* plot begins). With religion "hanging by a thread," Bentham was convinced that the best advantage of educational reform lay in the "diffusion of Truth," says Ogden, yet truth alone could not cure one of modernity's special ills, a disease "characterized by restlessness in retirement" and resulting from "insufficient intellectual stimulus in youth, maturity, and middle age." Copying Beardmore's obituary into his text, Bentham illustrates the disease in question. Ogden appends to the whole a title, calling it "The Sad Case of Mr. Beardmore." For the disease, he invents a name to match, dubbing it *"Beardmore's Blues"* (introduction cxliv, original emphasis).

John Beardmore, so the story goes, was an industrious man of humble beginnings, rising from clerk to partner in the brewery firm "Calvert and Co., in Red Cross-street, London." Apparently he was himself hardly haunted at all. Beardmore, his obituary explains, "had passed his grand climacteric with less visitation from indisposition of mind or body than happens to man in general." Yet neither "confirmed health" nor "independent property," an "amiable wife" or the company of friends, can sustain Beardmore after his retirement from business (*Chrestomathia* 85). He succumbs to "*désoeuvrement*," Bentham's word—for which "the English language furnishes no equivalent"—for a condition in which the mind sees "nothing to be done, nothing in the shape of business or amusement which promises either security against pain or possession of pleasure" ("Chrestomathic Instruction" n.p.). The moral of the story is clear enough: inactive men weaken, then perish. Yet in detailing how his "want of customary application" brought with it a "train of evils" with death as the caboose, Beardmore's story returns us to a by now familiar undercurrent of concern. "Beardmore's Blues" denotes an especially "Sad Case" in that it diagnoses a kind of mental paralysis, an "unworking," a "*taedium vitae*" from which no feeling can issue, and interest cannot penetrate (ibid.). A subject without a predicate, Beadmore foresees nothing but the promise of more of the same, a deadly decomposition that comes of having nothing to do with oneself. And it appears to be catching. Beardmore's Blues might be another, no less nefarious version of what, in the year of his death, afflicts *Persuasion*'s Anne Elliot, a case of nothing-left-to-be-done (or said) threatening to reduce her to unmarried, useless oblivion.

We shall return to *Persuasion* later. For now, it is important to see "Beardmore's Blues" as shorthand for a problem Bentham considered widespread, an "endemical disease" of the era (Ogden, introduction cxlv). As Bentham maintains, he who resolves "not to have anything to do with new words, resolves by that very resolution to confine himself to the existing stock of ideas and opinions, how great soever the degree of incorrectness, imperfection, error, and mischievousness which may in those ideas and opinions happen to be involved" (*Bentham's Theory* 140). Without new words, persons (and cultures) made sad cases indeed, committing themselves to intellectual graves. While "Beardmore's Blues" is Odgen's invention, a product of "modern methods of nomenclature" as he says, Bentham too was a "linguistic innovator" (introduction cxxxix). He may have had a beef against verbs—a grammatical form "he considered dangerous" (cxlii)—and distrusted personification ("usually regarded as harmless," but for Bentham an "[instrument] of delusion") ("Constitutional" n.p.). Yet Bentham saw linguistic innovation as a means of personal and national survival. Beardmore was no great intellectual, having "no relish" for the "dull sedentary investigations of abstract science," the classics, or moral philosophy; yet he grows fatally "conscious of a vacuum, that, alas! his want of intellectual resources rendered him utterly unable to supply" (Ogden, introduction cxlvi). Thus, says Ogden, Bentham "treats us to [Beardmore's] sad story in order to recommend [a] remedy," the "cultivation of the intellectual garden in general, and of the linguistic and fictional in particular" (cxlv).

This may seem a curious recommendation from someone who felt threatened by verbs. But Bentham's zeal for invention derived from a conviction that language (particularly legal) stood in desperate need of overhaul. As Angela Esterhammer writes, the idea "that language does not merely describe reality, but that it affects, shapes, alters, or constructs reality, appears regularly in linguistic, moral, political, and legal philosophy from the 1780s to the 1820s."[23] Committed to puzzling out how language authorizes the things it purports to exemplify (in legal discourse, the term means "to copy"), Bentham found it full of ghostly forms with no clear reference, pointing not to realities but to qualities of mind. Language is "the sign of thought, an instrument for the communication of thought from one mind to another." Further, it is "the sign . . . of the thought which is in the mind of him by whom the discourse is uttered." Language may be the sign of "other things and other objects," but "of this object"—thought—"it is always a sign, and it is only through this that it becomes the sign of any other object" ("Language" n.p.). Even in statements like "that apple is ripe" or "apples are good," where something other than the mind is the subject of discourse, "yet in neither of them is it the immediate subject." The apple is a "receptacle" into which the "imaginary, fictitious entity called a *quality*—is lodged" ("Logic" n.p., original emphasis).

Whether I describe my corporeal feelings (hunger, thirst) or objects external to me, in "both these cases," Bentham insists, the "immediate subject is no other than the state of my own mind—an opinion entertained by me in relation to the ulterior object or subject."[24] Less open to error in describing our physiological states, the attempt to describe things outside ourselves, even the sources of sensation, is more precarious: "from that moment," he says, "I am liable to fall." Exposition precipitates a fall into human sentiment, attitude, and perception; that "common" "infirmity" worsens the more "the state of the speaker's mind intervenes, precedes, introduces, and weakens the ulterior assertion which lies beyond it." Yet this infirmity, the ghost in the machine, is impossible to do without. Meaning may be subject to *désoeuvrement* the more language reflects a speaker's mind rather than whatever "lies beyond it," but it cannot be transmitted at all without expressing "the state[s] of [our] own mind[s]." Since language routes through sentiment the realities "ulterior" to it, fiction—and here I would add, sympathy—is, as Bentham concludes, "a necessary resource" (*Bentham's Theory* 71–73).

Bentham's excoriations on the subject of legal fictions are notorious. So charged with disapproval are the metaphors Bentham chose to characterize them that the whole business can seem quite laughable: legal fictions are the thief's pick-lock, the rattlesnake's fangs, the tiger's claws, a hatchet, a stealing power, an engine, a labyrinth, and "a syphilis, which runs in every vein, and carries into every part of the system the principle of rottenness" ("Scotch Reform" n.p.). Marjorie Stone has called his campaign against English legal fictions "more violent, more sustained, and in many ways, more far-reaching in its effects" than his assault on poetry, which he called "a more deceiving game than pushpin" (125). Obscuring the workings of the law, legal fictions corrupted the courtroom proceedings of which they were a common part. If the newly instituted policy of holding public hearings marked a step forward in the push for greater transparency, Bentham continued to insist that "[f]iction, tautology, technicality, circuitry, irregularity, [and] inconsistency" remained (Harrison 24). Targeting Sir William Blackstone's *Commentaries on the Laws of England* (1765–69), Bentham set out to show that legal fictions—along with all manner of procedural devices—clouded the processes they presumed to clarify by making it impossible to tell true statements from false. Louise Harmon explains it this way: a procedural legal fiction (the easiest to define) was "a false allegation of fact" that all participants acknowledged as false; it involved the pretense that a fact, *if* true, "would have led to a desired result under the existing rules of law" (2). An especially terrible legal fiction was that of civil death, whereby convicted criminals, losing their civil rights, effectively ceased to exist. For women, the law of coverture produced a similar effect. With no legal status after marriage, women became little more than ghosts.[25]

Yet legal fictions were a pernicious type of that more common category. Where Bentham would define a "fictitious entity" as an object whose existence "is feigned by the imagination, feigned for the purposes of discourse, and which, when so formed, is spoken of as if a real one," he writes in "Essay on Language" with the understanding that language flounders without recourse to things "as if" from life. It is "to language alone . . . that fictitious entities owe their existence; their impossible, yet indispensable, existence" (*Bentham's Theory* 15). Fictitious entities were not lies, but they were "impossible" in that they were real only to the mind. Fictitious entities (which were "indispensable") were therefore like legal fictions (which were not) in that both had utility: each imparted substance to imagined things, making it feel "as if" they existed. Describing Bentham's dilemma, Isobel Armstrong writes, as "[f]orms of words are substituted for arguments," they gain shape along with explanatory momentum; this in turn conceals from the listener "the nothingness" of the arguments that lie beneath (149). Legal fictions were objectionable because they were treated as if they described an extralinguistic reality when there was, in fact, "nothing" behind them.

Yet Bentham strenuously argues on behalf of the power of that nothing. Springing to life from nothing, fictions could change the course of human action, directly affecting our experience of the world. Thus, he worried about the efficacy of legal fictions in places like courtrooms, whose cases could produce damaging results. It was their portability into and out of different cases and contexts that raised Bentham's polemical hackles. While Blackstone worried that, without legal fictions, the general rule of law might get in the way of law-keeping, in Bentham's view the legal fiction was a "willful falsehood, uttered by a judge, for the purpose of giving injustice the colour of justice," one part of what Harrison calls "a whole system of artificial devices, developed in the interests of the class of lawyers" (24). Painting them with the Gothic colors of a remote and "venerable" past, Blackstone had characterized legal fictions as "difficult" but benign.[26] But for Bentham, their labyrinthine character served as reminder of the way fictions of all kinds systematically wormed their way into every aspect of language, which depended for its usefulness on the nothingness, the "as if," of fiction.[27]

Several critics have demonstrated the importance of fiction to the realism Bentham develops, and many more have noted his concern with pleasure and pain, yet it is sympathy that most effectively combines the two into a single project. For Bentham, on whom Smith's influence has long been recognized, sympathy was inextricable from the mental processes by which the real is substantiated, and fictional language the medium through which reality and feeling were frequently joined. As he saw it, the ability to represent other minds was a necessary precondition for understanding once reality was available only through discourse, and only insofar as discursive forms conveyed the pleasures and pains of its human practitioners. Describing that reality as one in which "real bodies move into presence by way of predication and representation," Iser depicts a set of conditions for which sympathy is paramount.[28] Like Smith, Bentham thought self-consciousness impossible absent the ability to turn oneself into parts of speech. Bentham tells a version of a story we heard in chapter 1, in which Smith describes the impoverished subjectivity of a man utterly deprived of social awareness. Lacking an "idea of other people," he could form no idea of himself; hence, he had no self at all (*TMS* 193). Making a nearly identical claim, Bentham suggests that without recourse to language, humans lose more than the ability to communicate. The "stock of [our] own ideas," he insists, "would in point of number [be] as nothing," one's thoughts "as flitting and indeterminate as those of the animals" ("Logic" n.p.). This might seem to be a claim about the priority of language, not sympathy, for human thought and expression, except that linguistic and sympathetic representation can now be understood as two versions of a parallel figurative act. For we find that a sympathetic imperative underwrites Bentham's premise that what remains "nothing" from an empirical standpoint is, from a practical perspective, real. The effort to form ideas of ourselves and others involves a social view of reality in conjunction with a sympathetic understanding of language use. Bentham would have agreed with two of Smith's most fundamental propositions: that I rely on the sympathy of others to grant substance to my ideas, which in turn enables me to feel real to myself; that in my sympathy with others, I rely on fiction to grant their feeling a reality it can have for me in no other way.

In this way, Bentham contributes to a new conception of verisimilitude, one in which the bare mention of things alone fails to capture what experienced reality is really like. In Armstrong's estimation, Bentham's theory of fictions proved to be a successful aesthetic theory because it attempted "to explain and understand the *effectiveness* of fictions"; it "neither consolidated pure representation" (the nominalist position) "nor identified the sign and the thing signified" (150, original emphasis). For Kenneth Burke, Bentham's fictions "fall under the head of *ethics* and *form* rather than *knowledge* and *information*"; because such fictions are concerned above all "with *action* and *attitude*," to understand them is to ask "how they *behave*" (185, original emphasis). Stressing the pragmatic bent of Bentham's theory of fictions helps us recognize its affinities with the historicizing, sympathetic realism we have been charting. Both emphasized social modes of understanding, focusing on how things work rather than what they are; both saw sympathy as integral to the way the mind uses fictions in constituting the real.[29] And for both, the project of representing reality was a deeply rhetorical affair. Burke ultimately concludes that Bentham's "great contributions to the study of persuasion were made almost despite of himself," but he credits Bentham with discovering poetry "concealed beneath legal jargon usually considered the opposite of poetry," which he showed to be "*applied poetry,* or rhetoric, since it was the use of poetic resources to affect judgments, decisions, hence attitudes and actions" (90, original emphasis). Bentham's theory of fictions, sharing historical space with Jane Austen's last novel, magnifies the rhetorical function of language such that realism now signifies what rhetoric always has—the force of human sentiment in generating the facts of life.

Turning to *Persuasion,* we will be keeping Bentham's fictions in mind. For we might say of nineteenth-century fictional realism that it, too, falls generally "under the head of *ethics* and *form* rather than *knowledge* and *information*" and is concerned with the effects that come of treating fictions as if from life (Burke 85). As Taylor Stoehr once suggested, the nineteenth-century novelists understood better than their eighteenth-century forebears that mimesis and verisimilitude can sometimes conflict, when "the rendering of once-familiar ways should turn out so faithful as to leave the reader no means of judging them against his own experience" (1276). It was not enough to pad stories with the particularities of objects, time, or place. These were just the sorts of details making novels like *Robinson Crusoe* feel foreign and archaic, naturalistic rather than realistic; they were overly attentive to actual fact at the cost of impressions, attitudes, and desires.

Moreover, as Bentham makes clear, the rising status of fiction raised the rhetorical stakes for novelists and lawyers alike. The novelist-as-lawyer analogy—the opening gambit of Scott's *The Heart of Mid-Lothian* and a common feature of novels in the period—draws the persuasive techniques of both professions into close proximity. As Scott's punning barrister asserts, the "inventor of fictitious narratives has to rack his brains for the means to diversify his tale, and after all can hardly hit upon characters or incidents which have not been used again and again," but he who draws his subjects from life finds "infinite" variety. "O! do but wait till I publish the *Causus Celebres*"—the celebrated cases—"of Caledonia," he announces, "and you will find no want of a novel or a tragedy for some time to come" (*Heart* 19, 21). To Bentham's mind, lawyers and judges misbehaved when they behaved like novelists, engineering fictions for the purposes of controlling fates. Before him, Smith had drawn a stark contrast between critics and casuists; the first (rightly) derived their moral guidelines from "ordinary way[s] of acting," while the latter were moral "grammarians" (wrongly) attributing grammatical precision to moral law.[30] For Thomas de Quincey, Catholic priests were "moral attorneys" who treated "every case of human conduct . . . as an exception, and never as lying within the universal rule" (50). By the beginning of the nineteenth century, the sympathetic realist novelists were preoccupied with the question of how to represent ordinary behavior morally without falling prey to "grammarian" tendencies. Key to their sympathy was the desire to be critics and casuists (in the best sense) at once.[31]

Perhaps it is not surprising, then, that Raymond Williams should cast Austen in similar light. Austen "guides her heroines, steadily, to the right marriage. She makes settlements, alone, against all the odds, like some supernatural lawyer, in terms of that exact proportion to moral worth which could assure the continuity of the general formula" (*English* 246). For Williams, Austen is a kind of moral attorney, coolly apportioning reward and punishment, perpetuating the status quo. Yet by continually attributing to Austen's novels a perfect, "absolute" style and fixed moral formulas, we obscure how much it matters in a novel like *Persuasion* that one be capable of imagining alternative endings, other selves.[32] It was an ability for which Bentham, too, apparently longed. In his *Memoirs*, Bentham craves an almost Beardmore-like undoing, writing "O that I could decompose myself like a polypus. Could I make half a dozen selfs, I have work for all" (*Memoirs* n.p.). Ogden takes this to be a fairly straightforward claim about Bentham's work ethic, a busy man's wanting for extra hands. But in turning to Austen, we will see that there are other reasons for desiring the decomposition of self. For Anne Elliot, it will be a sympathetic ability that can offer the potential for new life long after her own sad case has apparently been closed for good.

PART 2. *PERSUASION* AND THE SYMPATHETIC CASE
The Case of Anne and Wentworth

It was, perhaps, one of those cases in which advice is good or bad only as the event decides.

—Jane Austen, *Persuasion*

We begin with an ending that isn't one, in a conclusion that wasn't the first, at the finish of what would be Austen's last finished novel. Readers will remember, and perhaps remember as odd, that as *Persuasion* winds to a close—its lovers reunited, their romantic disorders finally set right—Anne Elliot has two conversations with Wentworth that provoke disagreement and reprisal. The first takes place in those few, electric minutes after the pen momentously drops and the lovers, come face-to-face on the street, are able at long last to "exchang[e] again those feelings and those promises which had once before seemed to secure every thing, but which had been followed by so many, many years of division and estrangement" (193–94). Their animated talk ranges briskly over "the little variations of the last week . . . and of yesterday and to-day," the scenes of jealousy at Bath and Lyme, the hard-won lesson of the Cobb, capped by Wentworth's description of the suffering he endured while believing Anne engaged to her cousin Elliot and "feel[ing]," as he puts it, "all the horrible eligibilities and proprieties of the match!" "Was it not enough to make the fool of me which I appeared?" he continues in escalating tones. "How could I look on without agony? Was not the very sight of the friend who sat behind you, was not the recollection of what had been, the knowledge of her influence, the indelible, immoveable impression of what persuasion had once done—was it not all against me?" (196–97). Recollection collides so forcefully with scenes of the present that it seems wonderful to Wentworth that the past should ever have been overcome.

Anne, of course, needs no reminding of "what had been" or of persuasion's terrible costs. Yet her response isn't lovingly to succor Wentworth's rattled nerves or to share his awe but, mildly, insistently, to berate him. She urges him to see the mistake he has made in failing to see the two cases as "different": "You should have distinguished . . . You should not have suspected me now; the case so different, and my age so different. If I was wrong in yielding to persuasion once, remember that it was to persuasion exerted on the side of safety, not of risk. When I yielded, I thought it was to duty; but no duty could be called in aid here. In marrying a man indifferent to me, all risk would have been incurred, and all duty violated" (197).

Later that evening, Anne finds herself still dwelling on that difference. Though she appears to be "occupied in admiring a fine display of green-house plants," she continues to muse over their earlier conversation, finally breaking her silence to say,

> I have been thinking over the past, and trying impartially to judge of the right and wrong, I mean with regard to myself; and I must believe that I was right, much as I suffered from it, that I was perfectly right in being guided by the friend whom you will love better than you do now. To me, [Lady Russell] was in the place of a parent. Do not mistake me, however. I am not saying that she did not err in her advice. It was, perhaps, one of those cases in which advice is good or bad only as the event decides; and for myself, I certainly never should, in any circumstance of tolerable similarity, give such advice. But I mean, that I was right in submitting to her, and that if I had done otherwise, I should have suffered more in continuing the engagement than I did even in giving it up, because I should have suffered in my conscience (198).

Given what we know of sympathy, one can spot in Anne's speech elements of Smithian design. In the most explicit, she summons an impartial spectator with which to evaluate her actions, adjudicating if not right from wrong then at least this case from that. Seeking to "regard . . . [her]self" in an impartial light, Anne compares then to now, weighing her felt suffering against the hypothetical pangs of conscience she otherwise might have experienced, finally judging her behavior good on these grounds. "Thinking over the past" means thinking about feelings felt and imagined, those real and those merely possible. The pain of the last seven years, Anne reasons, was easier to endure than the pain she "should have suffered" but did not, in an alternative reality she managed to evade (198).

For some, this is casuistry of a deeply flawed, if familiar, kind. Anne appears to justify an old decision solely on the basis of its happy, accidental results. But Anne is clearly waffling. "I must believe that I was right" turns into the stronger "I was perfectly right," easing into what some readers have regarded as an intolerable compromise: the possibility that maybe it's just "one of those cases" good or bad "only as the event decides." This last declaration has led to many a critical disputation on the subjects of moral relativism and "moral luck," but in fact Anne is doing here what she does many times throughout the novel, which is to deliberate upon—without settling—her own case.[33] Indeed, she suggests that Wentworth should be doing the same, or that if he is, he isn't doing it right, a suspicion confirmed in his reply to Anne's complaint that he should be able to tell the two cases apart. "Perhaps I ought to have reasoned thus," he tells her; "but I could not" (197).

But why now, after "all the surprise and suspense, and every other painful part of the morning" has dissipated, now that she is "happier than any one in that house could have conceived" (197), should Anne continue to debate the case? What does she do, or gain, by turning her history with Wentworth into a series of cases? We might begin our answer by remembering that the case of Anne and Wentworth covers an unusual expanse of time in this novel—unusual not because their romance is central (nothing odd in that) but because the case has already been decided when the novel begins. Anne Elliot, with her "claims of birth, beauty, and mind," was once engaged to Wentworth, but as she wasn't the sort of girl "to be snatched off by a stranger without alliance or fortune," she had long ago been "persuaded to believe the engagement a wrong thing." "A few months had seen the beginning of the end of their acquaintance," and though Anne's "attachment and regrets" lasted "for a long time" to come, "an early loss of bloom and spirits" is all that results (27–28). Loss and diminution define her. She is "too little from home, too little seen. Her spirits were not high" (18). She doesn't count and isn't thought of. Her "word had no weight . . . she was only Anne."[34]

Case closed.

But of course, it isn't. And Anne already suspects as much as early as chapter

4. For unlike Wentworth, who in his "recollection of what had been" considers it weighted down by "indelible, immoveable impression[s]," Anne frequently characterizes the past in terms far less rigid (197). Even before his surprise return to Somersetshire, Anne is convinced that she should have married Wentworth the first time around, that "under every disadvantage of disapprobation at home, and every anxiety attending his profession, all their probable fears, delays, and disappointments," she "should yet have been a happier woman in maintaining the engagement, than she had been in the sacrifice of it." "And this," we are told, "she fully believed, had the usual share, had even more than a usual share of all such solicitudes and suspense been theirs, without reference to the actual results of the case, which, as it happened, would have bestowed earlier prosperity than could be reasonably calculated on" (29).

Hindsight, as we know, will make these sentiments wrongheaded when Anne, in winning her man, is rewarded the patient daughter's due. As she seems in the end to believe, she may have been "perfectly right" all along; obeying the injunction against marrying a man with "nothing but himself to recommend him" might be proof that, for an Austen heroine, the woman one might have been is never preferable to the woman one becomes (27). We may have little reason to suspect that love's open declaration in this novel's final pages should do anything other than what it tends to do in novels like it, which is to close the book on all previous uncertainty once and for all.

How, then, to reckon the force of Anne's continuing refusal of endings? The passage above opens up many more plots than can be realized, the most obvious coiling around Anne's regret. The "happier woman" she "should yet have been" in marrying, notwithstanding the "probable fears, delays, and disappointments" of Wentworth's profession, is in many ways the ghost of doubt, a foreclosed possibility into which happiness seems at this point in the novel to have been forever interred. It isn't hard to see, given the real diminishment of her life, why Anne should imagine herself better off having married despite the consequences. What is strange is that she can "fully believe" this to be so "without reference to the actual results of the case," results she treats as more or less incidental, hardly different in kind from the "probable" results that, as it turns out, Wentworth's prosperity has proven wrong. The "actual results of the case" are made to seem surprisingly inconsequential: "*as it happened*" Wentworth grows rich despite all calculation, the narrator remarks, as though that fact, surely a bitter pill for Anne to swallow, were little more than a casual afterthought. This might seem wishful thinking, willful naïveté, were it not that Anne's speculations drive a wedge between the case and its results. For it is *as* a case that Anne can imagine for herself these improbable futures, alternative pasts—places and times outside the dreary certainty of manifest fact.[35] The facts of the case do not make this case, which continues to open up again, resurrected from the dead well before any hint that Wentworth's feeling will do the same. From its beginnings, *Persuasion* tells us that not even actual results need decide one's case for good.

The past is of course well-traveled terrain for the Austen protagonist, who with few exceptions (*Mansfield Park*'s Fanny Price is one) discovers, then corrects, an old mistake. Critics have been quick to point out, though, that since Anne doesn't err, there is nothing to correct; no revelation of prior wrongs can loosen the grip of the past on the present. Perhaps, as some have argued, the novel presents the past as something to be abandoned rather than fixed. In his deft account of novelistic memory, Nicholas Dames considers *Persuasion* a novel in which a "new horizon of nostalgia"—nostalgic forgetting—is most thoroughly delineated. "A leavetaking of home spurs a series of further leavetakings; a trauma rooted in the memory is ameliorated, judged, and left behind; former mistakes are canceled, former times periodized and then ended, stopped with a mental period; and what is left is a capacity for a communalized retrospect" (*Amnesiac* 71). Yet as the previous examples have begun to suggest, *Persuasion* is riddled with provisional forms and conditional grammars that keep history in suspension and cases pending.[36] Unsettling the happiest of endings, Anne seems almost perverse in her unwillingness to leave the past behind. Incredibly, she continues to treat her story as unfinished *after* the plot's romantic conflicts have been resolved. Incredibly, she imagines different circumstances for herself *after* Wentworth's avowal of love should have put all desire for such alternatives permanently to rest. Barely blunting the knife's edge of her critique in telling Wentworth, "I certainly never should, in any circumstance of tolerable similarity, give such advice" as that which had been given to her, Anne prepares to meet future versions of herself, caught in similar snares. Former times are not so much end-stopped as recirculated in alternative realities where, one hopes, things may turn out differently, and better.

That the case should be central to this project makes sense given what we know of its formal mechanics. Pressing into future times and places in which norms can be renovated, cases are places where old conclusions can come undone. Treating the past as a case, as a prompt for the unfinished business of imagining the people that one should have or might have been, Anne rewrites it into a subjunctive mood and a conditional tense, a grammar powerful enough to begin unraveling the fixed conclusions of history itself. Throughout the novel, this action will be tied to Anne's ability to reactivate her plot. The gap between what Anne thinks in chapter 4, that she was wrong not to have married, and what she decides near the novel's finale, that she was "perfectly right" not to have done so, isn't as great as it first appears. Both moments see Anne drawing the past out of closure and into something more like narrative suspense. And in both, Anne relies on the language of cases to accomplish goals with which we are by now familiar: to revive a formerly held attitude in order to fairly explain and asses it; to "fall" into objectivity in the effort to acquire, to define, a self. "[T]he natural sequel of an unnatural beginning" proves an apt description for Anne's character development as well as the novel's narrative arc (*Persuasion* 30). Predication marks the beginning, not the end, of her person and plot.

Consider the scene in which Anne cares for her injured nephew, Charles, while her sister Mary attends a dinner at which Wentworth will be a guest. Left behind "with as many sensations of comfort as were, perhaps, ever likely to be hers," the one consolation she manages to muster is her "utility to the child." Cold comfort that, and it doesn't last. "What was it to her if Frederick Wentworth were only a half mile distant, making himself agreeable to others?" Anne asks. Soon she is thinking about Wentworth's feelings, then imagining what she might have done had she been in his place. Launching into a warp-drive of conditionals and modal verbs, the result is a dazzlingly counterfactual grammar: "She would have liked to know how he felt as to a meeting. Perhaps indifferent, if indifference could exist under such circumstances. He must be either indifferent or unwilling. Had he wished ever to see her again, he need not have waited till this time; he would have done what she could not but believe that in his place she should have done long ago, when events had been early giving him the independence which alone had been wanting" (51).

There is judgment here, even despair, but there is also time travel, an uncertain wanting to know, which coincides with the lingering dread of knowing full well all that is over forever. The final phrase—"when events had been early giving . . . [what] alone had been wanting"—registers the enduring quality of past events, set in motion in relation to present desire in past perfect continuous tense. More spectacularly, if the many "should," "would," and "could haves" stretching out against fact into improbable futures and impossible pasts are tinctured with the sad knowledge of all that Wentworth might have chosen to do but didn't, their sheer numbers hint at the dormant power of feeling and desire to turn a past "could" into a future "still yet." For if love in combination with longing energizes this particular thought experiment, the exercise perpetuates a temporally mobile conception of self, an Anne who might have been (and might be) otherwise. Knowing full well that wishing alone cannot unmake it, Anne nevertheless refuses to let the past stay put.

Having begun in this way, the novel cannot resolve itself with the usual, tidy conclusions. And it doesn't. "Who can be in doubt of what followed?" the narrator asks as the pair finally acknowledge their love (199). But doubt steals back in. Anne in the end may be "tenderness itself," but "future war" clouds the horizon; the "glor[y] in being a sailor's wife" is checked by "the tax of quick alarm" (202–3). Anne's refusal, even now, to relinquish the most the painful aspects of her former life indicates an unwillingness on Austen's part to let the past be blotted out for the sake of present joy. Critics often describe Austen's plots as developmental, yet *Persuasion*—her only novel set contemporaneously—upsets temporal and diegetic expectations at every turn, beginning as it does with the conclusion of Anne's plot and framing everything that follows from it as a revision or readjustment to solutions that don't stick and endings that refuse to hold. Tony Tanner notes the "radical transformation or devaluation" in *Persuasion* of all the "normal sources of stability and order in Jane Austen's world" ("In Between" 237). More recently, Mary Favret has shown that the novel's "broken story" reflects "the structures of feeling demanded by war," set as it is in the tentative peace following Napoleon's apparent defeat.[37] Favret joins several other critics in arguing against the notion that Austen's depicted worlds are the parochial, sealed-off environs of middle-class fantasy. In the "pervasive anteriority" of Austen's novels and the many "could- and might-have-beens [that dwell] in [their] uncanny, inordinate detail," these critics find in Austenian form a record of historical time.[38] For history, as William Galperin suggests, is never confined in Austen to what actually happened. The past indexes not only what was but also what was once *possible*. Austen's fiction subtly refutes an empiricist, probabilistic logic in its orientation toward "something missed or bypassed that does not belong entirely to the realm of fantasy," "different course[s] of events that [are] merely foreclosed upon rather than denied" (Galperin, "Describing" 356, 359). In recording how such potentialities shape actual, mundane experience even when never coinciding with it, her novels frame reality through the display of unrealized potential, the "*something else* in all its ordinariness" that might have been but was not (380, original emphasis).

If *Persuasion*'s form provides a sense of what it feels like to live among the heightened exigencies of embattled, historical life, Austen brings sympathy to bear on that form and on that experience. Once the past is a field whose meaning is not rigidly dictated by closed-off actualities and completed events, perspectives taken and feelings felt in the present have a hand in determining its survival, modifying whether, and how long, it lasts. That possibility is central to how we should understand the particular force of Anne's imagining, thrown into bold relief against the stubborn memorializing of nearly everyone around her, all of whom go to great lengths to refuse time and whatever comes with it. Mrs. Clay, Elizabeth comments approvingly, "never forgets who she is"; Lady Russell, we're told, "never wished the past undone" (33, 29). Engulfed in "a general air of oblivion," the family practices a "perfect indifference and apparent unconscious-ness . . . which seemed almost to deny any recollection" (30). Change occurs but is almost universally unacknowledged; even Wentworth, saying to Anne "to my eye you could never alter," tells her a transparent if pleasing lie (196). Anne's dealings with the past are far less rigid; they must be so if she is to sympathize with herself. "Like Adam Smith," Michael McKeon writes, "Austen would have us understand that both self-knowledge and ethical sociability require the sym-pathetic internalization of the other's point of view as if it were one's own" (717). But Smith and Austen also saw that the other might include, along with other people, other versions of oneself. And it is in sympathy with herself that Anne Elliot helps us see that what Dames characterized as "communalized retrospect" is something that can be accomplished alone (71). Far from corrupting fellow-feeling, then, sympathy with oneself proves to be constitutive of it, begetting a migrant conception of self at once continuous with the past and not utterly determined by it. As we shall see, the self-fragmentation that makes it possible to sympathize with others also generates the conditions through which one har-monizes self with self—one's former lives with the life one is living, one's past with one's present, the possible lives one isn't living but might have, might yet.

Other Annes, Wentworth's Nut

> Anne, at seven and twenty, thought very differently from what she had been made to think at nineteen.—She did not blame Lady Russell, she did not blame herself for having been guided by her; but she felt that were any young person, in similar circumstances, to apply to her for counsel, they would never receive any of such certain immediate wretchedness, such uncertain future good.
>
> —Jane Austen, *Persuasion*

Being a character in Austen, Alex Woloch writes, means being "continually con-trasted, juxtaposed, [and] related to others" (43). Yet *Persuasion*'s Anne—a beleaguered heroine long familiar with feelings of isolation and irrelevance—often imagines herself, or her selves, past and present, in relation to other, alternative selves. In the passage above, Annes proliferate. Time thickens and spreads. There is the nineteen-year-old Anne, persuaded against her inclination, and also the Anne who thinks "differently" at the age of twenty-seven. These two Annes are shadowed by a third, an imagined "young person, in similar circumstances," whose life is and isn't like Anne's own. Thinking about this third, prospective Anne shifts Anne into the position held, in her own case, by Lady Russell. Taking her place, and improving on her advice, Anne imagines preparing for another Anne the prospect of an alternative future.

This merely possible, future Anne is one with whom we are already familiar, and on that score Anne is unwaveringly decisive. What she says here she will say later, almost verbatim: no new Anne, if Anne can help it, will reap the suffering of the old. The one thing about which Anne has zero uncertainty hasn't happened, and might never. Who can say whether another young person, similarly circumstanced, will approach her with such an appeal? Yet these Annes serve another function within the novel, in confirming the realism of the Anne we are left with at the end of the book. All of these Annes, all the Annes whom Anne is not, lend coherence and texture to the person she is now; they join with the persons she used to be in consolidating who she has become. We can almost imagine Anne rewriting Bentham's explanation of sympathy this way: "*There stands a woman, in whose behalf I feel myself strongly interested*"—perhaps adding, "for it is my strong interest in others that enables me to strongly 'feel myself.'" Critics of the novel have noted its commitment to rendering "what the presence of other people feels like," how it compares the experience of reading "to the influence of one person's mind over another's" (Pinch, *Strange* 139). Yet the novel also vigorously records another kind of intersubjective experience, arising in our routine confidence in those whose presence can, strictly speaking, never be felt. Anne's sympathy with merely imagined others prompts her to reach beyond present company and felt sensation to body forth those imaginary beings on whom her sense of self relies. Such acts of projection make the processes of sympathy intrinsic to the realist enterprise. The ability to imagine unseen people, alternative selves, is the foundation on which our sense of our own reality derives.

When Wentworth plays with numbers, the results are decidedly different. For him, what multiplies are nuts, not Annes (he later denies her change: "to my eye you could never alter"), and firmness, not modulation, is what matters most (196). They are walking near Winthrop when Louisa makes what turns out to be an ill-omened pronouncement. "When I have made up my mind, I have made it," she boasts, and Wentworth responds approvingly to the idea that minds, once "made up," do best not to change. "To have a mind such as yours at hand" is a happiness, he says, and prompted to make a speech in favor of "the character of decision and firmness," he exemplifies the point by taking the case of a nut: "Here is a nut . . . [to] exemplify,—a beautiful glossy nut, which, blessed with original strength, has outlived all the storms of autumn. Not a puncture, not a weak spot any where.—This nut . . . while so many of its brethren have fallen and been trodden under foot, is still in possession of all the happiness that a hazel-nut can be capable of" (74).

Still? Leaving aside the question of how much happiness a hazelnut is capable of having, we might wonder how much "character" can sustain a logic that proclaims "the worst evil of too yielding and indecisive a character, [is] that no influence over it can be depended on." Wentworth seems not to notice the faulty logic of championing a character at once obstinately unimpressionable—with a "firmness" incapable of "puncture" or "weak spot"—and dependably receptive to influence. More importantly, what happened to the nut? If this were another novel, and Louisa another girl, the nut would find its way to a treasure box, where it would nestle beside an old pencil and a bit of court-plaister. As it stands, after "catching [it] down" from its prominence in "an upper bough," and expostulating on its fine qualities at length, Wentworth apparently tosses the nut away, conscribing it to the common ground of "so many of its brethren," a fate it has till now managed to thwart. The nut—"beautiful," "glossy," "blessed"—is not so much fallen as pushed into destruction, where it is "trodden under foot" (74). Case cracked.

But, of course, it isn't. For if Wentworth's game of nuts is but an idle diversion, it marks a failure of imagination, yet another doomed attempt to make a case that sticks because its results need never change. Wentworth resembles no one more than Anne's father in his facility for making canons of cases, treating character as a behavioral law. Wentworth's casuistry might seem merely wrongheaded, disappointingly opportunistic in comparison to Anne's more nimble imagining, were it not for the way it echoes Sir Walter's expiations on sunburned, "mahogany" skin and freckles: comic but sobering reminders of what can happen when character is confused with plot (22). And that it is also nearly fatal tells us just how seriously we should take the case of the nut and the mind it nearly splinters. For, tellingly, a terrible literalization soon takes place: rushing to exemplify the rule of the nut, Louisa falls from an upper prominence, cracking her skull. From then on, the language describing her plot will continually rehearse Wentworth's ill-chosen figures of speech. Benwick bears a heart "pierced, wounded, almost broken!"; Louisa's is proclaimed no "desperate case" merely because her extremities remain unharmed (148). Surely no other logic than that epitomized in Wentworth's nut could declare with apparent relief, "Louisa's limbs had escaped. There was no injury but to the head" (94).

If we thought the fault lay in the contents of this case, not in the manner of its making, we should remember Anne's former schoolmate, Mrs. Smith (née Miss Hamilton), whose chief quality is a flexibility we are given reason to admire. She is destitute, ill, a shadow of her former self, but Anne finds that if "a more cheerless situation" cannot be imagined, "neither sickness nor sorrow seemed to have closed her heart or ruined her spirits." Astonished at her friend's capacity for gladness, Anne "watched—observed—reflected—and finally determined that this was not a case of fortitude or resignation only," displaying instead an "elasticity of mind, that disposition to be comforted, that power of turning readily from evil to good, and of finding employment which carried her out of herself, which was from Nature alone" (125). "Elasticity of mind" appears to accomplish for Mrs. Smith what it could not for the regrettable Beardmore, combining the benefits of work with the sympathetic ability to be "carried out" of oneself. But before long, what seemed commendable becomes proof instead of reckless incaution. As Mrs. Smith relays proof of Mr. Elliot's greed, Anne realizes that she has badly misjudged her cousin and her friend; mistaking tricks of evasion for "elastic" flexibility, she overlooked an unqualified "bitterness," and worse (168). In yet another revision of an earlier judgment, Anne finds that neither flexibility nor firmness gives the rule in a world where one's actions may be right or wrong only as the case decides. Mrs. Smith "did not want to take the blame herself" for the overspending that led to her poverty. More unsettlingly, she renewed her acquaintance with Anne for financial reasons only. Mr. Elliot having proved unhelpful in recovering a lost property, she sets her sites on the woman she thinks he loves. There's nothing inherently wrong with a woman's desire to survive economic ruin (money, as *Emma* bitingly quips, prevents girls from becoming bitter spinsters), but what cannot be so easily forgiven is the emotional legerdemain practiced on Anne. Hoping to "interest Anne's feelings" to the cause, it is only on discovering that a false report circulated the rumor of Anne's engagement that Mrs. Smith comes clean about her past (170). The language of feeling imparts to Mrs. Smith's scheme an especially sour note in that her "interest" is self-interest only. "Elasticity" in this case of "petty difficulties" signals little more than sneaking, if pardonable, guile (202).

Insisting that no single quality, no rule of thumb, is suitable for deciding every case, *Persuasion* plays roughshod with the notion of precedent, which is throughout the novel an urgent matter of representation. The novel's bounty of spills and prodigal returns, its tireless attempts at recuperation, all seem designed to measure Austen's awareness of just how pressing the issue of antecedents has become. In Austen's most mature and final novel, revision does not always lead to development, second chances to improvement; changes of mind and heart, if destined to alter everything coming before and since, do not always do so for the better. Louisa's romance with Captain Benwick, marred by injury and death, is, like most sequels, disappointing for both. The different modes of adjudication that the novel has so far explored come acutely into focus when Anne reads in Wentworth's letter that the rule of "true attachment and constancy among men" is, in his case, "most undeviating." Caught in "the first stage of full sensation," Anne finds herself desperate for "half an hour's solitude and reflection," "plead[ing] indisposition" in a hasty attempt at retreat. In the move from judge to "pleading" witness, Anne suffers what is arguably the most wretched (and common) effect of crowds in Austen's fiction, "the absolute necessity of seeming like herself" when seeming like oneself is the hardest thing of all (it leaves Anne looking "very ill"). Of course Anne isn't quite herself because she is filled with "an overpowering happiness" (191). But the difficulty of such seeming increases for another reason. Wentworth's revelation, altering the case, has forever modified who that self is and can become.

Anne's struggle to seem herself is exacerbated when Mrs. Musgrove, constitutionally hard-headed, orders a chair to fetch her home, loudly objecting that Anne mustn't walk because she has suffered a fall: "The chair was earnestly protested against; and Mrs. Musgrove, who thought only of one sort of illness, having assured herself, with some anxiety, that there had been no fall in the case; that Anne had not, at any time lately, slipped down, and got a blow on her head; that she was perfectly convinced of having had no fall, could part with her cheerfully, and depend on finding her better at night" (192).

The prose here is anxiously redundant, making it hard to rest assured that no fall has taken place, that there have been no new blows to the head. Mrs. Musgrove's incredulity—she hardly believes there has "been no fall in the case"—marks an exemplary sort of stuckness that is remarkably common in this novel peopled with amnesiacs, blockheads, and one-track minds.[39] Unable to picture Anne as other than felled, Mrs. Musgrove swaps her case for another, turning her into a second Louisa, another concussive, another attenuated life. She can only imagine Anne fallen into disability because there is only one category ordering her thoughts; thinking "only of one sort of illness" is itself a sort of illness, configured in terms of mental and narrative paralysis.

And yet there has been a fall in this case, as there are falls in every case. In this novel full of chance occurrences, some of the most inadvertent slips and spills are bound metonymically to more opportunistic forms of permanence, including the *longue durée* of history itself. The climactic letter-writing scene finds Captain Harville pronouncing himself "in very good anchorage" in conversing with Anne even as Wentworth's pen falls again, and again—"his pen had fallen down . . . the pen had only fallen"—into a history that retells the story of female inconstancy, again and again, because only men have written it: "the pen has been in their hands."[40] Neither history nor literature can decide the debate, for, as Anne submits, it involves "a difference of opinion which does not admit of any proof"; it is, rather, a matter of "circumstances (perhaps those very cases which strike us the most) . . . precisely such as cannot be brought forward without betraying a confidence, or in some respect saying what should not be said" (189). Blakey Vermeule has said of *Persuasion* that there are "no puzzles, no mysteries, no riddles, no clues, no charades, no blanks to be filled in," only characters who are "more or less suited to each other, as they more or less know from the beginning" (102). But the novel teems with cases that cannot be brought forward, blanks and nothings anticipating future filling-in. Obsessed as they may be with fine-tuning our ability to read other minds by observing bodily gestures and expressions, Austen's novels also demonstrate the need for a sympathetic capacity fiction was uniquely designed to cultivate—that of bringing to life the feelings and minds of those who have no presence and must forever escape our view.[41]

The Art of Knowing One's Own Nothingness

One could argue that Anne's moral compass shines so brightly in *Persuasion* because it is the only one in the novel.[42] Lady Russell assures Sir Walter that "it is singularity which often makes the worst part of our suffering," and Anne's singularity is nowhere in doubt (16). Even Wentworth, who isn't exactly clueless when it comes to ethical judgments, angrily vows to marry "any pleasing young woman who came his way, excepting Anne Elliot" (54). While it isn't unusual for novel heroines to enjoy a special status, it may seem wrong to argue that Anne's ethical strategies represent the sine qua non of Austenian realism, given that she seems an exception to the rule in a world dense with moral imbeciles. That her energies are directed toward self-reinvention may give the lie to any claim extending Anne's ethical reach beyond her own small life.

One passage in particular links Anne's habits to a wider ethical sociability, and represents her "nothingness" as an occasion for sympathetic awareness. She has just arrived at the home of her sister Mary, with whose family Anne is now made to live:

> Anne had not wanted this visit to Uppercross, to learn that a removal from one set of people to another, though at a distance of only three miles, will often include a total change of conversation, opinion, and idea. She had never been staying there before, without being struck by it, or without wishing that other Elliots could have her advantage in seeing how unknown, or unconsidered there, were the affairs which at Kellynch-hall were treated as of such general publicity and pervading interest; yet, with all this experience, she believed she must now submit to feel that another lesson, in the art of knowing our own nothingness beyond our own circle, was become necessary for her;—for certainly, coming as she did, with a heart full of the subject which had been completely occupying both houses in Kellynch for many weeks, she had expected rather more curiosity and sympathy than she found (39).

The "lesson" of Anne's "own nothingness" is clearly painful to learn, but Anne knows her own nothingness all too well even at this early point in the novel. Why is it "necessary" that she learn it again? Framed as a matter of feeling, the lesson is one of acknowledgment; Anne "feels" that lesson in feeling for herself as do those beyond her family circle—in feeling, that is, nothing at all. Austen's pronouns magnify that extension: the lesson of "*our* own nothingness beyond *our* own circle" gives Anne an advantage the other Elliots lack, a recognition of "how unknown, or unconsidered" their lives become after just three miles' distance (emphasis added). Expecting sympathy but receiving none leads Anne to a valuable, if difficult, insight. Fellow-feeling consists in the nothingness we all share in common.

Nothing is something Austen never stopped thinking about. As David Marshall notes, the word appears in various forms over 150 times in *Mansfield Park* (by my count, *Persuasion* comes in at around 140).[43] There are plenty of reasons for this, but one has to do with acknowledging the implicit claims others make on us. That obligation, *Persuasion* seems to know, is an ethical fiction with deep significance, an affective nothing binding the members of social groups. Vermeule may be right to claim that psychological and economic motives are nearly identical in Austen, whose novels depict "a system of resource allocation that requires intense mental dexterity to navigate" (191). But if *Emma* strikes the keynote of this particular truth about Austen's fiction, and "the problem of living in a small world" it repeatedly represents, *Persuasion* fits the pattern less snugly (Vermeule 185). For in returning us again and again to the thinking we do in the company of those we will never know, the feelings we share with those who feel nothing for us, it gestures toward a world large and widening, full of strangers and un-knowns. Moreover, if being nothing within one's intimate circles causes psychic pain, knowing one's own nothingness in relation to the greater world, Austen suggests, involves an "art." It may be just this dual recognition that Austen's realism hopes, in the end, to capture. Sir Walter Scott considered it a mark of Austen's genius that readers were happily incapable of distinguishing her prose from life. "It affords to those who frequent it a pleasure nearly allied with the experience of their own social habits," he wrote of *Emma;* "the youthful wanderer may return from his promenade to the ordinary business of life, without any chance of having his head turned by the recollection of the scene through which he has been wandering" (*"Emma"* 200). Perhaps Scott recognized as Austen's achievement not that her novels seem so true to life as to be mistaken for it, but that they reveal to us how much like (her) fiction life really is. Each affords us with an ambient sense of continuity and connectedness, a faith that we are all going along together, not because they make us feel something in particular but because they don't.

CHAPTER 3

Dickensian Sympathy

Translation in the Proper Pitch

PART I. HARMONIZING IN OTHER WORDS

We began our investigation of sympathy's formal protocols by focusing on its qualities of abstraction, noting sympathy's deep dependence on the strength or weakness of our ideas. "To conceive or to imagine" pain, writes Adam Smith in *The Theory of Moral Sentiments* (*TMS*), "excites some degree of the same emotion, in proportion to the vivacity or dullness of [our] conception" of it (9). Raising our feeling to a level that approximates the feeling of another first requires representation, for only as a "conception" does the other's feeling become vividly real to our minds. And though much has been made of the spectatorial elements of his sympathetic scene, when it came to portraying optimal sympathy Smith frequently turned to metaphors of sound. Sympathy at its most operative moments achieves a "concord" of different, yet coordinated, ideas and emotions, a "harmony of sentiments and affections," not an identical match (22, 19).When sympathy fails to develop, it is often the fault of bad "pitch": an off note or tonal misfire, a minor error in a major key (22). Though Smith uses the term loosely, its psychoacoustical properties are part of the appeal: "pitch" is subjective in that it involves a listener's (or reader's) perception, and it is objective in its concern with how the mind categorizes and orders a perceptual field. In Smith's account, excesses of pitch are usually caused by sufferers unable or unwilling to hold back, while the puny, half-hearted effort of some would-be sympathizers kills sympathy before it starts. A sufferer's "violent and disagreeable passions" impede the process by hindering our ability to feel "any thing that approaches to the same degree." Until he "flatten[s] . . . the sharpness" of its "natural tone," his feeling and ours will not "beat time" together (ibid.). Finessing variations tonal and rhythmic is simply what one must do to sympathize with others. One needs a good ear to make it work.

Given this, Charles Dickens's rowdy cast of characters, with their trademark noise and extravagance, seem so prohibitive of a Smithian brand of sympathy one might suspect they had been invented for the purpose of demolishing it. Peopling his worlds with all things loud, frenetic, and absurd, Dickens creates environments that seem inimical to the rational, well-mannered sympathy Smith prescribes, an up-tempo riot to Smith's slow jam. Dickens's characters speak at decibel levels painful even to read about. The most popular Dickensian mode of utterance is the "ejaculation," "astonishment" a common expression. Being shocked into or out of countenance is a frequent occurrence in a world where characters find it hard getting away from their own words (especially if Fagin is nearby, for he will likely repeat them). Verbal tsunamis spill forth from Mrs. Nickleby, Toots, Uncle Pumblechook, accosting their hearers. Flora Finching punctuates her sentences "with nothing but commas, and very few of them," until even they finally desert her—and so it goes, ad nauseam (*Little Dorrit* 166). Stifled, endlessly talked-to characters vent their frustrations on themselves: Mr. Pocket yanks his hair out; Caddy Jellyby stings her inky face with vinegar; infants and children, their flesh "notched memoranda of their accidents," tumble down stairs, brain themselves with nutcrackers, swallow pins, reach for scissors and fire (*Bleak House* 78). If a model of sympathy prevails in Dickens, it appears to be David Hume's, not Smith's. Humean emotional contagion, vibrating unstoppably from one body to the next, seems to animate the typical Dickensian text. If we are disinclined to sympathize with anyone whose pitch is off, or with displays of feeling any more robust than a trembling lip and moistened eye, it's hard to imagine getting very far in Dickens before manifesting a Smithian sense of disgust.

I wonder whether perhaps that isn't the point. For Dickens hardly expects us to sympathize with every blunderbuss and hysteric who comes our way; he knows very well that we cannot. Tears and treacle notwithstanding, Dickens presents us with a world in which sympathy is difficult to accomplish, precisely because it is all too easy to judge other people's sentiments preposterous and unfounded. A committed realist despite evidence to the contrary, Dickens defended himself in several of his prefaces against the charge of hyperbole, writing "IT IS TRUE," in the 1841 preface to *Oliver Twist*, of his presentation of Nancy Sikes (460), and issuing for *Little Dorrit*'s "extravagant conception," Mr. Merdle, a mock apologetic appeal to "common experience" and recent headlines (5). In so doing, he insisted that the real felt truly outrageous, and he wasn't alone in feeling this way. As Raymond

Williams argues, Dickens's London can be seen as "the physical embodiment of a decisive modern consciousness"; though they were gathered together in unprecedented numbers, London's citizens couldn't conceive of themselves as members of a unified group. "What was commonly seen, in immediate experience, was social dissolution in the very process of aggregation" (*Country* 239, 216). In "the great city itself, the very place and agency—or so it would seem—of collective consciousness, it is an absence of common feeling, an excessive subjectivity, that seems to be characteristic" (215). Affective disproportion characterizes this Dickensian landscape. Lacking in fellow-feeling, its inhabitants suffer damaging concentrations of self. Thomas Carlyle remarked balefully on how "hurried" men rushed past without noticing one another (in Froude 120), while Friedrich Engels described a "repellent and offensive" indifference, permeating an environment of "unfeeling isolation" (68–69). As Amanpal Garcha suggests, the "manic activity and fragmented social relations" of Dickens's London reflect "the temporal pressures [that] prevent individuals from forging meaningful connections" (119). To battle the problem of excess subjectivity, Williams claims, nineteenth-century thinkers sought to discover an "underlying" consensus: for Marx and Engels, "a new collective proletarian consciousness and self-consciousness"; for Dickens, "a practical underlying connection, in human love and sympathy" (*Country* 216).

Yet we might say that estrangement is the underlying condition and sympathy a way to combat it.[1] A fitful, difficult enterprise, sympathy is in Dickens less a stable human attribute than something perpetually to be worked at against sizeable odds. And in his novels, estrangement *in language* is the alienation most painfully felt. "Rhetorical through and through," language is the social medium his characters struggle hardest to share (Stewart, "Dickens" 140). Hardly anyone in Dickens's fictional worlds is at home in language, where sentences are forever shimmying from the grips of their users. Words sunder, shards of them sticking in the craw. Critics have been quick to point out the biting satire of Dickens's portrait of the Benthamite school, but a striking feature of *Nicholas Nickleby*'s Dotheboys Hall is that words there, as they had for Bentham, have come undone. Disjointed letters, "B-o-t, bot, t-i-n, tin, bottin, n-e-y, bottiney," comprise its grammar lesson, "noun substantive, a knowledge of plants" (100). The failure to cohere that Williams finds at the macro-level of the city is mirrored in the minutia of schoolroom grammar and syntax. Like Bentham before him, Dickens portrays these linguistic fragments as evidence of fractured human thought, but now they also symbolize a pronounced disintegration of human relations. Syllables cannot aggregate into words, words into sentences, or either of these into more than clamor and gibberish without sympathetic communication with others.

George Levine has said that it is "perverse" to apply to Dickens "a critical method that assumes the separation of language from its object," but we have seen that Bentham already made that assumption, finding "nothing" in even the most substantive parts of speech.[2] In fact, Dickens should remind us of Bentham in another way, for his characters frequently cannot speak, or even know their own thoughts, except through the mouths of others. What Williams characterized as a problem of excess subjectivity might therefore signal an opposite problem—or, rather, the same problem, differently described. Character tics, fixed behavioral patterns, endless verbal repetitions—these bizarre yet routine features of Dickensian character, in light of the sympathy this book describes, seem evidence of *partial* subjectivity. Signifying the failure of full subjective development, they are the diminished proofs of sympathy's absence. As we have seen, Smith had envisioned just this possibility. Deprived of sympathetic connection to others, he argued, a person could not acquire a self. Only by way of sympathy could he imagine a shareable, objective world; shorn of that ability, he was destined to live a one-note, mechanical life. In this section, I show that because Dickens saw modern, urban existence as an arena of pitch gone wildly awry, the forms of sympathy most needed were not unlike those Bentham prescribed: forging connection through efforts of syntax and paraphrasis, filling in others' broken sentences, completing their thoughts.[3] Where sympathy in Sir Walter Scott meant reconstructing the mentalities of those living in an absent past, Dickens's sympathetic reconstructions are aimed at the alien minds and foreign languages of the present. Sympathy with the living meant dwelling in their sentences rather than in their skins.

Baulked by Dickens

I think a man, young and perhaps eccentric, feigning to be dead, and *being* dead to all intents and purposes external to himself, and for years retaining the singular view of life and character so imparted, would be a good leading incident for a story.

—Charles Dickens, *Letters*

Characters in Dickens are fatefully, constitutionally baulked. They seize up and fail, swerve and stop short, are thrown away, disappointed, foiled, blundering, and heaped about the grave. Even the most exemplary are clipped and refraining, so successful at composing themselves they decompose, veering threateningly close to negation. Oftentimes they are women who, as Hilary Schor writes, have "chosen 'nothing' as their portion" (124). Yet if sparing, self-disciplining figures like Little Nell and Florence Dombey are to be admired for keeping themselves in check, that ability acquires a more sinister cast when transposed onto the masochistic energies of Dickens's villains—think of Bradley Headstone's spontaneous nosebleeds—or the radical self-abnegation of boys like Pip, who early in *Great Expectations* admits, "I was in mortal terror of myself" (14). In the case of Headstone, the "very dark expression" he wears cannot be precisely translated; "fierce, and full of purpose," its object is uncertain, and "might have been as much against himself as against another" (*Our Mutual Friend* 636). David Copperfield's birth is figured as the eclipse, rather than the origin, of his being. A "posthumous child," David is never free of the weird indeterminacy that dogs his story. "Whether or not" David "turn[s] out to be the hero of [his] own life, or whether that station will be held by anybody else," *David Copperfield* is an object with no clear subject, the life history of an indeterminate, unspecified life (11–12).

Being baulked, clogged, or otherwise choked up leads to the antic behavior familiar to Dickens's fiction, whose performative energies continue to be a popular critical subject. Dickens the theater-man is said to put everything on the surface, equating clothing with character, public face with private: his Veneerings shimmer, Gays delight, and Generals rule. The effect, as J. Hillis Miller sees it, is not only that a man's surroundings determine his life, but that the man seems less a person than a series of "gestures, roles, or functions," an actor of parts mostly unaware that the world's a stage and he is on it, pantomiming one imitation of life after another ("Fiction" 130). Miller's point is finally about Dickensian realism, which in his view doesn't pretend to represent a real life beyond language so much as expose that life's thoroughly conventional quality, its "stale repetitions" and increasingly "paler imitation[s] of the past" (139). The crucial thing isn't that the theatergoing, actor-obsessed Dickens wrote novels in which theatrical forms are overtly a part but that Dickensian theatricality reveals the "counterfeit quality" of realist mimesis, which never depicts life but only images (and images of images) of it (171). The openly symbolic or quasimetaphorical names of his characters boldly tell us that Dickens's are not real people but products of language. Thus, at his most authentic, Dickens portrays the "grotesque" comedy and "ephemeral violence" of the melodramatic stage: belonging to fiction, not nature, these posit a "time out of time created within art by the reference of each fiction to the near nothingness of other fictions" (ibid.). In sum, Dickens's artistry succeeds first by publicizing mimetic fraud and then by reveling in the "meaninglessness" of the fictional medium—ink or, in some of Cruikshank's sparer illustrations, not much of anything, "a blank place on the paper" (170).

From this view, Dickens would seem to have dispensed with sympathy's usual encumbrance by turning his characters inside out. We need no special powers of discernment to know what a man named M'Choakumchild is like (*Hard Times* 58), and we needn't peer into Uriah Heep's secret heart once we see him writhing "like a Conger-eel" (*David Copperfield* 569). A scene in *Our Mutual Friend* (1868), published late in Dickens's career, appears to confirm the point. Conceived as the story of "a man, young and perhaps eccentric, feigning to be dead, and *being* dead to all intents and purposes external to himself," the novel presents us with an early exchange between two lawyers, Mortimer Lightwood and Eugene Wrayburn, and Rogue Riderhood, a fishy fellow who has come seeking an affidavit against Gaffer Hexam, his rival in the river-dredging (and corpse-robbing) trade (Forster, *Life* 291, original emphasis). True to what Miller considers the law of Dickensian representation—the metonymic conjunction between persons and their environs—Rogue's slime perfectly indexes his moral essence, as well as his professional cast. Wearing "an old sodden fur cap, formless and mangey, that looked like a furry animal, dog or cat, puppy or kitten, drowned and decaying," Rogue insists that he gets his living "by the sweat of his brow," which, true to form, "pour[s] down like rain." To prove who he is, he need only point to himself. He is a "Waterside character" through and through (*Our Mutual Friend* 148, 150).

As expected, this is a moment of increased legibility, and what we see clearly is Riderhood's guile. The lawyers' questions, however, effectively dry him up:

"Now," said Lightwood, for the third time . . . what's your name?"

"Rogue Riderhood."

"Dwelling-place?"

"Lime'us Hole."

"Calling or occupation?"

Not quite so glib with this answer as with the previous two, Mr. Riderhood gave in the definition, "Waterside character."

"Anything against you?" Eugene quietly put in as he wrote.

Rather baulked, Mr. Riderhood evasively remarked, with an innocent air, that "he believed T'other Governor had asked him summat" (150).

Less at ease when they ask of his "calling or occupation" than he had been in stating his name and address, he is "not quite so glib with this answer," and by the time they ask, "Anything against you?" he is decidedly less free in his response. He is instead "[r]ather baulked" and pretends (as cover) to have heard "summat" else. The ruse seems only to secure his undoing. No "air," "innocent" or otherwise, is convincing for so oozy a figure as himself.

If we aren't exactly hard pressed to understand the purpose of Rogue's evasive tricks, we may well wonder why this city slicker should be shaken by questions so easy to evade. That he is nonplussed at all is strange. What sort of rogue baulks at telling a lie? Rogue's responses, we begin to notice, materialize not the mimetic congruence between outside and in (already obvious from his kitten cap and excessive schvitzing) but the mobility of his language, its ebbs and flows. Being baulked produces rogue language, "summat" with no clear origin or content. In this elemental scene of water and air, the text calls our attention to its speakers' competing modes of expression. When words travel, it suggests, we should study the conditions in which they move.

Here "glib," with its silver-tongued artful dodgery, seems the verbal antithesis of the arresting "baulked." The more baulked he is by the lawyers' questions, the less glib Rogue's replies become. The glib, the *Oxford English Dictionary* (2nd ed.) tells us, is easily pronounced and "easily swallowed," as in, plausible. Spilling unobstructed from one mouth (or throat) into another, glib words slide down like so many oysters; one can, we assume, barely feel them at all. "Baulked" connotes in its root form many things, including a grave-mound, a division, a ridge, something lost, a blunder, an omission, a stumbling block. Yet the two are not entirely different. Glib speech is effortless, but suspiciously so. It too marks a limit, taking a good thing too far. The glib implies a shameful lack of shame, and therefore of self-consciousness. Each is, in its way, thoughtless—the glib, since one suspects it isn't entirely forthcoming, the baulked because, dead on arrival, it isn't going anywhere at all.

The presumption is that it requires a sophisticated ear to avoid being taken in by the dangerous smooth talk of the flatterer, the rake, the parvenu, or the thief. But that lesson also comes with a warning, that the words we use may not be our own, that they can turn, or be turned, against us. For all the scene's metonymic clarity, for all that is worn on the sleeve, words are the least transparent, most thinglike of its parts. Others' thoughts can get inside us without our quite knowing it, on the backs of words as they slip in and out. Once inside, they can lodge there, interrupting our language's ordinary currents, halting its flow. The fear that others' words may be speaking us is uniquely tied, for Rogue, to spoken language. He isn't worried about writing. With an unshakeable faith in "the binding powers of men and ink and paper," he asks repeatedly to be "taken down" in print and is shocked at the lawyers' unwillingness to commit him to the written word (149). But Rogue has underestimated the difficulty of making words stick. Every time he opens his mouth, he grows more vulnerable to their two-way traffic. If the jig is up, it isn't only because the lawyers see through Rogue's pretense at sincerity—no great accomplishment in a world where the (wet) suit makes the man—or even because Rogue fails to see (and he hasn't) that his performance is being judged. For what we see here isn't a turning of insides out, but the reverse: self-consciousness sets in, interiority develops, as the other's words enter us. To open one's mouth at all is to risk semantic reconstruction by others. Rogue, being a rogue, fights back, repeating his point: "haven't I said from the first minute I opened my mouth in this here world-without-end-everlasting chair," he entreats, "that I was willing to swear that he done it?" (151). But staying on script affords him little power in controlling where his words end up—or which steal into him.

None of this seems to have anything to do with sympathy as we know it in Dickens or anywhere else. More typical is the idea that certain characters, the sympathetic ones, are baulked in a different way, wordlessly longing for someone to come along and understand all that they cannot say. Desperate for semantic aid, they are hardly to be confused with the Rogue Riderhoods lurking about. His character, his worry, is the opposite of theirs. He wants only to be minimally understood, taken seriously by the lawyers but inviolable to any keener penetration. Yet sympathy is in many ways the keynote struck in this scene of intersubjective travel, as Rogue fabricates an increasingly elaborate lie in which the sentiments of others play a significant part. At first, Rogue tries to make his case to the lawyers by claiming a personal conviction of Hexam's guilt ("[o]n the grounds that I knowed his ways"); failing that, he points to public suspicion ("[o]n the grounds that it's well understood along the cause'ays and the stairs that he done it"). From these proofs, he claims a certainty: "I have made up *my* mind," he says. But this, they tell him, amounts to "[m]erely nothing"; feelings cannot count as evidence or stand up in court (151, original emphasis). Rogue's willingness to swear an oath to his feelings only adds to the lawyers' evidentiary frustrations. As Mortimer says, "you only offer to swear to your suspicion, and I tell you it is not enough." Next, Rogue tries a different tack, claiming Hexam confessed to the murder directly: "he told me by his own lips," he says (151–52). But it doesn't stop there. The last piece of evidence he tries—arguing that the sheer knowledge of Hexam's deeds causes him an analogous guilt—offers sympathy as a proof. For Rogue's mind, he suggests, is pervaded by other people: "I was so troubled in my mind, that I wouldn't have knowed more," he exclaims. "Am I to have this trouble on my mind for ever? Am I never to throw it off? Am I always to think more of Gaffer than of my own self?" (152, 154).

Dickens levels a blow to Rogue's villainy by turning his words against him. "I do mind it, and I must mind it and I will mind it," which Rogue claims is true of his guilty conscience, is proof only of his greedy self-interest (153). The only man on his mind is himself. But Rogue's sham sympathy casts doubt on sympathy altogether, or at least on certain understandings of it. For Dickens presents as an issue of law one that had long concerned moral philosophy, the question of knowing how words and feelings become substantive, whether and when they can be taken as evidence. One question—how are we to know the other's mind?—turns into another: how are we to know what, or who, is in our own? For Dickens's minor characters, that question has seemed easy enough to answer. The lawyers' turning the tables on Rogue seems to prove Miller right by exposing a mimetic sleight of hand. Rogue is an idea, not a person; he's a blank onto which nothing sticks. Unctuous though he is, Rogue cannot even carry out his metonymic birthright, for various elements of the scene conspire to stop his flow. Twice seen to "chew" his wine before swallowing it, this Waterside figure, liquidated of content, looks to be a "character," nothing more (154–55).

Yet in framing the issue as a contest between mimetic fraud and fictional exposure, we risk underestimating the deep rootedness of sympathy in Dickens's language games. We might fail to see metonymic destiny unraveling with each slip of the tongue. For what emerges in the interrogation of Rogue—who are you, where do you live, anything against you?—is a subjectivity hanging in the balance between a self and others, his words and theirs. Rogue *is* a product of language, of fiction rather than nature, but the same is true of all subjectivity as sympathy understands it: whatever I am, whoever I become, unfolds in the persistently reoccurring gap between my understanding of myself and the self I imagine others understand me to be. The gap is necessary. To be stranded on one side of the equation is to risk total self-enclosure; on the other, environmental determinism. In saying this, I am in some ways only confirming what a number of recent critics have said regarding the structure of realist character, that its propulsion is fueled by the perpetual yet always unfulfilled desire to overcome the difference between who I am (or was) and who I still want to (or have) become.[4] Counterfactuals, character doubles, alternative lives—these become evidence that the processes of realist individuation, which prioritizes some characters at the expense of others, require the "submerged perspectives" of the latter, those "other possible stories" and potential lives that are "intertwined with and obscured by the main focus of attention" (Woloch 40). But we should see that this is the structuring desire of sympathy as well, which involves the same imaginative comparisons: of self to former, future, possible selves, of self to others, and to the self we imagine others see in us. Rogue's off-note, baulked utterance may signal his failure to connect (the lawyers hardly beat time with his mental rhythms), but it is also proof of a sympathetic understanding of character formation. Unsympathetic by any usual standard, even he gains something like interiority through modifications of pitch and degree, tonal shifts that yank him into subjectivity by way of intersubjective commerce.

Williams's excess subjectivity and what we described as subjectivity's stunted development now look to be versions of the same thing. In both, underdeveloped fellow-feeling, the failure to engage in sympathetic projection, results in a thickening of character for which some kind of thinning out is required. What we have elsewhere in this book called "sympathetic departicularization" is needed, a means of diluting overly condensed, mechanistic forms of life. The baulked utterance, suspended between intention, expression, and reception, thus makes us keen to a process of which Rogue grows increasingly aware. A lapse in character *produces* character, one which grows more recognizably human in becoming self-divided. This is true whether we like Rogue or not. Cutting through his undifferentiated damp, the baulked utterance is the sound-bite on which his subjectivity hangs. As Kent Puckett observes, such lapses in character do more than make characters "interesting" because they are "not fully resolved": they prevent them from being "monstrous," so indivisible, so utterly self-contained, as to be incapable of subjective experience (123–24). That proposition is consistent with the Smithian view. A person cannot so much as "think of his own character" without having first projected himself into the minds of others, and introjected their minds into his (*TMS* 110). Subjectivity requires self-difference, a departicularization that is itself the product of sympathetic thought.

Puckett describes as a crack in the teacup the minor flaw that, in interrupting form, undoes monstrous self-enclosure. Rogue is no teacup, but like many of Dickens's characters he is so particular as to seem entirely self-evident, so closed in upon himself that there is no telling outside from in. Yet we see in Rogue's "summat," and the many other chipped words and tonal glitches scattered throughout Dickens's fiction, that it only takes one rogue word (or sound) to convert monsters into men. If the move from glib unself-consciousness to baulked interiority sounds more than a little repressive to our modern ears, we should also register in it a powerful hope that the most minor verbal stumblings can help secure a self. This in turn explains why sympathy in Dickens's novels so frequently involves reconstructing other minds from the partial evidence of the sounds people make, words caught in the back of the throat, neither uttered nor entirely swallowed back. Reduced to the most basic units, in desperate cases down to nonce words and single, meaningless letters of type, Dickens's hyper-fictional, hyper-individual characters are only as human as the words other people can make of them. We feel called on to perform a kind of textual Heimlich maneuver, forcing up what cannot on its own be coughed out.

Thus Dickens reminds us of another idea Smith made central to his account of sympathetic understanding: that our feelings are dead to the reality outside us, remaining so until they are (if they are) reconstituted by others. For Dickens, language is as necessary for that reconstitution as it had been for Smith, words being the medium through which human sentiment passes from one person to the next. But Dickens has added a further, Bentham-like complication by dicing words into pieces, mortifying their progress.[5] Dickens's fantasy of a shared affective reality finds its clearest expression in language broken and bent out of shape. George Levine suggests that "Magwitch's click in the throat, heard in the first pages of *Great Expectations,* holds the secret of the novel, legible to us but not to Pip" (*Realistic* 47). But we might press that claim even further. For where words fail, a click or summat like it may be all we have to go on in bringing others (back) to life. Magwitch's click refuses to put into words that which the sympathetic imagination must make sense of once human language splinters into the otherwise meaningless noise of syllables torn apart.

Sympathetic Translation

Dickens is sometimes considered a "fanciful photographer," at once diligently recording and refashioning the landscapes on which he looked (Slater 11). It is as a "photographer" of modern, urban existence that his reputation as a realist rests. Even his "fanciful" departures from observable reality call attention to the conditions in which his characters live. Their attempts at escaping it reveal how bleak that reality is. As Garrett Stewart says of Dickens and the "imaginists" populating his fiction (Dick Swiveller, Jenny Wren), each manipulates, so as to wrest pleasure from, the "stiff, spent, [and] joyless" language dominating their beleaguered environments.[6] Thus, Dickensian prose, with its "expansiveness and profusion of phrase, with concision flouted in sentences terraced crazily with surplus detail, the constant foraging after metaphor, [and] all the tireless flights and flourishes": these "become occasions for a symbolic economy unknown to more chiseled and lapidary, less broadly spontaneous styles" (*Dickens* xiv). Stewart associates that linguistic flight with freedom, including the novelist's liberty to portray otherwise unmentionable subjects through verbal puns, homonyms, and syllogistic humor. Dickens's stylistic wildness contributes to a joyful celebration of semantic abundance.

At the same time, Dickens uses dialect and pronunciation to shore up all kinds of social distinctions, especially of class and moral character. Sometimes bad English isn't a symbol of imaginative emancipation. It's just bad. The Victorians, as Raymond Chapman observes, suffered from a pronunciation anxiety their eighteenth-century predecessors did not possess. As the gutsily titled *Enquire within upon Everything* proclaims, "few things point so directly to the want of *cultivation* as the misuse of the letter H by persons in conversation."[7] *David Copperfield's* Uriah Heep is one of the most villainous H-droppers in the Victorian canon, but his "umble" is also archaic, an "aping of a traditional pronunciation which was already moribund."[8] 'Eep's missing *H* designates him as lower-middle class and (the same thing) a copyist. In *Little Dorrit,* a London waiter calls out to a chambermaid, "Chaymaid! Gelen box num seven wish see room" (45). There's nothing especially poetical in this mangled bit of pronunciation, which serves primarily a mimetic purpose.

Good English can be bad too, a sign of Dickens's snobbishness. The best English speakers are often the most insipid. His protagonists speak, unfortunately, very well. Oliver Twist, who "always uses language literally," is easily the least critical favorite of Dickens heroes, in part because his English is so by the book.[9] As Arnold Kettle writes, we may be outraged by what happens to the boy as orphan and battered child, "but our entanglement in his situation is not really very deep" (117). Mr. Meagles, a more ambivalent figure, asserts repeatedly that "the English tongue was somehow the mother tongue of the whole world" and that foreigners were simply "too stupid to know it" (*Little Dorrit* 840). Dismissing a language he patently refuses to understand, he considers French, with its "allonging and marshonging," pure nonsense; it's "all bosh" (30, 840). Or take Simmons, a parish beadle in *Sketches by Boz,* whose ability to state the case "without a single stammer" sends a poor widow into the workhouse (18). The pattern is repeated in *Oliver Twist,* whose more nefarious beadle, Bumble, is "stupefied" at being ordered to remain silent, considering it an outrage against his profession: "[a] beadle ordered to hold his tongue! A moral revolution" (26). Sometimes the humor wickedly cuts both ways, as when in another of the *Sketches* a missionary back from the West Indies reports a dialogue he overheard there "between two negroes": mimicking their "broken English," he is met with wild applause (55). We can't be sure who to laugh at, or who did the breaking. Little wonder *Twist's* Grimwig spends so much time threatening to "eat [his] own head" (110).

We might recall that in Dickens's time as a parliamentary reporter he spent his days turning good English into bad, shorthand's weird tongue. For all the theatrical staginess of his fiction, and for all it might imply about the importance of visible performance, Dickens's parliamentary experience trained his eye and ear to the material conditions of language, perhaps especially to the clipped, compressed figures embedded in it. For all its exuberant verbosity, linguistic compression is also an important element of Dickensian fiction. The novels' readers aren't alone in facing characters entirely made of words—oddly abbreviated, part-human figures reduced to scraps of language, and an unfamiliar language at that.[10] *Little Dorrit*'s Arthur Clennam knows no more than we do how to attune himself to Mr. F's Aunt. Proper pitch she hasn't. "You can't make a head and brains out of a brass knob with nothing in it," she blurts with no apparent object (291). Like most everything she says, these words are "totally uncalled for by anything said by anybody," "traceable to no association of ideas." She may have "some system of her own, and it may have been ingenious, or even subtle," we're told, "but the key to it was wanted" (172). Knowing Mr. F's Aunt to be full of rage, or even that she directs it at Arthur, tells us next to nothing about how to comprehend her. We cannot even say that her emotions are transparent to meaning when we, no less than Arthur, haven't a clue what to make of them.

Given that communication without sympathy has come to seem impossible, we can begin to see why sympathy must perform what is ordinarily the translator's work. As Walter Benjamin understood it, translation is a "mode of intention," not an attempt at transparency; translations issue in an "afterlife" which repeats without copying an original source (73). A translation and its source do differ, but change occurs in both directions. For translation would be impossible, Benjamin insists, "if in its ultimate essence it strove for likeness to the original." In the "afterlife" of translation—"which could not be called that if it were not a transformation and a renewal of something living"—originals, too, are altered; the "mother tongue . . . is transformed as well." When translators try to preserve language from foreign influence, bad translations result, but they don't succeed by producing "a vague alikeness between adaptation and original," either; translation doesn't "necessarily involve likeness" at all (73–74). Word-for-word substitutions are, anyway, impossible. Idiomatic meanings, affective registers would fall away. Translation, Benjamin concludes, "is only a somewhat provisional way of coming to terms with the foreignness of languages" (75). A translator should strive to give voice "to the *intentio* of the original not as reproduction but as harmony" (79). His task is to "harmonize" different tongues (77).

Paul de Man suggests that the translator, not the poet, is for Benjamin the exemplary figure because translators, by definition, fail; they must "give up in relation to the task of refinding what was there in the original" (33). Because translations cannot merely copy a source, they provide provisional solutions to a foreignness at once mediated and preserved, by combining different tongues into what we might consider "proper pitch" rather than strict identity. And, as was true for the process of sympathetic understanding, failure is good: knowing that identical reproduction is impossible paves the way for dynamic "renewal," an "afterlife" studded with fresh potential. Translation achieves what seems an unattainable demand, fidelity *in* transformation, what Maurice Blanchot calls "an identity [forged] on the basis of an alterity." For this reason, the translator "is a strange man," the "eternal guest" of a language he neither owns nor fully inhabits (59–60). It is de Man's conclusion as well: translation demonstrates the irreparable strangeness of our own tongues.[11] Highlighting the disjunction between word and word, origins and afterlives, its pattern of relation is synecdochic and successive rather than metaphorical and simultaneous. Both source and translation "remain essentially fragmentary" (de Man 43).

Sympathetic translation of the sort Dickens portrays is indeed the work of strange men—and women—enlisted in similar kinds of metonymic labor, reconstructing others' sentiments from their sentences' fragmented parts. "The Doll's Dressmaker Discovers a Word," chapter 60 of *Our Mutual Friend*, illustrates the point through a particularly brutal version of the speech impediment. The scene involves the aftermath of a savage beating. Pummeled by Bradley Headstone, Eugene can no longer think clearly or speak for himself. At issue is his desperate, deathbed desire to take Lizzie Hexam as his bride; thus, "wife" is the word the doll's dressmaker, Jenny Wren, must discover. Despite the fact that "no spirit of Eugene was in Eugene's crushed outer form," that he considers himself "murder[ed]," drifts into and out of consciousness, cannot move his hand to place the ring upon his new wife's finger, and avows repeatedly that he "ought to die," Eugene manages to marry Lizzie (736, 738, 754). But he needs a sympathetic "interpreter" to do it:

> The doll's dressmaker, all softened compassion now, watched him with an earnestness that never relaxed. She would regularly change the ice, or the cooling spirit, on his head, and would keep her ear at the pillow between whiles, listening for any faint words that fell from him in his wanderings. It was amazing through how many hours at a time she would remain beside him, in a crouching attitude, attentive to his slightest moan. As he could not move a hand, he could make no sign of distress; but, through this close watching (if through no secret sympathy or power) the little creature attained an understanding of him that Lightwood did not possess. Mortimer would often turn to her, as if she were an interpreter between this sentient world and the insensible man; and she would change the dressing of a wound, or

ease a ligature, or turn his face or alter the pressure of the bed-clothes on him, with an absolute certainty of doing right (739).

Adept in piecing together remnants of cloth, Jenny stitches "close watching" to "secret sympathy" with the thin thread of "as if." Sympathy and watching are aligned but are not the same. Jenny looks, but as Eugene makes "no sign," there isn't much to see. Mortimer appears mainly to be watching her, "an interpreter" between their "sentient world" and the "insensible man."

Pressing her ear to the pillow, Jenny listens for whatever "faint words" might be falling out. Yet listening is something about which she and Mortimer have little choice. For there is "one word, Lizzie," which Eugene "incessantly repeat[s]," in "a hurried and impatient manner, with the misery of a disturbed mind, and the monotony of a machine." "Lizzie" he says, rolling his head about the bedcovers or lying "still and staring," "repeat[ing] it for hours without cessation"; he rises up like "a drowning man from the deep" to say it, only to "sink again" (739–40). "Lizzie" is a word cut off from the intents and purposes its speaker tries to give it. It is the deluge in which he drowns. "Tell me in a word, Eugene!" Mortimer cries, clutching his friend; somehow "Lizzie," muttered endlessly, isn't doing the trick. Staring blankly, Eugene figures narrative and psychic paralysis, "the only word [coming] from his lips" a word "millions of times repeated. Lizzie, Lizzie, Lizzie" (741, 739). He doesn't speak the word as much as it speaks him; then, he falls unconscious. What happens next is strange even by Dickensian standards. Jenny asks Mortimer a question, "Shall I give you a leading word to say to him?" "Oh, Jenny, if you could only give me the right word," he responds. Whispering into his ear "one short word of a single syllable," Jenny urges him to "Try it" (739). Hours later, Mortimer passes on the "leading word," and the insensible man is restored to language—and in the same instant, to life. Speaking in whole sentences ("I love you, Mortimer"), saying aloud what he has long struggled to say, Eugene announces, "If my dear brave girl will take me, I feel persuaded that I shall live long enough to be married." "He is conscious, Jenny," Mortimer assures the seamstress. "He knows his wife."[12]

There are many things one might say about this thoroughly triangulated scene, but one of its most astonishing features is the way words move into and out of the mouths of others. "Wife" is the most obvious of these. Having slipped from (because beaten out of) Eugene's mind, that word escapes him entirely. The closest substitute he tries fails, for "Lizzie" and "wife" are not yet synonymous. Given this strange concatenation of mental impairment and sympathy-as-word-supply, we might ask of Eugene what Roman Jakobson—in his famous essay on metonymy and metaphor—asks of the aphasic patient: what aspects of his language are impaired? In some respects, Eugene seems to suffer from the second type of aphasia Jakobson describes, for he is in need of metonymic assistance. "Contexture-deficient aphasia" leaves sufferers with a "contiguity disorder"; speechless but not wordless, they have lost the "power to propositionize," can provide the names of things but not their predicates. Having lost all grasp of grammar and syntax, the person afflicted with contexture-deficient aphasia manages to keep single words intact, but lacking syntactic contextualization they pile up ("Lizzie, Lizzie, Lizzie") into meaningless "word heap[s]." In aphasia of "selection," by contrast, "context is the indispensible and decisive factor" (Jakobson 85, 77). The sufferer responds coherently in conversation with others but has difficulty initiating dialogue. He is "reactive" rather than inventive, speaking easily only of the situation at hand; he cannot say "it's raining" unless he sees that it actually is. For one such sufferer, the word "bachelor" has become untranslatable. His metonymic, contextualizing capacities remaining intact, he freely describes rooms in his building known as "bachelor apartments," but when asked what a bachelor is, he cannot say.[13] Qualifications like "a bachelor is an unmarried man" escape him. Caught up in paraphrasis, he is unable to move from index to icon, metonymy to metaphor; describing what is nearby or part of the thing, he cannot name or define it. From a certain angle, then, Eugene resembles this man too. He lacks the inventive power to transform "Lizzie" into "wife."

Eugene's inability to speak one of nineteenth-century fiction's most powerful plot-enders magnifies the novelistic quality of this particular defect. Without the word "wife" this book could go on and on, like him, forever. Swapping that word for any other is no simple accomplishment. Indeed, reasons having more to do with social class and custom than with brain damage prevent Eugene from qualifying "Lizzie" as "wife." The words do not yet share what Jakobson calls "equational predicate[s]" (81). Their senses do not align. Yet Dickens turns this rather ordinary romantic plot device into a unique linguistic crisis. Eugene's contiguity disorder leaves him entirely estranged from semantic—social—context, trapped in communicative limbo. He is confined to a purely paradigmatic existence, a private vocabulary of isolated signs. Reduced to "infantile . . . one-word sentences," he lacks all ability of inflection; "oversimplification and automatism" are his only verbal powers (Jakobson 87).

In this condition, Eugene requires a sympathetic form of speech therapy, which Jenny and Mortimer must join forces to give. And this they do—not by copying his words or feelings, but by fitting new predicates to his desire, filling out his stunted, one-word sentences. The example of Fagin is instructive: merely repeating a person's words back to him, verbatim, is mocking and sinister but it is also symptomatic of the failure to propositionize, a refusal of social codes; sympathy manifests, alternatively, as a creative verbal and figurative force. Yet if Jenny's substitution of "wife" for "Lizzie," in joining the two into symbolic unity, proffers a metaphorical cure, it also has the significant effect of restoring Eugene to discourse. Her metaphor, her new paradigmatic equation, alters the dimensions of the available context, expanding its sequential and combinatory potential. This in turn restores Eugene to a living—a communal—syntax. And Jenny does all of this without feeling what Eugene feels. Sympathy occurs through the making of "equational predicates" rather than emotional equivalence.

Using Dickens to illustrate the symptoms of aphasia isn't new. Though his immediate point of departure was *Oedipus,* J. Hillis Miller clearly had Dickens in mind when he wrote that even ordinary speech "is like that of a brain-injured person who utters words different from those intended, or like the sounds made by someone with the sinister form of a tic that causes its victim to involuntarily bark like a dog or speak blasphemies of obscenities, as if he or she were a mechanical talking head" (*Reading* 25). That list reads like a compendium of Dickens characters, right down to Boffin's "bow-wow" and "quack-quack" (*Our Mutual Friend* 596). Yet the association was already clear in 1866, when the authors of "Aphasia," an article published in the *Spectator,* opened their discussion by quoting (or, rather appropriately, misquoting) *Dombey and Son*'s Mrs. Skewton and her botched rendition of the Koran: "one might almost be induced to cross one's arms upon one's frock, and say, like those wicked Turks, there is no What's-his-Name but Thingummy, and What-you-may-call-it is his prophet!" (461–62). Hers, the authors say, is an ordinary problem, a "tendency which more or less exists . . . in most declining and overfagged memories to make out their accounts in blank, as it were, and trust to the power of association in the minds of others to fill up the blanks correctly."[14] Starting sentences is easier for aphasics than finishing them. They "pull up short" as they "approach the predicate," failing "at the parts of the sentence where there is most need for attention and volition,—not because they lose the ideas, since they have the idea even vividly before them, but because they have lost confidence in their own power to pronounce the talisman which will recall it to other minds" ("Aphasia" 45). The typical sufferer is at once poetical and stricken with writer's block. She exercises "the most complete power over the organs of speech" but cannot "choose words appropriate to the thought in the mind"; in milder cases, "the patient can still describe by a periphrasis the object which he wishes to mention, but has to wander round it and indicate it by stray shots." One represents the moon as "that public light," acquaintances and friends as "new or old specimens" (44). It may be, the authors speculate, that the aphasic is unusually anxious about self-expression. He "strains . . . the nerves which are put in action when he interprets himself, *translates* himself to others" (46, original emphasis).

Aphasia is presented as an extreme version of an everyday, yet difficult phe-nomenon, the self-translation that expresses us to other minds. Because it is "sometimes carried to an extent and comes on with a suddenness," it has lately acquired "a name of its own." It is as if we are reading Bentham all over again: our words can easily feel strange, our thoughts estranged from us, the authors tell us; we must trust others to find suitable replacements, supplying "volition" to our sentences, "filling up" the predicates we have grown too tired (or unconfident) to supply ("Aphasia" 46, 44–45). It is easy to simulate the experience of apha-sia by thinking hard of a single well-known word. Zero in, and the word grows "opaque," "lose[s] its meaning." Stripped of grammatical context, it "sound[s] a foolish sort of word, not calculated to express meaning at all," as if it were an "illusion, an imposter, a sound which tries to make us believe that it will mean something to other people, but which will betray us and stultify us if we trust to it." The authors single out two "curious and characteristic facts" about this phe-nomenon. First, "the words which seem to come most easily and rapidly to the lips of the aphasic patient are rather exclamatory and interjectional than words of proper meaning"; words "of impatience, or anger . . . flow easily from lips which cannot express any connected sentence at all." "Criky!" and "Gemini gosh!" burst forth with as much forethought "as there is in a dog's mind between the noise at the gate and its own bark." According to one Dr. Jackson, such "swearing is, strictly speaking, nor [sic] a part of language" but "belongs to the same general category as loudness of tone and violence of gesticulation." Thus the second ob-servation, that such expressions, "being properly signs of emotion," are "nearer in their character to tears, smiles, and gestures than to words of coherent mean-ing." Elements of an affective vocabulary, conveyers of "tone," they are the "signs" and "character[s]" of emotion (45–46).

These medical specialists felt comfortable concluding that aphasics spoke a sentimental language that was, "strictly speaking," not part of any ordinary one. Emotional tones, they believed, were easily conveyed because emotions "need no recollection"; they are something one never forgets how to express (45). It was a trust into which these authors placed more faith than did Dickens, for whom "tears, smiles, and gestures" were signs in a sentimental vocabulary that could not be guaranteed to speak for itself. This may seem a strange claim to make given the ease with which feeling issues forth in the interjections common to aphasics and Dickens's characters alike. But the frustrations of both register the disconnection of language from feeling and thought, along with the insistence that we need others to express our minds and hearts. For sympathy, as Dickens understands it, is a matter of speaking through the other's mouth, and enabling others to speak through ours. Even the most private feelings are mediated through the language communities Dickens's characters inhabit; the most pathological figures are those whose feelings cannot be sounded back to them by others. Mrs. Skewton neither desires our sympathy nor likely deserves it, but her comic, angry straining for expression adds to our sense that linguistic disorientation is the common condition for which sympathy is the only practical cure. It may be most right to say that while all of Dickens's characters speak the language of feeling, that in this they have no choice, only some fully comprehend the collective nature of that enterprise. To be truly of the world means being able to finish other people's sentences for them, and to have them be willing to do the same for us.

PART 2.   FORM'S PROPER PITCH
Nickleby's Knuckles

In "He Stuttered," Gilles Deleuze describes the ways written texts become audible to readers. Authors can represent their characters' speech through dialogic tags, which "*say it without doing it*" (as in, "he muttered"), or by "doing it" through direct renderings of dialect and idiom. To these Deleuze offers a third option, a "*minor use* of the major language," made possible when writers make foreign languages of native tongues. "When *saying is doing*," Deleuze writes, " . . . the stuttering no longer affects preexisting words, but itself introduces the words it affects; these words no longer exist independently of the stutter, which selects and links them together through itself. It is no longer the character who stutters in speech; it is the writer who becomes *a stutterer in language*. He makes the language as such stutter: an affective and intensive language, and no longer an affectation of the one who speaks" (107, 109, original emphasis).

Stuttering language is atmospheric, "a milieu that acts as the conductor of words"; the stutter "grow[s] from the middle" of language, like grass rather than a tree. Mobile, it "roll[s] from right to left," "pitching backward and forward" across the text (108, 110–11). Stutters can happen even when individual words remain intact, through the proliferation of parentheses, rhymes, and repetition. The resulting "grammar of disequilibrium" pushes language "toward a limit that is itself no longer either syntactic or grammatical, even when it still seems to be so formally" (112).

Grammatically correct sentences, too, can stutter. A writer's processes of association and selection can create a *"form of content"* whose contents are impersonal yet affective and highly energetic. In such cases, stutters call forth intensities of feeling that emanate from and belong to language rather than to particular characters. Language that "brings together within itself the quiver, the murmur, the stutter, the tremolo, or the vibrato" then makes "the indicated affect reverberate through the words" (108). For Deleuze, the highest compliment one can pay to the stutter is that it achieves the sonority of music. D. H. Lawrence "made English stumble in order to extract from it the music and visions of Arabia"; Kleist, "by means of grimaces, slips of the tongue, screeching, inarticulate sounds, extended liaisons, and brutal accelerations and decelerations," made German into "a vertiginous music."[15]

Deleuze draws most of his examples from the Romantic, symbolist, and Modernist canons, bypassing much of the nineteenth century and the realist novel almost entirely. It's pretty clear into which of his categories Dickens would fall. Most of the time, Dickens "does it"; he warps the language of "the one who speaks." When Dickens appears in *Essays Critical and Clinical,* it is as a negative example. Herman Melville's "Bartleby, the Scrivener" is singled out as exemplary in part because it isn't Dickensian. Beginning as if it were an English novel set "in Dickens's London," Melville's story goes on to undermine all the usual narrative and symbolic formulas Dickens keeps intact. "Bartleby" stutters by speaking the politest English: "I prefer not to," the clerk's perfectly grammatical signature, neither belongs to Bartleby nor expresses him. The phrase "open[s] up a zone of indetermination or indiscernibility in which neither words nor characters can be distinguished" (Deleuze 76–77). It abolishes reference, even figurative kinds; it cannot be metaphorized; it isn't metonymically secure. Such expressions, in "the *boom* and the *crash,*" push language to "to its outside, to its silence" (112–13, original emphasis). By "doing it," Dickens forecloses on these formal possibilities; he relegates the stutter to isolated characters, putting it into the mouths of inarticulates.

To reconsider that idea, we might look to *Nicholas Nickleby* (1838–39), a novel with many clerks, one an apparent mute. Employed by the malevolent Ralph Nickleby, a businessman and moneylender, Newman Noggs is tall and poorly dressed, goggle-eyed and "cadaverous" in appearance. Adopting a "fixed and rigid look," Noggs "render[s] it impossible for anybody to determine where or at what he was looking" (24). This is one of several survival skills. Carolyn Dever calls Noggs "a secret agent" who "work[s] both sides of the fence," navigating Ralph's immoral world while plotting to upend it (3). To do so, he has made himself hard to read. While the "expression of a man's face is commonly a help to his thoughts, or glossary on his speech," we're told, Noggs's countenance, "in his ordinary moods, was a problem which no stretch of ingenuity could solve" and "nobody but himself could possibly explain" (*Nickleby* 32). But he's not talking. It is his custom to "fall into a grim silence, and [rub] his hands slowly over each other, cracking the joints of his fingers, and squeezing them into all possible distortions" (24). When Nicholas meets him, he first supposes Noggs is deaf, then ill, finally deciding that the man's problem is liquor. "[W]ithout uttering a syllable," Noggs stares horribly, "thrust[ing] his hands under the stool and crack[ing] his finger-joints as if he were snapping all the bones in his hands." It is a posture he frequently adopts, bones grinding, eyes "looking in no direction whatever" (54, 384). He isn't saying much, but wherever we find him, Noggs is making noise.

The tremolo of language pushed to its limits this isn't, for it isn't language, quite. These gestures seem stark evidence of repression, proof of what John Kucich calls "the nineteenth-century cultural decision to value silenced or negated feeling over affirmed feeling, and the corresponding cultural prohibitions placed on display, disclosure, confession, assertion."[16] For Kucich, that prohibition is a sign of something even more ominous, a "systematic deflection of desire away from any relationship to collective identity." The politically progressive, "fusional energies" of the communal group are replaced entirely, in his account, by internalized, wholly individual ones. Victorian novels, including those by Dickens, do portray repression as the fulfillment of a social duty, "explicitly presenting its anti-individualism as a surrender to collective will," but isolated subjectivity, not community, results.[17] Repression, as Kucich describes it, is a version of Raymond Williams's excessive subjectivity, and both have corollaries in nineteenth-century critiques of Dickens's fictional method—in what George Henry Lewes saw as Dickens's antisocial retreat into "hallucinatory" isolation or in the "hunchbacks, imbeciles, and precocious children" with which, griped Henry James, Dickens filled his novels, despite their having no correspondence to natural people or existing types.[18] Kucich shows repression to be a sometimes pleasurable thing, not entirely unlike those childish enjoyments that Lewes found in Dickens in great supply, but even pleasure severs the Dickensian subject from the world, by way of "euphoric enlargement" (*Repression* 22).

Yet we might ask, along with Christopher Lane, whether experiences of the self are strictly "private affair[s]," for we know that, from a Smithian perspective, they are decidedly not (*Burdens* 34). One proof that they weren't so for Dickens, either, may be in the way his texts stutter by creating emotional through-lines that, cutting across character, join feeling to formal modes of critique. Affects belonging to no one in particular stutter through the typical Dickensian text; private subjectivity breaks down as the stutter moves from one person to the next. Not even *Nickleby*'s knuckles are body-bound. Cracking in weird echoes and discordant rhythms, knuckles strike on tables and against noses; they tap midair on the hands of the benign businessman Charles Cheeryble, one of a pair of toothless twins (432). Another set belongs to a "diminutive boy, with his shoulders drawn up to his ears, and his hands planted on his knees," sitting "with evident dread and apprehension" in a room at Saracen's Head Inn (44). One of several "hollow-eyed, small-boned little boys" about to enter Dotheboys Hall (47), he "screw[s] up a couple of knuckles into each of his eyes" as if anticipating a lesson whose full impact he only begins to foresee: the family Squeers considers it their business "to get as much from every boy as could by possibility be screwed out of him" (45, 96).

Even the tyrannical Mrs. Squeers—"no grammarian, thank God"—is in on the act, and in a more double-jointed sense. "What do you think of him?" asks the paternal Squeers with regard to Nicholas Nickleby, his recent hire. "Oh! That Knuckleboy . . . I hate him," she replies (107). She isn't shy about using the phrase to Nicholas's face, either. "What do you say, Mr. Knuckleboy?" she asks at dinner, doling out slices of meat (91). A key scene shows Squeers justifying the cost of hiring Nicholas by comparing himself to a West Indian slave driver. The latter "is allowed a man under him, to see that his blacks don't run away, or get up a rebellion," he says, "and I'll have a man under me to do the same with *our* blacks." Mrs. Squeers grows vicious, saying, "He's a nasty stuck-up monkey, that's what I consider him." Young Fanny, untroubled by "scholastic matters," then wonders aloud "who this Knuckleboy was that gave himself such airs." "Nickleby," her father explains. "[Y]our mother always calls things and people by their wrong names" (108).

It may seem counterintuitive to move in this way from free-flying Deleuzian asyntax to the obvious brutality of tyrants. Having already noted that, in Dickens, how one speaks is indicative of how one thinks, feels, and lives and is thus a measure of moral worth, pointing out the callousness of a Squeersian dialect may merely be redundant, a stutter of the least welcome kind. Yet Dickens brings this semantic violence directly to bear on the notion of the inviolable self. Deleuze's artist stutters so as to destroy the self, but *Nickleby*'s stutter destroys a different object, the fiction of subjective isolation. Rippling into and out of the novel's many vocabularies, *Nickleby*'s knuckles make the social basis of character explicit: nobody escapes their touch. Some critics have claimed that, like *Oliver Twist*, another early Dickens novel, *Nickleby*'s bifurcated structure safely seals off the good, middle-class characters, protecting them from the harm striking everyone else, and the fates of Nicholas and Kate do seem the products more of birth and fortune than of circumstance.[19] Yet that very security comes under attack. Mrs. Squeers isn't exactly wrong to consider Nicholas a "Knuckleboy." Calling him by the wrong name is right, a translation both terrible and true. As Robert Tracy remarks, the heroic Nicholas is "most unlikeable," exhibiting disdain for those around him, especially his companions in the theatrical way (161). Though he laughs when a fellow actor calls him a "puppy" and a "Slave!" he also knocks him down for it, and Lenville isn't the only one bearing the brunt of his fists (*Nickleby* 363). Nicholas's knuckles screw many times into others, including Squeers, whose philosophy of life comes in this way to sock him back. As Squeers tells Ralph, "Mortality itself, sir, is a wisitation. The world is chock full of wisitations; and if a boy repines at a wisitation and makes you uncomfortable with his noise, he must have his head punched" (695).

The Squeersian creed depicts a landscape ghostly and unstable; one never knows when (or whom) the next "wisitation" will hit. As John Bowen argues, in this novel obsessed with money and market forces against which no form of privacy is immune, Dickens is "determined to generalize," to understand the larger forces at work in bringing horrors like the Yorkshire schools to life ("Performing" 160). Dickens's way of "transcoding" details from scene to scene operates in the service not of overblown particularization but of another form of departicularization, the "mutual implication" of seemingly disparate parts. Connecting those elements of the text that are differently valued or put to opposite moral purpose, the novel makes certain terms "utterly promiscuous," applying in some form or another to nearly every character; "lady" and "gentleman," in their profusion, push the divide between gentility and nongentility "to the point of meaninglessness" (Bowen, "Performing" 165). *Nickleby*'s knuckles, in a similar way, carry a bone-cracking violence into nearly every setting, including the artist's. Chapter 31, shot through with "the sound of Newman's knuckles," begins with Noggs feigning to mend a pen with "a rusty fragment of a knife" and ends with Miss La Creevy trading in her "black-lead pencil" for a "mother-of-pearl fruit knife" and "lunging as she spoke" (384–85, 388). Much of the novel's language lunges in this "wisiting" way. Nearly every hand clasps a knife—Mantalini, Lillyvick, Tim Linkinwater, John Browdie, Squeers, Snawley, the Crummleses, the baron, the Lord of Grozwig, the Cheerybles, Mobbs's stepmother (who passes her knife on to a group of missionaries), a murderous journeyman shoemaker. Even Mrs. Kenwigs handles knives, wishing "more than once that private society adopted the principle of schools," requiring that everyone supply his own (169). The nickel-less Knuckleboy isn't the only one with a chip on his shoulder or a weapon in his fist. The novel's metonymic surplus and dizzying puns produce compound fractures and compound nouns, of which the "pen-knife" is only the most graphic. Together they portray a collective consciousness both singular and self-divided, a world in common and at war.

The word "sympathy" appears in one form or another some thirty times in *Nickleby*, more than in *Bleak House, Great Expectations*, or *The Old Curiosity Shop*, yet we cannot appreciate its full importance if we consider it a virtue reserved for moral innocents. For sympathy is in Dickens a formal concern, a way of modulating the text's tonal—and moral—registers. Swimming through Dickens's alphabet soup, spinning words into loose affiliation before splitting them apart into new alignments, we are called on to bring tonal changes to bear on ethical and textual judgments. Mrs. Squeers is neither sympathetic nor likely conscious of her pun, yet her bad English, monkeying around with names, joins a comic pattern that keeps far more serious semantic issues in play. For what, indeed, is Nicholas—puppy or punk? Monkey or slave driver? Who or what can correctly be called "slave"? Her joke splinters tone in at least two contrasting directions—humor and moral outrage, laughter and disgust. Carolyn Dever suggests that *Nickleby*'s melodramatic extremes crank up the emotional volume so as to make the middle ground between them, emotional "ambivalence," more visible (7). Both she and Joseph Childers comment that the Cheeryble brothers are "too good to be good," proof that extremities of all kinds should be considered suspect (Childers 61). The novel enacts a model of subjectivity in which discrete individuality is, for better or worse, a fiction. Believing oneself an individual is a luxury few can afford; those who are individual are utterly abject. Not for nothing does Dickens kill off Nicholas's surrogate (and Ralph's actual) son at the moment when his paternity, and surname, is revealed. Smike cannot be a Nickleby, not even a Knuckleboy; he doesn't survive the translation. The prospect of becoming a Nickleby "unnerves . . . as much as it comforts" the boy whose personal history "includes no mother, no father, not even a wire monkey—just a room" (Dever 10).

Nickleby's narrator is, by his own admission, caught in a representational dilemma of which sympathy is the crux. He tells us in no uncertain terms that sympathy is a formal matter, one of balance and degree. Leveling his critique against a "diseased sympathy" that expends itself on "out-of-the-way objects" while ignoring those closer to home (a complaint later reprised in *Bleak House*'s satirical portrait of philanthropy for Borrioboola-Gha), the narrator explains, "There are many lives of much pain, hardship, and suffering, which, having no stirring interest for any but those who lead them, are disregarded by persons who do not want thought or feeling, but who pamper their compassion and need high stimulants to rouse it." And so it is "with the one great cardinal virtue, which, properly nourished and exercised, leads to, if it does not necessarily include, all the others. It must have its romance; and the less of real hard struggling work-a-day life there is in that romance, the better" (213). The immediate point is that Kate Nickleby must stand in for every other girl employed at Madame Mantalini's shop, then for every other suffering, laboring girl. Her story, told in detailed isolation, ignites readerly interest in ways that all the others, told in "sum and substance," cannot. The narrator, clearly angry at this state of affairs, raps our collective knuckles for failing to notice all that is "constantly within the sight and hearing of the most unobservant person alive" (ibid.).

Yet this, like so much of the business of this novel, is a speculative gamble. Dickens seems just as angry with himself for caving in to romance at realism's expense. The narrative's tone is unstable, shifting from shaming admonition to satire. "The more romance, the better" can hardly be the rule in a book laden with suicides, murder, brain damage, and infant phenomena painful to smile at. Well aware that he is himself to blame for the novel market's heavy trade in "high stimulants," Dickens insists that his romance is rooted in life, real hard and struggling, in "dullness, unhealthy confinement, and bodily fatigue" (213). But the balance is precarious and prone to failure. Rendering sympathy involves a careful finessing of degree, a continual jogging between high stimulants and low. Even in this early novel, Dickens recognizes realism as the difficult achievement of sympathetic proportion. In concert with the reader's keen listening, it results from the proper pitch of form.

George Eliot felt that Dickens might have provided "the greatest contribution Art has ever made to the awakening of the social sympathies" had he not failed to give his characters psychological and emotional depth ("Natural" 111). But Dickens affiliates psychology with form in so unremitting a way as to insist on the inseparability of their connection, and on the social, sympathetic basis of both. He puts the sympathetic imagination to use in navigating form's portrayal of a social psychology laden with moral weight.[20] Private emotion is not Dickens's principal object, which is, rather, the formal mechanism through which feeling can best be consolidated and shared. The novel's narrative knuckling reproduces that larger structure in miniature; like knuckle-cracking, it builds and releases tension, builds by releasing the tension it seeks to undo. To say, then, that sympathy underwrites *Nickleby*'s "form of content" is to suggest that the feelings of individual characters are peripheral to sympathy's more broadly social and structural importance. Stuttering along in its noisy way across an uneven grid of affective values and moral judgments, the novel evokes readers' sympathies each time they confront its endless variations on a word, its moral-acoustical fits and starts.

Little Dorrit's Dress

"Altro!" he shouts, or perhaps stutters, "altro, altro, altro, altro—an infinite number of times" (*Little Dorrit* 25). The Italian speaker is John Baptist Cavalletto (translated literally from "Giovanni Baptista"), a man whose signature is his signature word, one that is, "according to its Genoese emphasis, a confirmation, a contradiction, an assertion, a denial, a compliment, a joke, and fifty other things," and which becomes "in the present instance, with significance beyond all power of written expression, our familiar English 'I believe you!'" (23–24). Moments later—"Al-tro!"—that word is "an apology," standing for "Oh, by no means!" (27). If there was any doubt about the foreignness of language, of even "our familiar English," it doesn't survive *Little Dorrit*'s opening scene, set "thirty years ago" in a Marseilles prison. Overseeing the whole is the rootless Monsieur Rigaud (later Lagnier, then Blandois), an "insinuating traveler" and Dickens's most cosmopolitan villain; in the background, "Hindoos, Russians, Chinese, Spaniards, Portuguese, Englishmen, Frenchmen, Genoese, Neapolitans, Venetians, Greeks, Turks, descendants from all the builders of Babel, come to trade at Marseilles" (15, 460). Words cannot be trusted in this landscape of linguistic confusion. Rigaud, his hands lacerated by scratches, is hardly to be believed when he claims that his wife committed suicide. The gentler Cavalletto, "a poor little contraband trader," is caught because "his papers are wrong" (24).

Words, we quickly discover, are the contraband most often traded in this novel. Cavalletto's favorite, "Altro," quickly enters into other mouths. "What's Altro?" asks the rent collector, Pancks, on hearing it in Bleeding Heart Yard. Mrs. Plornish, Cavalletto's self-appointed translator, happily explains it as "a sort of general expression," which Pancks immediately adopts—"Why, then Altro to you, old chap. Good afternoon. Altro!"—then proceeds to go on saying it, so that "it became a frequent custom" for the two men to exchange it back and forth: "Altro, signore, altro, altro altro!" (325). That word bears a heavy expressive burden for the poor, injured Italian, for whom it is a kind of linguistic passport, easy to bandy about because it can mean almost anything. Not so English, which gets harder to comprehend the more its native speakers try to impress on him "the appalling difficulties of the Anglo-Saxon tongue." Speaking "in very loud voices as if he were stone deaf," the Bleeding Heart Yarders—"by way of teaching him the language in its purity"—consider Cavelletto one of Captain Hook's "savages," Friday to their Crusoe. Mrs. Plornish, "especially ingenious in this art," and convinced of her "natural call towards the language," thinks herself "a very short remove indeed from speaking Italian" in telling him "Me ope you leg well soon" or explaining to Pancks "in her Italian manner," "E glad get money . . . . E please. Double good" (323–24). As one critic notes, the so-called pure language "turns out to be nothing more than the strung-along substantives and uninflected verbs of pidgin English—the language of condescension," "English made un-English"; the Yarders "believe that Italian is simply English with a fractured word order," English minus the *h* (Edgecombe 280). Even the (sometimes) beneficent Meagles "addresses all individuals of all nations in idiomatic English" with the expectation that they are "bound to understand it somehow" (*Dorrit* 37). Having "lost [his] pleasant interpreter"—his daughter Pet—to marriage, Meagles needs, as he says, "a deal of pulling through": "I stick at everything beyond a noun-substantive," he tells Arthur. Unable or unwilling to pronounce the Italian's name, Meagles calls him "Caval-looro" instead (551–52). Life, the narrator comments in a subtle pun, is "up-hill work for a foreigner, lame or sound" (322).

A story of prisons and echo-chambers, *Little Dorrit* centers thematically on issues of containment and escape and is bound up in questions of language and memory, of how things disappear or carry on.[21] Henry Gowan is no exception in describing ordinary life as "pass[ing] the bottle of smoke, according to rule" (424). Full of locked doors and barred windows, the novel is equally obsessed with the fragile boundaries separating remembering and forgetting, what lasts from what doesn't. Contemplating Cavalletto's imprisonment prompts the narrator to consider others like him and what goes on inside their "noble hearts," a subject about which "no man think[s]": "not even the beloved of their souls," nor less the "great kings and governors, who made them captive, careering in the sunlight, [with] men cheering them on." "[G]reat personages" are remembered, their "sounding speeches" becoming the memories that "polite history, more servile than their instruments, embalm[s]" (29). Forgetting is a problem, but so too is embalming memory, and history "servile" and "polite" is just what results when Dorrit, the child-king, assumes his title. The Father of the Marshalsea grows vain, punctilious, and demanding, greeting new inmates with "a kind of bowed-down beneficence"; the other prisoners minister to his needs with "overcharged" "pomp and politeness," delivering tithes disguised as "tributes" (81). A "gentleman" and "ed'cated" like one, the petulant Dorrit lords over them all because he is fluent. As the turnkey brags, "As to language—speaks anything. We've had a Frenchman here in his time, and it's my opinion he knowed more French than the Frenchman did. We've had an Italian . . . and he shut *him* up in about half a minute" (79).

Little Dorrit presents 1820s London as a place where words have been emptied out. Translation is not the answer in this late novel, where English is a tool for imposing silence. If the Marshalsea is where many things remain unspoken, the Circumlocution Office is a paper prison, all red tape and paper trails, with messengers running about with "plenty of forms to fill up" but nowhere to take and no one to read them. Visitors, told to "keep on writing," are stopped in their tracks "with a minute, and a memorandum, and a letter of instructions, that extinguished [them]" (130–31, 120). Inside its walls, men like Daniel Doyce, an engineer with a labor-saving invention, are denied patents; outside, things aren't much better. The family business from which Arthur resigns has long been in decline; Meagles's fortunes have fallen; Mr. Plornish, plasterer, is unemployed; the Bleeding Heart Yarders live in a perpetual state of "arrears," their debts un-discharged.[22] "All such things as jobs," says Mrs. Plornish, seem "to have gone under ground" (152).

In this suffocating environment, hearing loss is a considerable problem; with no one listening, words have nowhere to go. Mr. Dorrit is one of the worst offend-ers; he hears only what he wants to, for he hears "with the ears of his mind" (645). That wonderful phrase is indicative of the novel's many forms of sound-proofing, good and bad. The Clennam house is a tomb where "street noises," along with "whistling, singing, talking, laughing, and all pleasant human sounds," are shut out, leaving Affery "feel[ing] as if she were deaf" (195). Other sounds are se-questered inside. "There never was such a house for noises" Affery says of the "rustlings and stealings about, trembling, [and] treads" others seem not to hear (720). At Casby's, another vacuum, things are "silent, air-tight," "stifled" as if "by Mutes in the Eastern manner," their tongues forcibly cut out (159). Mr. Merdle, his own tongue "stiff and unmanageable," speaks hardly at all; there are "black traces on his lips where they met, as if a little train of gunpowder had been fired there" (642). As Plornish sees it, there are "many thousand Plornishes" living in the same impoverished condition, failing to secure a living wage, unable to air their grievances or place blame.[23] Within striking distance of the Office, that great

wheel of government, all are equally shut out, all "playing sundry curious variations on the same tune, which were not known by ear in that glorious institution"
(158).

The ability to hear anything at all can seem a moral good in such stultifying
environments. Clashing with one's environment means falling out of harmony
with the tone it sets. The best people have keen ears and careful timing; the
worst tune things out or fail to get the proportions right. Daniel Doyce speaks
in "a quiet deliberate manner, and in that undertone which is often observable
in mechanics who consider and adjust with great nicety." Plornish tries hard to
"balance his sentence[s]" (137, 157). Little Dorrit is practically bionic in her ability
to recognize people's footsteps, as she does when Arthur crosses the Iron Bridge.
Rigaud, conversely, seems most criminal not because he is a murderer but because "whatever he did, he overdid, though it were sometimes by only a hair's
breadth"; even his laugh is "diabolically silent" (380–81). Mrs. Merdle enjoins her
husband, a swindling banker, to be "more *degagé*, and less pre-occupied" with
business: "it is not the tone of Society, and you ought to correct it" (419–20). The
two have been discussing when, if ever, it is appropriate for a man to scream.
Of the Marshalsea, Fanny tells her sister, "there certainly is a tone in the place
to which you have been so true, which does belong to it, and which does make
it different from other aspects of Society" (264). Amy then confides to Arthur
that the prison's "tone and character" are her own (280). This becomes a problem once the Dorrits recover their wealth. "You—ha—habitually hurt me," Mr.
Dorrit complains in his stuttering way; "[t]here is a—hum—a topic . . . a painful
topic, a series of events which I wish—ha—altogether to obliterate . . . . You,
Amy—hum—you alone and only you—constantly revive the topic, though not
in words." Wordlessly, Amy sounds the painful tones her father wishes "blotted
out" (502–3).

"Prunes and prism" is the novel's shorthand for the problem, a nonce phrase
made for repeating, which Mrs. General instructs the Dorrit girls to mouth ow-
ing to the pretty form it gives their lips. The habit of mouthing senseless words is
spreading throughout Europe. As Amy says of the society of travelers into whose
company she is thrown, "[a] certain set of words and phrases, as much belonging to tourists as the College and the Snuggery belonged to the jail, was always
in their mouths." It isn't simply that Amy considers Europe "a superior sort of
Marshalsea," a refined prison into which English debtors flee, but that both are
prisons of language, echo chambers of hollow words. Aphasia has gone viral:
"hosts of tongue-tied and blindfolded moderns" can be found "carefully feeling
their way, incessantly repeating Prunes and Prism in the endeavor to set their

lips according to the received form" (536–37). Nor is England immune. Young Ferdinand Barnacle remarks often on the empty "forms of speech" keeping "the game alive" (591). Mrs. Merdle's prunes-and-prism expresses nothing but her iron will. "In the grammar of Mrs. Merdle's verbs," we're told, "there was only one Mood, the Imperative; and that Mood has only one Tense, the Present" (583). Meanwhile, the boozy Tip acclimates himself to the family's newfound wealth by turning every word into a money transaction. Slurring his words in the effort to talk the talk, he sounds "as if some of the money he plumed himself upon had got into his mouth and couldn't be got out" (837).

Lionel Trilling felt the novel one in which Dickens's "characteristic delights are not present in their usual force": "the imagination of *Little Dorrit*," he said, "is marked not so much by its powers of particularization as by its powers of generalization and abstraction," perhaps the best for which one can hope in a world where the mind is a prison, incarceration "the ineluctable condition of life in society" (292, 282). Dominated by a single moral idea, the novel is "only incidentally realistic," Trilling argues; "its finest power of imagination appears in the great general images whose abstractness is their actuality"—Merdle's patriotic suppers, the Circumlocution Office—or whose littleness, in the case of Little Dorrit, symbolizes "the negation of the social will" (293). More damning is James Kincaid's assessment of the novel as caring only for a handful of individuals, "silent, static, [and] tomb-like," who are rescued from the hordes by an "elevation into metaphysical marshmallow-land" ("Blessings" 17). Kincaid views the novel as a bitter rant demonstrating a "complete lack of interest in or curiosity about the lives of others" (18, 20). Both critics describe problems of proportion, whereby Dickens cynically preserves a select, "Little" few from the engulfing forces of the general will—from social reality as we have come to define it. Little Dorrit may be "the best of Amys," but Dickens's worry in this novel isn't how to make one toiling dressmaker stand in for all the Amys like her (256). There aren't any. The novel's characters are so utterly sealed off from life's eager movements, its embodied noise, that there is nowhere to go but further in: we "never leave prison, we never leave home, we do not forget—or we better not," as Kincaid says ("Blessings" 19).

Yet neither explanation accounts for the novel's constellation of floating signifiers, words and phrases which do not neatly correspond to anything in the fictive world. Here, even more than in *Nickleby*, floating signifiers raise the issue of translation while emblematizing the impossible task of translating the sentiments of one language (or person) into those of another. In so doing, they call attention to the central failure the novel depicts, that of customary English forms—English ways and syntax—that no longer get the job done. Daniel Doyce must travel to foreign shores, where things are managed in a "most uncivilized and irregular way," to finance his invention (702–3). Acting with "characteristic ignorance . . . on the most decided and energetic notions of How to do it," only a foreign "Power, being a barbaric one," can provide the resources he needs, because it is unshackled by English customs. Back home, the acid Mrs. Merdle, champion of How Things are Done, contrasts "Society," where everything is done according to form, to "the public," a realm of "Savages" (258). Formal barbarism, semantic savagery, not doing (or saying) it right: these are the foreign powers set against a deadened English language and culture, systems upon which even the tiniest units of language might wreak havoc.

If we are convinced that the littlest Dorrit is, more than anyone, hermetically preserved against a contamination that threatens but cannot penetrate her protective seal, we should remember that "Little Dorrit" is, next to Altro, the novel's most mobile signifier. "*She's* nothing," says Affery when Arthur inquires after the girl "almost hidden in the dark corner."[24] "It's no one in particular" the girl later says of herself (192). But "Little Dorrit" is the kind of nothing-in-particular that means many things, depending on who is saying it. Fanny, a "fair smuggler," hints at the contraband nature of the name being bandied about (531). In her more generous moods, she admires Amy for thinking only "of the dinner or the clothes"; when angry, she calls her a "prevaricating little piece of goods" (264, 391). Little Dorrit, seamstress, is continually associated with clothes and piecework, most often with her "shabby dress," which "must needs have been very shabby to look at all so, being so neat" (68). Her name and her "slight spare dress," "usual plain dress," are so often mentioned together that we can understand why Arthur, failing to recognize her love, sees only a "devoted little creature with her worn shoes, in her common dress" (67, 109, 404). Amy encourages the equation. Describing herself in one of her Italian letters as "the little shabby girl . . . from whose threadbare dress you have kept away the rain," she describes in yet another dreaming of herself "as a child learning to do needlework," dressed with "the patches on my clothes in which I can first remember myself" (495, 579–80). In Venice, she imagines herself at dinner draped a dress she owned at eight years old, and wore "long after it was threadbare and would mend no more" (580).

More bizarrely, Flora gives the name "Little Dorrit" to one of her *own* dresses, begun by Amy but left unfinished once her financial circumstances changed. "Such a needle as herself" was worth more than "half-a-crown a-day," Flora tells Mr. Dorrit, reminding him to his great consternation of his daughter's paid labor;

"the very dress I have on now can prove it and sweetly made" (648–49). On part-ing from the seamstress newly rich, Flora proclaims with characteristic flourish: "God bless you and may you be very happy and excuse the liberty, vowing that the dress shall never be finished by anybody else but shall be laid by for a keepsake just as it is and called Little Dorrit though why that strangest of all denominations at any time I never did myself and now I never shall" (438). Flora's semantic sav-agery is among the most pronounced in all of Dickens's fiction, yet "Little Dorrit" is a "denomination" that is "strange" even to her.

Who or what can be a Dorrit (never mind the "Little") is of course an impor-tant issue in its own right. *Nobody's Fault,* the novel's original title, speaks to that rampant social malaise that, in Trilling's view, made the novel so overwhelm-ingly abstract, but it also hints at a pressing empirical concern, the impossibility of finding lost origins. There are some important exceptions. Pancks discovers the Dorrit family fortune by finding "two exactly similar names, even belonging to the same place" (Dorsetshire), then connecting the patrilinear dots (432–33). And "Little Dorrit" is, as Amy reminds Arthur, "the name you gave me," and the one she instructs others to use: "I told [Pet] that the name was much dearer to me than any other, and so she calls me Little Dorrit too" (578). But Flora is right. "Little Dorrit" *is* a strange denomination, strange in its denominations. When Ar-thur thinks of "Little Dorrit," he thinks of figures and blanks: "he began to miss her and to find a blank in her place" before Little Dorrit leaves England (340). Afterward, he finds "what a large place in his life was left blank when her familiar little figure went out of it" (543). Arthur spends many pages of this novel trying to fill in blanks. It is his bitter inheritance. Dying "with [a] pencil in his failing hand, trying to write some word . . . to which he could give no shape," Arthur's father has only a near-mute son—no Jenny Wren—at his side, and as a result the shapeless figure goes missing for good (63). Haunted by a "secret remembrance" of an unnamed wrong, a blank where a word ought to have been, Arthur becomes a man possessed by someone else's memory, heir to an unrecoverable vocabulary lost to the past's "gloomy vista," "bare" and "blank" (62, 180).

But "Little Dorrit," a phrase of his own invention, is a more capacious kind of blank, another "Altro," a word it echoes and whose features its shares. Pancks refers to the injured Italian as "little Altro," and what is true of "Altro" seems also to be true of "Little Dorrit," for it too is a "highly condensed conversation," a for-eign phrase and an emotional shorthand used for telegraphing affective content that cannot easily be slotted into an existing vocabulary or grammar (607, 325). Flora considers "Little Dorrit," the dress, a "keepsake," but it is a curious memo-rial at that, standing as it does for what "shall never be finished" (438). It is worth noting that the Latin *dēnōminātiō* denotes a metonymic "change of name" that in turn implies a meaning surplus: metonymic meaning-by-association, rather than metaphorical identity, issues in polysemic abundance. Metonyms are fugitive, indirect, promiscuous, changed for things arbitrarily related to them. And like the dress, metonymy remains unfinished; it is partial rather than whole. Flora's grammar thus calls attention to the contraband phrase's metonymic power: "Little Dorrit" is a substitute name whose array of uses remains unfixed. For Amy and Arthur, that nonparticularity has special value. Well before their feelings are identifiable as love, "the phrase had already begun, between those two, to stand for a hundred gentle phrases, according to the varying tone and connection in which it was used" (186–87). "Little Dorrit" is to them what "Altro" is to those who use it, a denomination whose associations remain appealingly unstable. Its meaning depends on the "varying tone" and "connection" of its use.

If Dickens's verbal acrobatics seem less dizzyingly abundant in *Little Dorrit*, the novel nevertheless exploits language's tonal capacities for moving between, and yoking together, different conceptual levels, often with the purpose of bringing them into weird alignment. "Fidelity in alterity," Blanchot's phrase, captures the preferred activity of Dickensian tropes. As Garrett Stewart notes, one of Dickens's favorite rhetorical forms, syllepsis, connects two incongruous actions together by a single verb, producing "a syntax of two minds at once."[25] When Miss Bolo goes "straight home in a flood of tears, and a sedan-chair" (in the *Pickwick Papers*), the formula orients its verb simultaneously in two, apparently antagonistic directions, toward the literal and toward the figurative and abstract (482). In *Little Dorrit*'s more somber world, where prepositional comedy of the Pickwickian variety is less pronounced, words seem too anemic to leap so robustly from one predicate to the next. Yet the smallest of words and phrases carry enormous semantic and tonal burdens, producing similarly plural effects. "Altro," the most double-dealing, alerts us from the beginning to the possibility of hearing otherwise by always pointing away from itself. Common in musical contexts, the word indicates an acoustical echo that doubles without repeating an original sound. Stainer and Barrett's 1888 *Dictionary of Musical Terms* defines "altro" as "other," "another," and "others," where it signals an answering-back of one note or musical pattern in another key.[26]

"Little Dorrit," altro's rhetorical double, has accrued by the end of the novel more tonal variety and affective meaning than Arthur can recognize. His romantic second chance is framed as an awakening to tones that have long fallen on deaf ears, for Arthur's perceptual blockade has made him impervious to the language of emotion, which is to him a foreign tongue. For this emotional mute,

the association between feeling, word, and coin is explicit. Arthur is a man marooned, keeping the "locked-up wealth of his affection and imagination" hidden
away like "Robinson Crusoe's money," "exchangeable with no one" and going
"to rust" (165). Not even prison's long hours of self-reflection bring clarity to the
man who is a stranger even to himself. The exasperated John Chivery cannot by
the strongest of innuendo convince Arthur of Amy's love and finally resorts (at
great personal cost) to spelling it out. Stupefied, Arthur rereads Amy's letters,
noticing "a sound in them" that he hadn't heard, their "many tones of tenderness" (763–64). That sound brings with it a creeping realization of the extent of
his self-suffocation. "Was there no suppressed something on his own side," he
wonders, "that he hushed as it arose?"(754). If aural deficiency is a symptom of
Arthur's refusals of affection and self-understanding, his dawning capacity to
catch the emotional tones embedded in Amy's sentences is proof that his heart
and hearing are in sync and on the mend.

But there is still another necessary step. For in this novel, the past's grip on the
present is so thoroughly uncompromising that it takes more than music to undo
its terrible effects. A climactic scene finds Little Dorrit back in the prison cell
where Arthur, long having nursed paternal feelings for her, has taken her father's
place. "Light of head with want of sleep and want of food," Arthur feels his mind
"going astray"; he hears "fragments of tunes and songs, in the warm wind, which
he knew had no existence" (788). Waking from a fever, he notices the fragrance
of flowers, then "a quiet figure" dressed in black. "It seemed to draw the mantle
off and drop it on the ground, and then it seemed to be his Little Dorrit in her
old, worn dress. It seemed to tremble, and to clasp its hands, and to smile, and to
burst into tears" (789). A sentimental homecoming, it seems, as Arthur rouses
himself to ask, "Is it possible that you have come to me? And in this dress?" "I
hoped you would like me better in this dress than any other," Amy replies. "I have
always kept it by me, to remind me: though I wanted no reminding" (790).

Initially soothing, this vision soon prompts a different reaction. Little Dorrit's
old, worn dress signifies not the comforting continuity of past and present but
their insurmountable difference. It becomes a "mirror" reflecting to Arthur how
"how changed he was" (789). He considers the change irrevocable. As he tells
Amy, if only he had "read the secrets of [his] own breast more distinctly" in the
days when "this was [her] home and when this was [her] dress," he would have
"other words than these" to pledge. Now, he thinks, it is too late. Never dream of
"who I might have been," he demands (793–94). Little Dorrit's dress signifies a
bygone opportunity, a foreclosed future. It marks only how old and unmarriage-
able he is.

Little Dorrit has a more than daughterly affection for the would-be father to whom she ministers, for some pages, in a motherly way. There's something undeniably creepy, because incestuous, about these foster-relations, yet such substitutions are also a means through which new kinships can be built. Since homelessness and disaffiliation affect nearly everyone in the novel, surrogacy of some kind (good or bad) is a part of nearly every emotional relationship presented in it. In its most promising form, that surrogacy follows a sympathetic representational logic: taking the place of a missing parent, filling in the emotional blanks left by an absent natural tie, is a way of making do for abandoned children reared in unnatural environments. Such emotional surrogacy requires a high degree of inventiveness for those burdened with task of replacing feelings lost without having been possessed in the first place. Sympathy with others must make it possible for them to rekindle emotions they never had. Not surprisingly, such a sympathy requires a mnemonic and linguistic savagery: a way of fracturing the calcified meanings and associations that, barnacle-like, have made memento mori of words and embalmed human speech.

Consider Little Dorrit's strange mnemonic formula, "I have always kept it by me, to remind me: though I wanted no reminding." If asserting that Amy never forgets, the phrase also registers a bold repudiation of memory, announcing, "I need no reminding" along with, "I want to be reminded no more." At the same time, the word "reminding" highlights the role others play in remembering for us. To remind of something is to "recall [it] to another person's mind," to cause someone to "remember or think (again)."[27] The phrase, like the dress it describes, is a strange reminder, working as it does to offset the ideal of memorial and linguistic permanence. Fanny was right to call "Little Dorrit" (the girl, the dress) a "prevaricating little piece of goods" (391). That phrase repurposes language so as to undo the fixed meanings of the past; those who do otherwise are dressed in dust. Like Cavelletto's "carv[ed] flowers," "Little Dorrit"—girl, phrase, dress—crafts a substitute nature in an invented vocabulary culled from the scraps at hand; in putting Arthur in mind of what he has never felt, "Little Dorrit" (girl, phrase, dress) invites him to overcome all that he has (324). "At no Mother's knee but her's [sic]" had Arthur "ever dwelt in his youth on hopeful promises, on playful fancies, on the harvests of tenderness and humility that lie hidden in the early-fostered seeds of the imagination," the novel tells us. Only "in the tones of the voice that read to him" does he find "memories of an old feeling of such things, and echoes of every merciful and loving whisper that had ever stolen to him in his life" (LD 848). "Little Dorrit" (girl, phrase, dress) stirs the "echoes" of sounds Arthur has barely (if ever) heard. Her "tones" are the psychoacoustical medium through which he begins to recalibrate his emotional life.[28]

There is something to be said for "actuality in abstractness" when emotional atrophy combined with empty talk has made more precise communication impossible to manage. As we have seen, this is sympathy's central premise, as it is what makes reality shareable despite our inability to confirm or know other people's particular emotions firsthand. Adam Smith reserved sympathy for those for whom we do not share stronger affective bonds, but the organization of *Little Dorrit*'s romantic plot—with its desire for harmonic attunements, its fascination with the tonal capacities of words to inflect emotional content—suggests that, for Dickens, sympathy is the psychoacoustical foundation out of which affective ties of many kinds may be built. Fellow-feeling there is the stuff of echoes and whispers for those deprived of natural affection, a surrogate but powerfully felt emotional experience supplied, secondarily, by others. Bentham had argued that a user's state of mind was the one thing of which his words were always a sign, but the inhabitants of *Little Dorrit*'s fictional world must depend on others to make their minds known even to themselves. An important and not unwelcome conclusion we can draw from this is that our sympathy with others must do more than unveil shrouded feelings that cannot otherwise be expressed outright. We need instead a more inventive sympathy, one in which others make entirely new feelings, new realities, available to us.

CHAPTER 4

Not Getting to Know You

Sympathetic Detachment

PART I. SYMPATHETIC DETACHMENT

Of the metaphors used to characterize nineteenth-century literary realism—its ethos and methods—the mirror is arguably the most persistent. Holding mirrors to nature, the realists are said to offer reflections of and on the world by concentrating uncommon attention on common objects and rendering them without exaggeration. For the English novelists, however, realism involved more than fidelity to the actual. Form was for them a moral matter. The mirror and the method it figured were morally satisfactory insofar as a novel tempered its presentation of sordid fact with reflective distance. At this, the French were miserable failures. Members of a "cult of the ugly," displaying a "tenderness for crime, [an] admiration for lawlessness [and] the avowed principles of distortion," the French realists were routinely pilloried in the English press for assaulting readers with crass realities unleavened by disinterested judgment (Blaze de Bury 395–96). According to Mme. Blaze de Bury, Victor Hugo's "unbounded compassion for all suffering" distorted even our sympathy by releasing a "torrent of pity for all misfortune, all disgrace" (397). Hugo's aesthetic crime, a failure to set margins, had moral consequences for readers unable to distinguish one suffering from the next. As Blaze de Bury laments, the French think, but they are not "thoughtful": "thinkers of thoughts" though they are ("the business of their life is to think"), they refuse to "vulgarly appl[y]" thought to action. "It would be a mistake," she concludes, "to call the French a thoughtful race" (410). The English realists, by contrast, saw themselves as ordering the real through the reflective, moral machinery of conscience. Declaring her mirror "defective," George Eliot explained in *Adam Bede* that if her portrayals were sometimes "faint or confused," their outlines "disturbed," this was because the novel was the product of a double re-flection: "a faithful account of men and things as they have mirrored themselves in [the] mind" (159).

When Adam Smith spoke of mirrors, he too was interested in the distancing effects of representational doubling. It is not only that we strive for intimacy in sympathetic encounters, by mirroring other people's feelings in ourselves, but that others act as mirrors through which to envision our own reflections, seen as if through their eyes. Striving to inhabit other minds, we hope to gain something like a narrator's perspective on ourselves: impersonal and faithfully rendered, viewed at a remove. As we know, in *The Theory of Moral Sentiments* (*TMS*) Smith calls upon the "impartial spectator" for this purpose, naming that "great judge and arbiter of [our] conduct" the "tribunal" of our "conscience" (130). Impartial spectatorship involves reflection in several senses. Simulating impersonality in the effort to reflect upon the situations of others also enables a "survey our own sentiments and motives" as they might seem from the outside (110). Impartial spectatorship is "impartial" precisely because it is social. And it is thoughtful, gauging in an imagined, approximate way the impressions we leave on other people and those they imprint in us. Encouraging us to consider how others perceive us, Smith places sympathy's mirror "in the countenance and behavior of those [we live] with," where it is "always mark[ing] when they enter into, and when they disapprove of [our] sentiments" (ibid.). The legitimacy, the very real-ity of subjective experience, requires this outside confirmation. Imagining what others see involves self-difference; subjectivity emerges from that divide. The im-ages in sympathy's mirror are the products of a virtual, social reality: they reflect what we think others think of us.

Eliot has long been crowned the doyenne of Victorian sympathy, yet sympathy in her novels is surprisingly rare. *The Lifted Veil* has seemed to some a story that calls sympathy directly into question, rendering impartial spectatorship a cruel joke by granting its preening, unlikable protagonist superhuman insight into others' minds. A hapless stray apparently having lost his way en route to a Gothic tale (perhaps Charles Dickens's "The Haunted Man"), Latimer harbors a mental power that would make him an odd member of Eliot's high realist canon were it not that clairvoyance aptly figures a problem facing the realist novelists. As Gillian Beer suggests, for post-Romantic writers the "ethic of realism," "paying respect to things as they are, accepting the objectivity of objects," when combined with the ethic of sympathy "resulted in near intolerable pressure on the receptive or penetrating consciousness from the external world." Eliot sought ways "to prevent herself from being deafened by the insurgency of objects and of others"

("Myth" 100–101). Fidelity to the real, added to the mandate to occupy (and be occupied by) other points of view, was increasingly portrayed in the later decades as a futile, even dangerous, project that could drive ordinary people into pathological states. As Suzy Anger maintains, Latimer shares a strong resemblance to other Eliot characters, more likeable and realistic than he but still "fail[ing] dismally" in their efforts to sympathize with others (121). Unlike those who see him suffering from surplus sympathy—a capacity that, to his horror, can't be turned off—Anger finds in Latimer "knowledge devoid of sympathy." *The Lifted Veil* is "not a story about the impossibility of distinguishing between projection and empathy," she writes, for Latimer's lack of sympathy (not his knowledge) makes "clairvoyance a hell for him" (126). Latimer's disease appears to be French in origin. Privy to transparent minds, he's a realist but not a sympathetic one. He thinks, but isn't thoughtful about, other people's thoughts.

As Anger sees it, Smith's account of sympathy "comes closer to Eliot's than does Hume's," since unlike Hume's more "mechanical and mimetic" sympathy, Smith's requires willful effort (113). She situates Eliot in a philosophical tradition that stresses the link between the representational thinking requisite to sympathy and that needed for objectivity in general, noting, for instance, that for Leslie Stephen in *The Science of Ethics* (1882), "the only way we can make up an image of the objective world . . . is by summoning perceptions we are not currently experiencing" (Anger 115). And because he held that objectivity stipulates thinking that we hold our thoughts in common with others, Anger credits Stephen with the idea that sympathy produces reality: because objective knowledge "depends on shared understanding with others," sympathy is "essential to the ability to know anything at all" (116). Yet both Hume and Smith had characterized sympathy as the mechanism by which the mind processes reality. Like Stephen, they held that sympathetic, representational thought lent coherence to our sensations, "fram[ing] them into anything that can properly be called knowledge."[1] The words are Stephen's, but Hume and Smith shared the sentiment: sympathy is the framing device which makes the idea of shared reality feel like fact. "Sympathy and reason," Stephen writes, "impl[y] the other. I cannot reason about another man except in so far as I can rehearse his motives; I cannot feel for him except in so far as I can regard my feelings as representative" (230). Smith would have agreed, since for him, too, reason and sympathy held the real together by way of mutual reflection: reason depended on the imagined habitation of other minds, while sympathy began with reason's assumption that others think as we do, that they are "going along with" us (*TMS* 83).

In what follows, the desire for sympathy and the difficulty of getting it will be bound up with questions of omniscience, a technique many nineteenth-century novelists trusted to foster sympathy in readers. At base was the presumption that by knowing more and seeing further into others, we better identify—and so sym-pathize—with them. Yet though Richard Strang once declared all of Eliot's narra-tors omniscient because they treat every character's consciousness as significant, by the time Eliot began her campaign of making sympathy the realist novel's moral imperative, that trust was on the wane.[2] She shares her worry with Joseph Conrad and Henry James not only that omniscience prohibits sympathy but also that sympathy is diminished by the requirement that we strongly identify with, or know, the sentiments of others. Critics of *The Lifted Veil* continue to debate the le-gitimacy of Latimer's clairvoyance as well as the extent to which clairvoyance and omniscience are analogous, and the relation of both to free indirect discourse, considered by some a "compromise" between first-person (limited) narration and a "full omniscience" that is, in practice, hard to pull off (Levine "Literary" 19). For our purposes, the precise technical distinctions between omniscience, telepathy, and clairvoyance will matter less than the presence of omniscience (or something like it) in figures who ought not have it, first-person narrators and realistic char-acters alike.[3] Describing what she calls "third-personish free indirect discourse," Adela Pinch finds Eliot tinkering with the rules governing narrative perspective in order to represent a variety of mental experiences, as (for instance) that of "soundless words that feel like thinking, thinking understood as cut off from the ordinary world of speech" (*Thinking* 157). In a similar vein, I begin this chapter by suggesting that through characters displaying unsettling "third-personish" forms of omniscience, Eliot sought to disentangle sympathy, identification, and knowledge. Chipping away at the belief that we sympathize most with those whose hearts and minds we know best, her novels suggest that certain ways of knowing cancel sympathy by rendering imaginative thinking obsolete.

Latimer isn't alone among nineteenth-century narrators whose failing to be sympathetic is inextricable from his knowing too much. Jill Galvan writes that Latimer's "fault turns on the exercise of sympathy"; Eliot demonstrates "her well-known preoccupation with this state of feeling in its spurious formulation," for Latimer "ironically reverses this emotion." His sympathy "fuels his egotism rather than his altruism."[4] Galvan, Terry Eagleton, and others call Latimer's ap-parent clairvoyance into question, arguing that one "advantage of interpreting Latimer's paranormal faculties as false" is that it "return[s] *The Lifted Veil* to a realist mode, resolving the story's seeming eccentricity within George Eliot's canon."[5] This approach assumes that the story is realist to the extent that Lat-imer invents or falsifies the events in question. Yet just as Latimer cannot be said to "reverse [the] emotion" of sympathy (since sympathy is not an emotion), *The Lifted Veil* need not be considered realist only insofar as Latimer is proven to lie or to suffer from ethical madness. For as a first-person narrator beset by third-person problems, he literalizes a common feature of nineteenth-century realist fiction, omniscient narration's "inside view," then subjects its celebrated liaison with sympathy to devastating critique. Cursed by omniscience, Latimer loses the distance requisite to sympathetic understanding; knowing with certainty what others think and feel turns out to be, as Smith had foreseen, one of the worst impediments to sympathy imaginable. Critics who seek to disprove Latimer's clairvoyance in order to argue that the novel is realist, or who maintain that the novel cannot be realist because Latimer's clairvoyance truly exists, fail to appreciate that the novel's investment in realism corresponds to this bringing of omniscience, horribly, to life. *The Lifted Veil* does not so much evince doubt about the efficacy of sympathy as demonstrate a growing distrust that omniscience was an ideal way to secure it. It is not knowledge without sympathy, but realism without sympathy, that Eliot is most at pains to prevent: a reality become unbearably close because it is bereft of sympathetic abstraction.

Eliot's Omniscients

> [T]here is a loving laughter in which the only recognized superiority is that of the ideal self, the God within, holding the mirror and the scourge of our own pettiness as well as our neighbours.
>
> —George Eliot, *Impressions of Theophrastus Such*

In *The Lifted Veil*, Helen Small suggests, Eliot's style "acts as a mirror" for Latimer's "double consciousness": as he recounts coming to see into other minds he adopts a narrator's perspective of himself (xiii). In detailing the progress of his "abnormal sensibility," and in describing the "mental processes going forward first in one person, and then another," banging in his mind with the "loud activity of an imprisoned insect," Latimer moves between narrative levels (*Veil* 13). His language is at once "warped by emotion" and "oddly neutral, scrutinizing itself from a distance" (Small xiii). Insight into other minds draws Latimer's attention to the workings of his own, and to the challenge of accurately narrating what goes on inside it. The story that results is not simply autobiographical; rather, it is a detailed record of his mental movements and an account of how thinking others' thoughts impacts the stories one tells. Even seeing the future, what Latimer calls "prevision," involves anticipating how others will think, feel, and behave. "Prevision" and "insight," his two superhuman capacities, are mutually informing rather than distinct powers; as he says, "my prevision of incalculable words and actions proved it to have a fixed relation to the mental processes in other minds" (13). Infiltrated by the thoughts of others, Latimer can even seem responsible for their actions. They speak the lines that are already in his head.

Through the twinning of these powers, Latimer reprises and pathologizes the phenomenon described in chapter 3, whereby finishing others' sentences was a powerful means of sympathizing with them. *The Lifted Veil* reproduces that experience to quite different effect. Latimer's first prevision, of a city he has never seen, coheres just as his father is "called away before he had finished his sentence," leaving Latimer's mind "resting on the word *Prague*."[6] Here and elsewhere, a trailing sentence, many of them marked by ellipses, opens the door for paralyzing, not sympathetic, insight. The most stunning instance occurs in conversation with his brother, Alfred:

> I had never allowed my diseased condition to betray itself, or to drive me into any unusual speech or action, except once, when, in a moment of peculiar bitterness against my brother, I had forestalled some words which I knew he was going to utter—a clever observation, which he had prepared beforehand. He had occasionally a slightly-affected hesitation in his speech, and when he paused an instant after the second word, my impatience and jealousy impelled me to continue the speech for him, as if it were something we had both learned by rote. He coloured and looked astonished, as well as annoyed; and the words had no sooner escaped my lips than I felt a shock of alarm lest such an anticipation of words—very far from being words of course, easy to divine—should have betrayed me as an exceptional being, a sort of quiet energumen, whom every one, Bertha above all, would shudder at and avoid (18).

All the elements of sympathetic translation are there, including the speech impediment, but they are now cause for alarm. Filling in his brother's sentence in a fit of pique, Latimer reacts jealously, then immediately dreads exposure—though he desires exposure as well. There is more than a little wishfulness in this failed Romantic poet's fear of seeming "an exceptional being" possessed of preternatural semantic powers, and he is sorely disappointed when his companions treat his divination as a gaffe: "as usual," Latimer has overestimated "the impression any word or deed of [his] could produce on others"; no one gives "any sign of having noticed [his] interruption as more than a rudeness, to be forgiven [him] on the score of [his] feeble nervous condition" (ibid.). The fear of divulging his godlike ability is crushed by the bitter realization that those around him barely notice. They take his feat as further proof of his fragile, all-too-human status.

As many critics have noted, this is an author's anxiety. Neil Hertz reminds us that Eliot "broke off" writing *The Mill on the Floss* (1860), her most autobiographical fiction to date, in order to write *The Lifted Veil*, "a fiction that purports to be the autobiography of its narrator" and is modeled on Rousseau's *Confessions.*[7] Calling Latimer a "fleeting avatar of the Rousseau of the autobiographical writings," Hertz considers him an avatar for Eliot as well, or for an author's concerns about her work's reception and staying power, her words' real-life effects (51). More to the point, Latimer sounds like the implied author legible in Eliot's other works. He speaks with "those shrewd, arresting metaphors" characteristic of Eliot's third-person narrators; the effect is to bind "the uncanny or supernatural elements of [his] story to a set of larger concerns about the nature of narrative time" (Hertz 59–60). And he seems capable of making things happen simply by thinking about them. As Hertz points out, readers may legitimately wonder whether or not Latimer's words kill his brother. With what he calls "criminal indiscretion," Latimer asks Bertha Grant, at the time his brother's fiancée, if she will love him once they are married; simultaneously, Alfred is fatally thrown from his horse (*Veil* 27).

For Thomas Albrecht, Latimer's clairvoyance is "an implicit figure for realist art" because, by providing "access to the sentiments of large numbers of people," it makes him "a stand-in for the reader or viewer, and also, in another sense, for Eliot herself and for the artist in general."[8] Yet many readers view the story as a refutation of realism's mimetic commitments. Though it "raises the question of what the relationships between art and life are, might be, and should be," says one, its meaning "is not to be arrived at by any reference to the tenets of realism" (Swann 40). A "reader trapped in the book of life," Latimer's future is known to him from the beginning. His existence, unlike ours, "has form"; his is the story of art, not life (Swann 47–48).

Yet we might reach the opposite conclusion, that the tenets of realism are as central here as they were to most everything Eliot wrote. An almost identical set of representational issues troubles the lonely, erudite narrator of Eliot's other strange, rejected book, *Impressions of Theophrastus Such* (1879). From the start, Eliot's critics found *Impressions* insulting; it was either an inside-joke between two polymaths (Eliot and George Henry Lewes) or a failed experiment in citational humor. Riddled with untranslated quotations and obscure allusions, its wit depends on a breadth of classical and continental knowledge enjoyed by a select few. Theophrastus does not as fully literalize the "novelist's imaginary ability to predict the future or read minds," but his resemblance to someone who does and can, the antihero of what is widely considered her most anomalous novel, suggests that Eliot had *The Lifted Veil* in mind when she set out, once more, to dramatize a narrator's life (Hertz 56). Theophrastus isn't omniscient, but he is too knowing for his own good. As Nancy Henry suggests, the book meditates on the relation between the general reading public and members of an intellectual coterie, with unpromising results. "By the end of her career," Henry writes, Eliot "had concluded the author was an outsider as measured against the 'ordinary reader' and was likely to be misunderstood" as a consequence (xxxii). Yet already in *The Lifted Veil*, the resemblance between highly knowledgeable authors and overly knowing, third-personish first-person narrators is uncomfortably apparent. Outsiders looking in, Theophrastus and Latimer are depicted as scholars who have spent too much time alone with their thoughts. As would later be true of *Impressions*, Latimer is full of "quotations" others fail to hear or appreciate (*Veil* 16). The tales these men tell of themselves defy ordinary autobiographical expectations, for neither can narrate his life using conventional first-person modes of address. As Henry suggests, Theophrastus only glancingly reveals himself, doing so by describing "the habits of other persons" (xviii). His status *as* a character is continually scrutinized, as he seems a being unlike the rest. "No man can know his brother simply as a spectator," he says (*Impressions* 4). Yet spectatorship defines him, the fraternity of fellowship is elusive. Though "continually in society, and caring about the joys and sorrows of [his] neighbours," Theophrastus stands apart. As he says, "I feel myself, so far as my personal lot is concerned, uncared for and alone" (6).

Omniscience and its more human offshoots—genius, erudition, rare knowledge—come at a heavy price. Yet even as both men pine for human company, each harbors a deep and associated fear, that others will see in him what he cannot (or doesn't want to) see in himself. Embracing the narrator-philosopher's perspectival distance represents for both of them an anxious attempt at disowning character so as to disable others' capacity to reveal it. That's because "character," for them, is equivalent to commonness, not just in the happy, universalist sense (the humanness we all share) but in terms of limitation, partiality, embodiment. As Audrey Jaffe has argued, omniscient narration represents the fantasy of the subject who is never an object, a being who transcends "the boundaries imposed by physical being and by an ideology of unitary identity"; but for this reason, omniscience cannot exist at all without the contrast supplied by character, whose boundedness it seeks to evade (*Vanishing* 6). We might add to this dilemma that

being a character means becoming the object *of sympathy* in the fullest sense—
being impersonated by others, serving as the objects of their mental reflections,
figuring in the stories they tell. If impartial spectatorship is the mechanism for
achieving the objectivity Theophrastus, philosopher of humanity, most desires,
it also operates by turning everyone else into narrators bent on embodying us.
Sympathy is as necessary for narrative authority as it is dangerous on character-
ological grounds. Promising a philosophic escape from the limitations of self, it
threatens to make Theophrastus and Latimer human, and banal.

In *Daniel Deronda*, Leona Toker finds a "choreographic," Smithian form of
sympathy at work, in which feeling is "redistributed" between different persons
rather than "pooling" or "blending" in such a way that collapses those persons
together: "each subject steps in and out of the other's position" but does not
merge entirely with him (123–24). No such distributive control is available for
Latimer, powerless as he is to police the boundary between self and other; worse,
his omniscience, rather than securing a narrator's impersonality, suggests that
he too is an open book. Theophrastus's central anxiety in the opening chapter
of *Impressions*, "Looking Inward"—that we are easy to penetrate because more
like others than we care to believe—has already been realized in *The Lifted Veil*.
The most awful thing Latimer finds in peering with "microscopic vision" into
others is their "fatiguing obviousness" (*Veil* 14, 29). Surveying the "web of their
characters," he discovers in their "intermediate frivolities" and "suppressed egoism" a "struggling chaos of puerilities," a dismal collection of "vague, capricious
memories" and "indolent make-shift thoughts" (14). The story's central horror,
as Gillian Beer remarks, "is the horror of littleness" ("Myth" 97). Similarly, while
Theophrastus counts himself among the deluded with greater (if insincere) mod-
esty, announcing "[d]ear blunderers, I am one of you," he also "winces at the
fact" and, citing everything from Virgil to Bulwer-Lytton, sets about putting his
superior knowledge on display (*Impressions* 4). "If the human race has a bad
reputation, I perceive that I cannot escape being compromised," he says, adding
this half-hearted appeal: "[l]et me at least try to feel myself in the ranks with my
fellow-men" (5–6). Desiring fellowship, both he and Latimer jealously protect
their separateness. Each fears having his mediocrity—his realism—confirmed.

This narrative discomfort registers as a sympathetic dilemma; a full and impersonal comprehension of the human situation is achievable only by way of
human situatedness. Asserting himself full of "unconscious weaknesses," Theophrastus thus claims to be as little and as petty as everyone else, riddled with the
selfsame "labyrinthine self-delusions" and "pitiable illusion[s]": "it is not that I
feel aloof from you," he writes, for "the more intimately I seem to discern your

weaknesses, the stronger to me is the proof that I share them" (4–5). Turning to a metaphor familiar to us from *The Theory of Moral Sentiments,* he insists that others are the glass revealing our "self-ignorance," the "mirror" through which we judge ourselves.[9] Reflection in others helps us achieve "mental balance," he explains. For if "a squint or other ocular defect disturbs my vision, I can get instructed in the fact," but only from a perspective outside ourselves can we "remedy" the "inward squint" (9). On guard against "self-partiality," keeping watch for "what touches the feelings or the fortunes of [his] neighbors," Theophrastus sounds positively Smithian in aligning the social mirror with impartial spectatorship, calling on "the ideal self, the God within" (10, 13). It is the first step in satisfying a "permanent longing for approbation, sympathy, and love" (6).

We might see this desire for sympathetic objectivity, a "God within," as affording a secular, humanist solution for a narrative as well as for a moral dilemma. As Beer suggests, fiction "in the second half of the nineteenth century was particularly seeking sources of authoritative organisation which could substitute for the god-like omnipotence and omniscience open to the theistic narrator" (*Darwin's* 149). Narrative authority in *Impressions,* centered on the character sketch, seems driven by the hope that giving shape to human types and social categories grants reality a coherent shape, creating the continuities that make the lot of ancients seem parallel to our own. But there's a catch. As he tells it, other people take "the length of his upper lip" and projecting chin as proof of Theophrastus's poor intellect; they "judge the quality of [his] speech" before he utters a word (*Impressions* 7–8). Even friendly acquaintances load him with "all kinds of personal outpouring," talking "unreservedly of their triumphs and piques," yet they resent it when he does the same, exhibiting "signs of a rapidly lowering pulse and spreading nervous depression" when Theophrastus opens similar floodgates (11). Though he confesses to having petty weaknesses and submits them to "loving laughter," the "well-founded ridicule" of others is far harder to bear (13). Not "averse to finding fault with myself," he remarks, "I like to keep the scourge in my own discriminating hand" (6). Some would say you can't get more Smithian than that.

If the ability to know the contents of other minds no longer seems supernatural by the time we get to Theophrastus, it is still, as it was for Latimer, a kind of curse, for now others can turn us into characters and so know (or claim to know) us better than we know ourselves. "I am obliged to recognise that while there are secrets in me unguessed by others," Theophrastus writes, "these others have certain items of knowledge about the extent of my powers and the figure I make with them, which in turn are secrets unguessed by me." They are aware of "certain points in me" that escape "my most active suspicion."[10] We are all but guaranteed to "manifest some incompetency" plainly legible to (if only projected by) others, which we cannot predict and of which we know no more "than the blind man knows of his image in the glass" (5). Sympathy and knowing are again at odds. Wondering about "the figure I make" in other minds, Theophrastus worries that he is overly legible, embroiled in plots to which he is blind. He worries about what kind of character he is or will become. Sounding more than a little like Latimer, he admits to monitoring his thoughts "with peculiar alarm" lest his "philosophic estimate of the human lot in general" should turn out to be "a mere prose lyric," expressing his "own pain and consequent bad temper" (13). Theophrastus's book of life, he fears, may turn out to have but one diminished, prosaic subject—himself, just a character after all.

"Uncouth monster[s]" of the sort David Hume lamented having become, Latimer and Theophrastus seem erstwhile embodiments of the skeptic who, in carrying reason to its full conclusion, finds philosophical rigor incompatible with ordinary life (*Treatise* 1.4.7:172). Not that either is quite up to the task. Hume's skeptic understands the world's metaphysical illusions for what they are; the result is the "forlorn solitude" of a man at sea (ibid.). His story, though, has a happy ending. Reentry into the world is as easy as a game of backgammon, a fireside chat; mundane sociability warms and eradicates reason's chills, so that one finds himself, as Hume cheerily affirms, "absolutely determin'd to live, and talk, and act like other people in the common affairs of life" (ibid. 175). Properly sympathetic understanding is both sentimental *and* detached: customary feelings and habits provide comfort and stability, even as the real remains the object of skepticism, to be viewed from a critical distance. Detachment of this kind is just what Latimer cannot achieve despite his isolation, for he fails to complete the sentimental side of the dialectical equation. Identity with others—transparency to their thoughts—halts the process at the point of disillusionment. His curiosity vitiated, there is nothing to compel a Humean change in mood. The "white noise" through which "common life keeps going" has grown audible—buzzing insects, "grating metal," a "ringing in the ears not to be got rid of" (Duncan, *Shadow* 120; *Veil* 14, 18). In a passage all but copied into *Middlemarch*, Latimer describes his "preternaturally heightened sense of hearing, making audible to one a roar of sound where others find perfect stillness" (*Veil* 18). Knowing others' thoughts before they express them makes for a special kind of agony. It's bad enough to be "perpetually exasperated" by others' "self-complacent belief[s]," worse still to find them "not in the ordinary indications of intonation and phrase and slight action . . . but in all their naked skinless complication" (14–15). Latimer cannot interpret anything because, everything being "naked," nothing is held back. "Intonations" of phrase are stripped of nuance when one knows in advance what speakers intend their words to mean; "slight action" affords no delicious ambiguity when "skinless" and lain bare.

John Picker describes *Daniel Deronda* as the novel in which Eliot most fully explores the components of that "roar of sound" and the "potential for it to unite or confound."[11] He notes that Eliot and Lewes owned several books by the German natural philosopher Hermann von Helmholtz, including *Sensations of Tone* (1868), which discusses the phenomenon of "sympathetic vibration," for Eliot a "crucial sonic metaphor for the psychological and emotional tendencies and vulnerabilities" of her characters (88). Waiting for a "recurrence of [his] new gift," Latimer initially longs for a "reawakening vibration" to thrill him and, like any aspiring Romantic poet, references plucked strings, heart-chords, and thrumming, even posing for a painting of a dying minstrel (*Veil* 11). And Eliot affirms that "true knowledge of our fellow-man . . . gives us a fine ear for the heart-pulses that are beating under the mere clothes of circumstance and opinion" (*Scenes* 257). But in *The Lifted Veil*, "true knowledge" and "a fine ear for the heart-pulses" converge in such a way as to call the affinity between knowing and fellow-feeling into question. Careful listening is one thing, being pummeled by noise another, and though neither Latimer nor Theophrastus merits the praise Eliot bestows on characters less puerile and self-involved, their shared constellation of fears—of alienation from others and loathing for their suffocating proximity, a hostility toward and a desire for connection—suggests that there is something disastrous to well-being (and to art) of unmediated access to the heart-pulses beating in every other life. Hoping to remain "incognito," Eliot confessed in June 1859, a month before *The Lifted Veil* was published, "Talking about my books . . . has been so bad to me that I should like to be able to keep silence concerning them for evermore. If people were to buzz round me with their remarks, or compliments, I should lose the repose of mind and truthfulness of production without which no healthy books can be written. Talking about my books, I find, has much the same malign effect on me as talking of my feelings or my religion . . . The only safe thing for my mind's health is to shut my ears and go on with my work."[12] The need for shutting one's ears returns more than a decade later, when the narrator of *Middlemarch* remarks, "If we had a keen vision and feeling of all ordinary human life, it would be like hearing the grass grow and the squirrel's heart beat, and we should die of that roar which lies on the other side of silence" (182). A sympathetic art, like sympathy itself, depends on abstraction—a modicum of visual distance and a quantity of quiet.

Theophrastus expresses the artist's dilemma in terms of sympathy's double bind. One diminishes the self in the effort imaginatively to share sentiments that must also be kept at bay. Natural egoism disables our ability to inhabit fully the perspectives of anyone else; it is also what shields us against overwhelming perceptual and moral demands. "Examining the world in order to find consolation" for injuries and slights, Theophrastus writes, "is very much like looking carefully over the pages of a great book in order to find our own name, if not in the text, at least in a laudatory note: whether we find what we want or not, our preoccupation has hindered us from a true knowledge of the contents." To read (or write) in this way limits us to the "stupidity of a murmuring self-occupation." True to form, however, his words double back, condensing into a double-sided pun: "I had the mighty volume of the world before me," Theophrastus remarks, "the struggling action of a myriad lives . . . each single life as dear to itself as mine to me" (10). The book of life awaits reading—if only one can shut the "mighty volume" up.

Theophrastus goes on to weigh life's "conversational reticences" against the author's "garrulousness on paper," his ability to vent in writing what, in person, must be held back. Yet even in print, Theophrastus keeps others at arm's length. Fresh from publishing a work in Cherokee—which, like *Impressions,* hardly anyone can read—he relishes the "delightful illusion" of an audience both "nearer [his] idiom than the Cherokees" and farther away: "I imagine a far-off, hazy, multitudinous assemblage," he says, "making an approving chorus to [my] sentences and paragraphs." "The haze," he adds, "is a necessary condition": "If any physiognomy becomes distinct in the foreground, it is fatal . . . I shudder at this too corporeal auditor, and turn toward another point of the compass where the haze is unbroken. Why should I not indulge this remaining illusion, since I do not take my approving choral paradise as a warrant for setting the press to work again and making some thousand sheets of paper unsaleable? I leave my manuscripts to a judgment outside my imagination, but I will not ask to hear it, or request my friend to pronounce, before I have been buried decently, what he really thinks of my parts" (12). Cherishing this one "remaining illusion," Theophrastus voices a weariness with the ideal of transparency to others, knowing their thoughts about us and having them know ours. In print as in life, a "too corporeal auditor" depletes fellow-feeling, "pronounced" judgments are less preferable than the "hazy" tones of a disembodied, distant "chorus."

One gets the sense in these passages that Eliot is dealing with a difficult truth, that sympathy operates by way of figures rather than facts and is fed less by knowledge than by gaps in knowledge, things we cannot (or don't want to) experience firsthand. And though identification can mean many things besides an exact identification between self and other, there are throughout Eliot's work strong indications that the most powerfully moral sympathy arises in relation to those whose separateness remains at least partially intact. When Latimer makes this case, we are invited, despite his flaws, to believe him. Wrong though he is in clinging to the fantasy that Bertha loves him, there is something deeply tragic about living in a world where little to nothing is kept under wraps. Even Bertha considers his emotional crippling the result of having had the last of his illusions shattered. Accusing him of being "bitter against other clairvoyants, wanting to keep [his] monopoly," Bertha suggests that Latimer needed no special power to gauge her true feeling, despite having a mind his preternatural insight cannot penetrate. Clairvoyance confirms what he already knows. The biggest blow he suffers is Theophrastan, the "complete illumination" of self-delusion, the "negation" of all he "delighted to believe" (Veil 32). Adam Bede suffers the same disillusion. In his rosy view of Hetty Sorrel, Adam "created the mind he believed in out of his own" (Bede 319). Likewise, Latimer "created the unknown thought before which [he] trembled," treating it "as if it were hers." Bertha's "coy sensibilities" are the self-made inventions bitterly confirmed, not discovered, by his insight; the "common objects" and "petty devices that preceded her words and acts" are signs he intentionally misread (Veil 32). Though he seems genuinely horrified by the "systematic" totality of her hatred, Latimer is most stung by the mundane simplicity of it (and here too he sounds like Adam Bede—or Adam Bede—on Hetty): there are no "hidden" "landscape[s]" in Bertha's secret soul, no sublime emotional conflict, "only a blank prosaic wall" (ibid.). This understanding chills him into a kind of waking death. "Toward my own destiny I had become entirely passive," he writes, "for my one ardent desire had spent itself, and impulse no longer predominated over knowledge." Simply put, once knowing makes imagining all but impossible, he is left with "no desires" at all (33).

With death imminent, Latimer pauses near the end of his tale to anticipate its reception:

> That course of our [married] life which I have indicated in a few sentences filled the space of years. So much misery—so slow and hideous a growth of hatred and sin, may be compressed into a sentence! And men judge of each other's lives through this summary medium. They epitomize the experience of their fellow-mortal, and pronounce judgment on him in neat syntax, and feel themselves wise and virtuous—conquerors over the temptations they define in well-selected predicates. Seven years of wretchedness glide glibly over the lips of the man who has never

counted them out in moments of chill disappointment, of head and heart throb-
bing, of dread and vain wrestling, of remorse and despair. We learn *words* by rote,
but not their meaning; *that* must be paid for with our life-blood, and printed in the
subtle fibres of our nerves (34, original emphasis).

The paragraph presents a critique in miniature of realism's "summary medium," of sentences that "compress" the long, prosaic years of human life, to be
judged well or badly in response to syntactic incentives. There is a pronounced
hostility toward authors who "epitomize the experience" of their fellows in too-
calculating a grammar, and toward readers sheltering in "neat syntax" against
the rote tedium of suffering life. There is also an acknowledgment that narrators
have little choice but to squeeze out all that even "well-selected predicates" cannot
hold. Words condense visceral realities "paid for" in kind by, and through, others.
Such is the representational dilemma Latimer (and Eliot) is most concerned to
name, in what amounts to a reciprocal act of transfusion built from a sympathetic
realist premise: authors abstract "life-blood" into language, but they must also
impel readers to turn "print" (back) into "nerves."

Middlemarch is said to exemplify Eliotic sympathy at its best, in a heroine
whose "sympathetic motive" is the "current . . . in which her ideas and impulses
were habitually swept along" (80). Yet it too contains a figure whose pervasive,
third-personish mentality others repeatedly run up against. Henry James said of
the novel that Eliot's "marvelous *mind* throbs on every page," but it is Rosamond
Vincy whose mind concerns us here.[13] For although many readers have noted the
similarities between Rosamond and Bertha Grant, both cold-blooded blondes,
Rosamond most resembles Latimer in her display of a marvelous mental power.
A "thoughtless girl" with "no consciousness" that her "action[s] could rightly be
called false," Rosamond's self-centeredness seems typical enough for a spoiled,
pretty girl (*Middlemarch* 326, 627). She isn't thoughtful, to be sure, but Rosamond thinks—so much so that she is in a sense nothing *but* mind, practicing
a brutal form of single-mindedness. "Educated to a ridiculous pitch," a "sylph
caught young and educated at Mrs. Lemon's," she is a rarefied yet formidable
force, having "a Providence of her own" (157, 150, 248). Coolly annihilating all
discordant ideas and perspectives, she is unsympathetic not (like Bulstrode) for
her hypocrisy, but for quite an opposite problem. Rosamond can never be of two
minds. She assimilates all minds into her own.

Consider what happens once she gets it into her head to marry Lydgate:

> To Rosamond it seemed as if she and Lydgate were as good as engaged. That they
> were some time to be engaged had long been an idea in her mind; and ideas, we

know, tend to a more solid kind of existence, the necessary materials being at hand. It is true, Lydgate had the counter-idea of remaining unengaged; but this was a mere negative, a shadow cast by other resolves which themselves were capable of shrinking. Circumstance was almost sure to be on the side of Rosamond's idea, which had a shaping activity and looked through watchful blue eyes, whereas Lydgate's lay blind and unconcerned as a jelly-fish which gets melted without knowing it (255).

Lydgate hasn't a chance against the "shaping activity" of Rosamond's unshrinking will, which can endow an "idea in her mind" with "more solid kind[s] of existence." So aggressive is her mentality that it considers every "counter-idea" immaterial, the will of others no more than a shade passing across her sun, dissolved as easily as it (apparently) is to "melt" jellyfish without their knowing it. Rosamond is nothing if not "mindful"—full of the "more solid" materials of her own mind, and not much else.

She is like Latimer in this way. What she thinks, she gets, filling her book of life with ideas that harden into fact and shrinking the rest into "mere negative[s]" (255). She begins composing one chapter in particular from the moment Lydgate arrives in town. Having first "woven a little future" for the pair, Rosamond then manifests every aspect of their romance: each subsequent scene plays out "just [as she] had contemplated [it] beforehand." Deciding that "a stranger was absolutely necessary to [her] social romance," she easily fits Lydgate ("altogether foreign to Middlemarch") into her scheme; on the hunt for a man with good connections, she finds him "suddenly corresponding to her ideal" (109–10). In case we were inclined to overlook its more sinister aspects, Eliot borrows a term from *The Lifted Veil*'s playbook in giving a name to Rosamond's narrative control. Though the "basis for her structures had the usual airy slightness," she is "of remarkably detailed and realistic imagination when the foundation had once been presupposed ... There was nothing financial, still less sordid, in her *previsions:* she cared about what were considered refinements, and not about the money that was to pay for them" (110, emphasis added). Equipped with a "realistic imagination," Rosamond makes solids of air. Her "previsions," much like Latimer's, materialize the very ends of plot.

David Carroll sees Middlemarch as full of "monsters, vampires, and assorted succubi" tracking down their creators, with Lydgate (as Dr. Frankenstein) pursued by an "inflexible monster who submits him to his own experiments of maceration and control" (84, 85–86). Rosamond's inflexibility *is* monstrous, but largely so because it is a narrator's in human form. Her mind succeeds in doing what Lydgate's can't, exerting a monologic power over plot that guarantees her something like a narrator's infinite life. More Victor than Victor's creation, hers is a colossal ego that just won't quit. Her closest analogue is Lydgate's former paramour, the French actress Madame Laure, whose account of her husband's death exerts such mastery over plot that it's as if all plots are hers for the taking. Having first told Lydgate, "My foot really slipped," Laure then claims, "*I meant to do it*," finally asserting, "I did not plan: it came to me in the play" (43–44, original emphasis). Rosamond is, like Laure, "an actress of parts," but both women write their own scripts; with a narrator's ability, each places all parts, all plots, at her disposal. Indeed, Rosamond is most narratorlike in seeming not quite to have a character: she "acted her own character, and so well," we're told, "that she did not know it to be precisely her own" (109). Jettisoning anything that doesn't fit her script, she exercises an uncanny level of control over fates other than her own. One of the last things we hear of her is that, before dying, Lydgate began thinking of her as "his basil plant," for "flourish[ing] wonderfully on a murdered man's brains" (782). An embalming herb, basil is a fitting emblem of Rosamond's vampirism, as well as of her narrative authority.[14] Other minds—in this case, that of a consummate empiricist—are the food feeding her insatiable (French?) art.

Amanda Anderson has argued that outsider figures like Latimer, regular presences in the period's fiction, are the representatives, however unlikely, of a Victorian ideal, the attitude of detachment. Alongside their isolation and bitter refusals to connect, Anderson finds a vital mode of critique: from their alien perspectives, conventional novelistic remedies—domestic security, romantic union—are revealed as being in their own way dangerously self-contained (*Powers*). The detached may be sick and cynical, but their flaws are mirrored in perspectives that only seem innocuous—the provincialism, say, of kindly men with circumscribed vision, like *Middlemarch*'s Mr. Brooke. This doubling of perspectives ostensibly opposed—rootless aloofness as reflected in hypersituated localism, a cultivated cool in relation to infuriating mental littleness—offers evidence of what Anderson calls a "form of critical cosmopolitanism," whereby novelistic form critiques the perspectives it contains.[15] Suspicious of itself, a novel plots against its own ends by incorporating views critical of the perspectives it appears to embrace. Incongruities of form work to undermine the stated ideals a given novel otherwise seems unquestionably to endorse.

Eliot's example helps us see how, by late century, one might rely on the protocols of sympathy to enact just such a critique, leveled against one of the novel's most established modes of address. Extreme closeness breeds extreme inaction, even rage. Latimer hails from a region of mind-sharing that Smith's theory of sympathy had tried hard to repudiate, where we are powerless to control what sentiments enter in. Advocating sympathetic forms of detachment through portrayals of intimacies too close to bear, Eliot turns realist form against itself. That her most visionary artists suffer from powers usually reserved for third-person narrators suggests that she was deeply aware of sympathy's limitations when the ideal of intersubjective communication turns into brainless, effortless reproduction at best and, at worst, fatal absorption. Latimer's problems of proximity, mirrored in the social critic Theophrastus, demonstrate the difficulty of enacting that critique at the level of character. The one alienated by a toxic closeness with those around him, the other by an erudite worldliness that forestalls local connection, both suffer from perspectival extremes that make sympathy impossible. Eliot's final novel contains yet another instance. For Daniel Deronda's sympathy—"plenteous" and "flexible"—"fall[s] into one current with that reflective analysis which tends to neutralise sympathy." He, like Latimer, is a "medium" catching the flow of other minds, unable to distinguish his from theirs. "[In] danger of paralyzing in him that indignation against wrong and that selectness of fellowship which are the conditions of moral force," Daniel's sympathy leaves him unmoored, "without fixed local habitation to render fellowship real" (*Deronda* 364, 321, 365). It subjects him to an alienated passivity that looks to those around him like a form of omnipotence. Hans Meyrick considers him "an Olympian who needed nothing" (181).

As Anderson and others demonstrate, Eliot's best characters stand apart from, so as to reform, the attitudes and environments they inhabit. Eliot would have seen this oscillation between proximity and distance, and the possibilities for critique it enables, as sympathetic in both design and intention. Aligning Latimer's diseased, involuntary omniscience with Rosamond's single-minded narratorial power, and the many-mindedness of Daniel's self-canceling sympathy, Eliot suggests that only a sympathy that maintains a separation between self and other enables ethical choice, the ability to decide which sentiments to endorse and which to let die or resurrect. Form proves a training ground for sympathetic detachment, guiding readers to take on a variety of perspectives they need not fully inhabit. Mortifications of various kinds fall to those denied the capacity to stand back. Eliot's portrayal of characters bereft of sympathy, who haven't the power to give or receive it, suggests that fellowship with others depends on our being able to think "along with" them without falling helplessly susceptible their thoughts. In that class of characters who seem most like her in their narrating and authorial prowess, yet least like (or liked by) her in their deficit of fellow-feeling, Eliot critiqued a proposition fundamental to the literary realism of her time: that sympathy flows from unimpeded access into other minds rather than resulting from the difficult thinking taking place in the gap that separates them from us.

PART 2. GROUPTHINK IN CONRAD AND JAMES
Conrad's Hollow Men

Joseph Conrad was nearly forty when he published his third novel, *The Nigger of the 'Narcissus'* (1897), and the preface he wrote for it six months later is generally seen as a vindication of sorts, written "to justify a career" (D. Smith 56). It is also an artist's statement famous on the order of *Middlemarch*'s "pier-glass" passage, Eliot's optical parable of an "eminent philosopher" who dignifies dull reality by "lifting it into the serene light of science." Candles, Eliot writes, are like egos: both produce "flattering" optical illusions when held up to a disordered surface, the scratches on polished steel, or a random series of events. Such "illumination" tricks the eye into finding a center that isn't there, "concentric circles round that little sun" (248). Conrad, likewise, compares the artist to "the thinker or scientist" who "seeks the truth and makes his appeal," and for whom art becomes "a single-minded attempt to render the highest kind of justice to the visible universe, by bringing to light the truth, manifold and one, underlying its every aspect."[16] The artist seeks, "in the aspects of matter and in the facts of life, what of each is fundamental," their "one illuminating and convincing quality." But where the thinker "plunges into ideas" or scientists into facts, the artist "descends within himself" to find "the terms of his appeal" (Conrad, preface xlvii). Not "dependent on wisdom," art awakens our "capacity for delight or wonder"; the artist's object is "the sense of mystery surrounding our lives" (xlviii).

Art achieves its purpose by way of "temperament," a vague concept that might be better called "sympathy," for it is contextual, social, and aligned with moral feeling. Giving new life to "old, old words" involves the appeal of "one temperament" to every other, "whose subtle and resistless power endows passing events with their true meaning, and creates the moral, the emotional atmosphere of the place and time."[17] This idea complicates the optic philosophy with which Conrad is usually credited. Committed though he is to helping readers "hear," "feel," and "before all . . . to *see*," Conrad's "temperament" refers to a moral-emotional "atmosphere," situated in time and space (preface xlix, original emphasis). In Ian Watt's estimation, the term "denote[s] the idiosyncratic mixture of elements in the total personality which controls its response to sensory, emotional, intellectual, and aesthetic experience." It thus requires a "kind of seeing [that] must presumably operate through the temperament or the imagination rather than through the eyes" (*Conrad* 82–83). "Temperament," like sympathy, orders random events by suturing experience to a powerful yet impersonal current of feeling, a fellow-feeling borne of "dreams" and emotion, "aspirations" and "illusions," that binds "all humanity" together, "the dead to the living and the living to the unborn."[18]

Conrad's preface emphasizes art's affective power, advancing an aesthetic theory for which sympathy is central, but it introduces a claustrophobic novel that treats sympathy as sham, the "moral trick" practiced by the ship's crew, leaving them "inexpressibly vile and very much pleased with [them]selves."[19] F. R. Leavis declared the great achievement of *Heart of Darkness* to be that "[o]rdinary greed, stupidity and moral squalor are made to look like behavior in a lunatic asylum"—both "normal and insane"—and *The Nigger of the 'Narcissus,'* too, presents a normal world shot through with lunatic feeling from which no one is immune (176–77). William Deresiewicz considers the novel "divided against itself," its "form fractured," its "announced ideology undermined by deeper currents of feeling" (206). These currents of feeling are deep in large part because they are shared. In 1897, Conrad responded to a review published in *The Daily Telegraph* comparing *Narcissus* to Stephen Crane's *The Red Badge of Courage,* saying that while Crane dealt "with the psychology of the mass—the army," he "had been dealing with the same subject on a much smaller scale."[20] Downsized though it may be, groupthink aboard the *Narcissus* produces a sensory overload whose psychic and emotional effects cannot be guarded against. The summons to readers to see, hear, and feel is practically burlesqued in a novel that subjects its crew to an "incomprehensible and disturbing" "gibberish of emotions," an agony of "hollow, moaning, whistling sounds" and "vague mutter[s] full of menace"—subjects them, that is, to James Wait and the emotional drama unleashed by his pretending to die, then dying, and subjects us to the crew's confused strategies for dealing with both (119).

As many critics have noted, Conrad appears to turn the Victorian ideal of sympathy on its head. Full of sympathy and the worse for it, the crew are "demoralised" by Jimmy for the ironic reason that he leaves them "highly humanized, tender, complex." They "sympathise" with his "repulsions, shrinkings, evasions, delusions—as though [they] had been over-civilised, and rotten, and without any knowledge of the meaning of life."[21] As the narrator admits, the men hold fast to the admittedly false belief that they deal charitably with the sick man by feeling for (or with) him, when in fact he is little more than a dark mirror illuminating their self-absorption, "the latent egoism of tenderness to suffering [that] appeared in the developing anxiety not to see him die" (109).

The strand of criticism most pertinent to what follows deals with the novel's "gross violation of point of view" (Mudrick 72). Bruce Henricksen defends the practice—a "wavering . . . between the omniscient and the personal and between the plural and the singular"—as a formal reflection of theme, the "opposition between a world viewed communally and one viewed from the perspective of a particular interest."[22] As he and others point out, the novel moves (sometimes inexplicably) between different perspectival and temporal registers, alternating from a third-person voice, referring to everyone on the ship as "they," and a first-person plural voice who speaks in terms of a "we," only to end up, in its final pages, with a first-person singular narrator, separate from the rest, who twice says of the others, "I never saw them again" (136). Such shifts have caused a variety of logistical and interpretive problems for readers. Henricksen considers the whole a fulfillment of Conrad's optical purpose: "[f]ormal consistency is violated in the interest of surveillance, an interest Conrad announces in his preface when he states his intention to make us see" (785). Watt, too, sees such formal discrepancy as affirming Conrad's values ("on the whole traditional, if not authoritarian," he says, "but at least they are real values, and they are really there") (Conrad 82). In his view, the novel's "plurality of voices" achieves a Yeatsian "emotion of multitude": Conrad turns away from "the ever-increasing separateness of the individual and towards discovering values and attitudes and ways of living and writing which he could respect and yet which were, or could be, widely shared."[23] The "emphasis on repetition and balance of sound and rhythm" becomes the formal expression of Conrad's "controlled exaltation," brought on by "the prospect of the laborious but triumphant monotony offered by the endless tradition of human effort" (83).

Readers may recognize in "controlled exaltation" elements of a Smithian brand of emotional management. Yet criticism of the novel invariably pits monotonous-but-triumphant work against anarchic sympathy, or at least against those feelings associated with it. The "sentiment of pity," Watt says, "proves much more dangerous" than does the crew's resentment toward Jimmy for his apparent, galling unwillingness to work (Conrad 104). Pity threatens worker solidarity inasmuch as Wait "imperiously exploits the crew's sympathy" and insofar as his demands for quiet and bed rest make their ordinary entertainments—nightly talks, Archie's concertina—off limits. In the remaining silence, Watt argues, James Wait is internalized, becoming "the obsessive object of their private thoughts" (105). From this perspective, the crew, when they aren't working, think too much, and overthinking is the cause of their collective emotional trouble. Against those who consider Wait "an emissary from some spiritual chamber of horrors," Watt sees "an irrational projection of [the crew's] own dangerous fears and weaknesses": "behind the mysterious and menacing authority of a St. Kitts' Negro," he writes, "there is only a common human predicament."[24] More startling than anything Jimmy is or does is the revelation that emotional identification with one's fellow man threatens society. Even the novel's "only act of total sympathetic understanding," Captain Allistoun's decision to enforce Wait's lying-up, is at once a beneficent gesture protecting Jimmy from a terrible, inevitable truth and the match igniting the crew's revolt. Condemning him to civil death, the compassionate lie ends in near mutiny, the "most violent attack on the solidarity of the social order of the *Narcissus* as a whole" (108).

Narcissus makes good on Smith's idea that sympathy denotes "fellow-feeling with any passion whatever"—no matter how terrible—"of which the mind of man is susceptible" (*TMS* 10). The crew feel acutely because they sympathize with insufferable abundance—insofar, that is, as Jimmy figures as both the origin and object of their collective emotional life. Yet they do not feel what Jimmy feels, nor do they share one another's sentiments in any unified way. The sympathetic tendency they manifest most is a desire for subjection to an impartial judge, an impersonal conscience with which to constrain and organize feelings and thoughts otherwise threateningly erratic. As used as they are to following the orders of their commanding officers, however, they experience a pronounced difficulty in determining which elements of this sentimental authority originate outside themselves, which are impartial and which are not. Much like the narrator, who is (sometimes) a member of the crew and (sometimes) their distant judge, the shipmates are never sure what they see in the mirror of others, an impartial view of the self or an egotistical projection routed through false fronts. The sympathetic splintering of the self that Smith portrayed as the engine of self-consciousness turns here into a desperate effort to pin the self to others—or, more precisely, to pin the awful responsibilities of self-consciousness to someone else, someone with the power to make our decisions for us. Christopher Lane has suggested that Conrad investigates the "vexed, uncertain boundaries of selfhood" so as to direct our natural animus toward others to the ends of social critique.[25] As he writes of *The Secret Sharer* (originally called "The Other Self"), what's "typically Conradian" is "the ensuing tension between individual disbelief in collective life—including despair at what humanity is capable of doing—and narrative insistence that society is, at bottom, all we have" (*Hatred* 165). Aboard the *Narcissus,* feeling "highly humanized" follows from a collective desire for emancipation from the responsibilities of moral choice and action (*Narcissus* 110). Yet rather than internalize Jimmy, the crew externalizes itself through him. He becomes the subject, not the object, of their thoughts, the "total personality" setting the tone and controlling the whole (Watt, *Conrad* 82). Their disabling social fantasy, in other words, is inspired by sympathy more so than misanthropy: by the belief that others can be held accountable for our sentiments so that we don't have to be.

Early reviewers complained that *Narcissus* was all incident and atmosphere, with "no plot and no petticoats," as one *Academy* contributor put it (Zangwill 95). Arthur Symons griped in the *Saturday Review*, "there is almost endless description of the whole movement, noise, order, and distraction of a ship and a ship's company during a storm, which brings to one's memory a sense of every discomfort one has ever endured upon the sea. But what more is there?" (97). In the twentieth century, J. Hillis Miller describes Conrad as "habitually call[ing] attention to the conflict between the qualitative aspects of things and the interpretation of what is seen into recognizable objects" (*Poets* 24). Conrad represents the "culmination of a development within the novel" in which the attempt to recover an absent God is abandoned for "a human world based on interpersonal relations" (5). The ship's crew, living on the watery margins of the world, where "nothing was distinct and solid," are desperate for something steady, something *to* steady that most "restless" of phenomena, the "thoughts of men" (*Narcissus* 114). That desire manifests overtly once they have spotted land. "For the first time that voyage Jimmy's sham existence seemed for a moment forgotten in the face of a solid reality," the narrator says (115). But land cannot satisfy the craving. Jimmy dies, and his death, "like the death of an old belief," shakes "the foundations of [their] society," leaving them once again unmoored (123). Not even this ironclad proof of Jimmy's illness calms the crew. His demise, and the certainty that comes with it, leaves them foolish and exposed. "Doubt survived Jimmy," bringing fresh revelations of their surrender to a self-invented Providence. He "took away with himself the gloomy and solemn shadow in which [their] folly had posed, with humane satisfaction, as a tender arbiter of fate." What's left is "common foolishness; a silly and ineffectual meddling with issues of majestic import," men no better than "a community of banded criminals disintegrated by a touch of grace" (ibid.).

Watt describes the crew's fascination with Wait as a "demoralising absorption," an identification so total that it is only interrupted when the storm gives them "other things to think about" (*Conrad* 107). Yet it would appear that in their efforts to sympathize with Jimmy, the crew seeks to avoid thinking, to eliminate it altogether. At one point, the narrator considers the possibility that thoughts might travel without it. A "heavy atmosphere of oppressive quietude" engulfs the ship in the days following Donkin's miscarried revolt; the "problem of life" has by now grown "too voluminous for the narrow limits of human speech." Hanging wet clothes to dry "with the meditative languor of disenchanted philosophers," the crew has lost all use for words, but their thoughts seem to be enjoying a life of their own. For,

> in the confused current of impotent thoughts that set unceasingly in this way and that through the bodies of men, Jimmy bobbed up upon the surface, compelling attention, like a black buoy chained to the bottom of a muddy stream. Falsehood triumphed. It triumphed through doubt, through stupidity, through pity, through sentimentalism. We set ourselves to bolster it up from compassion, from reckless-ness, from a sense of fun. Jimmy's steadfastness to his untruthful attitude in the face of the inevitable truth had the proportions of a colossal enigma—of a mani-festation grand and incomprehensible that at times inspired a wondering awe; and there was also, to many, something exquisitely droll in fooling him thus to the top of his bent (Narcissus 109).

These thoughts may be "muddy," but they move. They, and the "bobbing" Jimmy, are all that does. Though the "unprosperous breeze" seems unequal even to the task of drying laundry, a "confused current" of thoughts rocks the ship, run-ning in an electric way "through the bodies of men" who seem less to think than to cling to them, the "black buoy" to which they are chained. Moreover, Jimmy's one, awesome fiction, his "untruthful attitude" toward truth, dominates every thought despite being by now an obvious lie. So much so, in fact, that thinking seems unnecessary to its survival: Jimmy's "attitude" requires embodiment, not belief. Most of the crew holds as fast as he does to what the narrator calls Jimmy's "obstinate non-recognition of the only certitude whose approach we could watch from day to day" (109). It cannot be quite right to say, then, that thoughtful sympathy and unthinking work are pitted against one another, for the men work hard to perpetuate—by embodying—a thought in which none believe, one that buoys them up without their having to think it. Captain Allistoun's offhanded slur against the crew, "a crazy crowd of tinkers! Yes, tinkers!" seems a wry joke on the thin line—an aspiration, a mere h—separating two kinds of life, the life of the (thinker's) mind from embodied (collective) action. Where, the novel appears to ask, does the origin of ethics lie? Even that most ethical act, the Captain's telling a compassionate lie, is done unthinkingly. "I thought I would let [Jimmy] go out in his own way," he says before amending that statement: "Kind of impulse. It never came into my head" (100).

Being driven by thoughts without having to think them up is like being a char-

acter in someone else's book. And, from this first, the novel's setting is a linguistic landscape, a sea of sound wherein the "feverish and shrill babble of Eastern
languages" combines with "the masterful tones of tipsy seamen," their "brazen
claims," "profane shouts," "howls of rage and shrieks of laments" gradually sub-
siding into "a subdued buzz of expostulation" (6).The members of the crew, all
"growling voices" and "bursts of laughter and hoarse calls," cannot at first be distinguished from one another, their conversation unattributable noise: "All were
speaking together, swearing at every second word" (6–7). When Old Singleton is
singled out, he is engrossed in reading Edward Bulwer-Lytton's *Pelham, or the Adventures of a Gentleman* (1828), which he "spell[s] through . . . with slow labour,"
"lost in an absorption profound enough to resemble a trance" (8). The tattooed
patriarch only seems unlike the rest in his savage silence, for like them he is lost
in words, "as ever unthinking" and (we're told twice) "absorbed" in a book (22, 7).
The sight of Singleton "lost in the serene regions of fiction" prompts the narrator
to shift from participant-observer to third-party critic, pondering the effects of
Bulwer-Lytton's "elegant verbiage" on childlike, emotional men: the "popularity
of Bulwer Lytton in the forecastles of Southern-going ships is a wonderful and
bizarre phenomenon," he says (12, 7). Bulwer-Lytton's dandified worlds, he feels,
must seem incredible to the ship's crew; yet they too are "beings who exist beyond
the pale of life" (7). As Lane reminds us, Bulwer-Lytton was a career misanthrope,
authoring essays like "On the Want of Sympathy" (1835) and "The Sympathetic
Temperament" (1862) in an apparent repudiation of Smithian society; taking
interest in others, he felt, was something one "force[d] [one]self" to do.[26] At the
same time, the horror represented in these essays is often that of the "thwarted
solitude" of a mind ceaselessly penetrated by others (*Hatred* 49). Being "absorbed"
in reading Bulwer-Lytton, especially in these crowded conditions, might involve
confronting one of sympathy's more frightening prospects, the possibility that
others do our thinking for us, that with our thoughts we are never alone.

   As if in answer to the narrator's musings, James Wait appears on the ship a
living book and an embodiment of narratorial power—seemingly omniscient,
semivisible, the inky blackness into which the crew immediately become dissolved. Singleton has barely "shut his book" when a being, his name "all a
smudge," comes treading in from the dark, a still, inhuman presence, "calm,
cool, towering, superb" (12, 16). In a voice remarkable for its "soft precision,"
Jimmy announces, "I belong to the ship," but it is clear that he stands apart from
the rest, "as if from his height of six foot three he had surveyed all the vastness
of human folly and had made up his mind not to be too hard on it" (16). Jimmy
seems to the crew an all-knowing avatar of judgment, "right as ever" and impos-

sible to refuse; as their suspicions of him grow, Jimmy's narratorlike power only increases. Projecting their fears and fantasies onto Wait turns him into a delusional omnipotent, a stubborn man "absurd to the point of inspiration," "so utterly wrong about himself that one could not but suspect him of having access to some source of supernatural knowledge" (109). Excluded from full participation in the novel's "we," he is the outside that utterly defines them, a causal force with whom the "universe conspired."[27] Even what Wait doesn't know is seen as evidence of his superhuman status. He is "outrageous—belonging wholly neither to death nor life, and perfectly invulnerable in his apparent ignorance of both" (117).

The crew's conspiratorial desire makes Jimmy, in the end a "child frightened by the menace of being shut up alone in the dark," more powerful than he is by turning him into the author of their actions, the idea riveting their attention, and the conscience that controls their thoughts (120). They figure themselves "obsequious sycophants" in the service of his "glory," a deathless power living "within him with an unquenchable life" (110). Jimmy, as they see it, sets the temperament aboard the ship; he is the omnipotent author whose norms determine the mood, an atmospheric engine distributing justice. He seems to so influence the "moral tone of their world" that it was "as though he had it in his power to distribute honours, treasures, or pain," as if he could confer "eternal reward[s]" (110). It is important to see that Wait's monstrosity grows from the monstrous perspective of a hydra-headed narrator Watt describes (only half-jokingly) as "a veritable Pooh-Bah of perscrutation" (*Conrad* 66). Yet serious scrutiny is just what that narrator hopes to avoid by heaping that responsibility onto the "[o]ne lone black beggar amongst the lot" (*Narcissus* 100). The more Wait is saddled with that burden, the less personlike he becomes. He grows "immaterial like an apparition," "fascinating as only something inhuman could be" (110). Conrad himself saw fit to describe Wait as "the center of the ship's collective psychology and the pivot of the action," both the ship's and the novel's center of gravity, but also, he adds, "an imposter of some character"; "in the book," Conrad writes, "he is nothing."[28] Donkin expresses the same sentiment, telling Wait, "Yer nobody. Yer no one at all!" (119). Even Jimmy, uncertain of the weight he carries, appears "distrustful of his own solidity" (110). He behaves "like a man in hiding" and considers himself "lighter than the husks," an "empty man—empty—empty," someone whose "inside was gone" (89).

We have seen that omniscience is a narrative effect evolving from the tension between "a voice that implies presence" and "the lack of any character to attach it to," between "a narratorial configuration that refuses character and the characters it requires to define itself" (Jaffe *Vanishing* 4). Omniscience represents a specific fantasy, that of access to knowledge "no one knows" (9). Accounts of the transition from Victorian to modernist fiction often associate the former with certainty, the latter with uncertainty, so that Victorian omniscience—the intrusive stuff of external commentators—gives way to radical uncertainty, the deep plunges of Jamesian psychological depth. Yet omniscient novels of the nineteenth century, as Jaffe notes, frequently represent the display of knowledge, not possession of it. It is hard to imagine a novel in which the display of knowledge, without knowledge, more firmly registers. With an "imposter . . . character" at the center of its collective psychology and composite narration, *Narcissus* gives us reason to suspect that this harrowing tale of sympathetic overidentification offers a canny study of the limitations of omniscience, suggesting that there is no egoism quite so large, no sympathy quite so corrupt, as that which insists on burdening others with the responsibility for our feelings, turning others into the authors of our sentiments and, therefore, our moral action (Conrad, "To My Readers" xlv). Consumption kills Jimmy, but his humanity is first denied by the crew's persistence in making him appear to be beyond knowledge, so wrong about himself he is right in ways no person ever could be. The crew dehumanizes Jimmy, and themselves, by contriving in apparent sympathy with him to impart to him an omniscient authority. They confer to him a highly dubious honor, an outrageous knowledge no mere person could ever possess.

His foray into an omniscience attributed to Jimmy, but which Jimmy never has, exacerbates the narrator's sense of his own folly; it also suggests that Conrad experiments with narrative perspective in order to put the ethical limitations of omniscience on display. Alexander Gelley makes a similar point on behalf of Henry James's *The Sacred Fount* (1901). That novel's "I" narrator also lacks the traits "typically associated with a fictive character" (he has no name, physical description, or past). He seems less an "agent of mediation within the diegesis" than a formal principle come to life, "a means of disclosing the creative process *in actu*" (58). One gets that impression in part because, like *Narcissus*, *The Sacred Fount* centers around a colossal enigma that is never solved, growing harder to unravel the more the narrator fixes his attention to it. The more he tries to root out others' secrets, the more insistently he recruits them into his narrative formula, the less substantial they—and he—become. In the end, he suffers a complete undoing, and is forced, as is Conrad's crew, to "concede the hollowness of the narrative that he has constructed" (59).

Conrad admired James, sending him a copy of *An Outcast of the Islands* in October 1896 with a "pretty dedication" in the flyleaf (Conrad, *Letters* 54). James later expressed delight in Conrad's descriptive powers, and the two began a literary friendship. Watt portrays Conrad during this period as James's disciple, a lesser writer making an amateur's mistakes. In *Heart of Darkness,* he says, Conrad lets his protagonist "muddle out the meaning of his own experiences as best he can," adding that such "total subordination to the subjective limitations of the vision of one particular character is very different from James."[29] As Watt has it, James was at this time developing his signature style of indirection, a narrative perspective that avoided "both the intrusive authorial omniscience of earlier fiction" and "obtrusive detachment." Unlike Conrad, James "retained a discreet form of authorial narrative, and both his selection of a particular registering consciousness, and the terms in which he presented it, implied the author's full understanding of that consciousness" (*Conrad* 204).

Watt has novels like *What Maisie Knew* (1897) in mind when describing the "sympathetic and authorially-endorsed closeness" Jamesian narration invites, a measure of his success at countering both "the refrigerating tendency of third-person narration" and an equally problematic Conradian absorption (*Conrad* 204). He clearly isn't thinking of *The Sacred Fount,* a novel Leavis declared senile and one that might best be described, with a phrase lifted from Conrad criticism, as cultivating "resentful solidarity" with others from whose thoughts one cannot get away.[30] As Sharon Cameron writes, "*The Sacred Fount* victimizes characters by the tyranny of thinking" and victimizes readers "because there is no place outside the thinking mind . . . where one could assess the status of what is being thought," no safe distance from which "to think about thinking" (160, 162). James ups the ante when it comes to writing a plotless novel, exchanging Conrad's ship for an island-like country estate visited by a man with a "ridiculous obsession," an "immersion, intellectually speaking, in the affairs of other people" (*Sacred Fount* 72). Critics have called the novel vampiric, but here it serves as our final example of late-Victorian cynicism about the consanguinity between sympathy and immersion in others—especially when extreme proximity makes them all but impossible to distinguish from ourselves.

Emotional Eating in Henry James

When R. P. Blackmur took stock of James criticism in 1942, he found that with "a single exception, the other critics who have dealt with James have either ignored *The Sacred Fount* or dismissed it as a flat failure." The exception, Wilson Follett's "Henry James's Portrait of Henry James," argued that the novel wasn't a novel but, in Blackmur's words, "a fictional presentation of James's philosophy of fiction."[31] For Harry Thurston Peck, this was itself a problem: in fictionalizing his philosophy of fiction, James had sunk "into a chronic state of peri-phrastic perversity" (442). Rebecca West's swipe against the novel is the most notorious: a "week-end visitor," she says, "spends more intellectual force than Kant can have used on *The Critique of Pure Reason* in an unsuccessful attempt to discover whether there exists in certain of his fellow-guests a relationship not more interesting among these vacuous people than it is among sparrows." The book offends in its portions and proportions, a problem built into its core. Its "morbid analysis of thought and phrase and look and gesture, and then analysis of analysis," is at once over-extended and trivial, feeding on itself while leaving readers hungry (in Edel 3). According to another reviewer, just getting through it required an iron stomach. Those who succeeded, he sarcastically remarked, must feel the same "strenuous contempt" for easily digestible fiction "as some ostrich, blandly assimilating a breakfast of telegraph wire, must feel for such poor-spirited creatures as demand an effeminately eupeptic diet of green things or hay" (Anonymous 355).

Claiming that the story "worries one like a rat nibbling on a wainscoting," West wasn't alone in thinking that James overdoes it, and in an oral sense. The more admiring Marian (Mrs. Henry) Adams complained that it wasn't that James "bit off more than he could chaw but that he chawed more than he bit off" (in Blackmur 328). For Edel, the novel demonstrates that "[i]n the complex play of human relations persons do develop dependencies, do make emotional demands upon each other which can feed or even destroy their own lives" (7). At the heart of it all is the sacred fount, a mechanism through which affective and intellectual energies are exchanged. Oscillating between sustenance and deprivation, it is "like the greedy man's description of the turkey as an 'awkward' dinner dish," James declares. It "may be sometimes too much for a single share, but it's not enough to go around" (*Sacred Fount* 34).

Despite the sentiment that "it is hard to think of an occasion in a novel of James when a real taste is tasted or a real smell smelled," James in this novel puts the mind in the mouth, chewing away—viciously—at crumbs (Chatman, *Later* 30). As many commentators have noted, this isn't the sort of thing one would expect. Sharply distinguishing between literary and culinary taste, James chas-tised readers "for whom taste is but an obscure, confused, immediate instinct" and who believed that "a novel is a novel, as a pudding is a pudding, and that our only business with it could be to swallow it" ("Future" 243). But the difference between the two might not be so neatly drawn. As Jennifer Fleissner contends, novels like *In the Cage* present us with a choice between two options, refined taste and brute necessity (the "aesthetic" and the "everyday"), only to press beyond both with the suggestion that the body might be "granted an aesthetic life of its own" (39). James's "savorers," as she calls them, are eaters who "excessively, even perversely [insist] on wringing all possible pleasure from the meagerest morsel, precisely *as a result of* the evident recognition that more may not follow" (51, original emphasis). Their ratlike nibbling is perverse only from a perspective that can afford to ignore that possibility. Savoring expresses both gustatory refinement and the likelihood of want.

A novel of emotional eating, *The Sacred Fount* never lets us forget that the other side of feast is famine. "Whether you batten or are battened upon," as Blackmur put it, "you tap the sacred fount" (346). That possibility makes the novel's touted vampirism all the more curious. The plot, inasmuch as there is one, involves the narrator in a days' long investigation of a theory sparked by observations he makes at Paddington Station while awaiting his train. Though the narrator knows Grace Brissenden, he fails to recognize her on the platform; she appears years younger than her husband Guy while he, not yet thirty and more than ten years her junior, looks "quite sixty" and unaccountably fatigued (*Sacred Fount* 29). The narrator concludes that it is the usual dynamic of all couples for one to sap the energies of the other while the second is drained; "it's the deepest of all truths" that those on the losing end share a "fellow-feeling of each for the lost light of the other" (66, 122). Something similar, he decides, must account for yet another surprising revelation, the rise in intelligence of the formerly idiotic Gilbert Long. The narrator's goal throughout the weekend will be to discover who among them is the food on which Gilbert's intelligence feeds. "One of them always gets more out of it than the other," the narrator remarks; "one of them . . . gives the lips, the other gives the cheek" (66). Grace Brissenden, a prime example, is "bloated" from "eating poor Briss up inch by inch" (58, 60). And yet, the narrator remarks, if he has often seen "the fat grow thin and the thin fat," he has "*not* seen . . . the stupid grow clever"; thus, he adopts Grace as his collaborator in ferreting out who supplies Long with "a mind and a tongue" (22–23). Whoever that person may be, he or she is the sacred fount, energy source and emblem of the Darwinian logic that governs it. Combining nutrition and starvation, it reminds us of the harm that even sparrows do. For when in nature we perceive a "superabundance of food," Darwin darkly explained, we "do not see, or we forget that the birds which are idly singing round us mostly live on insects or seeds." In the effort to live, they are "constantly destroying life" (*Origin* 53).

We might expect this concatenation of food, sex, and death to seethe with erotic tension, but though one critic dubs the sacred fount a "hyperbolic euphemism for the reservoir of sexual energy," there isn't really much sex to speak of—no mean feat considering vampires are afoot (Stein 375). These vampires haven't much bite. As Joseph Halpern writes, it is a "de-Gothicized and toothless vampirism, to be sure" (53). What gives? For most critics, the answer has something to do with the artistic process, with the James-on-James microscopy of the narrative's self-remarking.[32] Gillian Beer claims that the Jamesian artist "must create by means of a counter-fiction which will contain that which is not to be contained. Through the geometric image of the circle or the round framing eye of the microscope or telescope, a readable focus is achieved and inquiry can be both initiated and brought to a conclusion" (*Darwin's* 145). But James ruthlessly pokes fun in this novel at the notion that the artist and the scientist-philosopher are one. Claiming "an extraordinary interest in [his] fellow-creatures"—"most men," he avers, haven't "half so much"—the narrator fancies himself a keen student of humanity. His interest "breeds observation," he says, "and observation breeds ideas" (108). Yet in what seems a sly (if inadvertent) riff on Hume, the narrator makes Gilbert Long, "a fine piece of human furniture," the focus of painstaking, fruitless inquiry (17). Though the narrator pursues his case in a quasi-scientific, inductive fashion, he admits to enjoying in "the fruit of [his] own wizardry" the artist's pleasure in making things up (97). "I struck myself as knowing again the joy of the intellectual mastery of things unnameable," he says, "that joy of determining, almost of creating results" (151). He associates these intellectual pursuits with a totalizing power of vision. Convinced that Briss considers him "his providence, his effective omniscience," he imagines himself intervening to "avert" Briss's "inexorable fate" (123). "I saw what I saw, I felt what I felt," he explains of his quest for a saving omniscience; "one couldn't know anything without seeing all" (108, 122).

Though the sacred fount is the narrator's invention, a theory he at first eagerly spreads around, the more he tries to fix people's behavior in accordance with the laws that govern it, the more chaotically they behave. As he grows increasingly aware, the fount's design is asymmetrical, its effects difficult to control or predict. Contemplating Long's extraordinary gift of gab, the narrator considers whether, "in these strange relations" he tracks, "the action of the person 'sacrificed' mightn't be quite out of proportion to the resources of that person." The sacred fount needn't strike a balance. It is "as if these elements might really multiply in the transfer made of them" so that a "borrower" can find himself "in possession of a greater sum than the known property of the creditor" (49). The first to identify the sacred fount, whose law he admits to "exaggerating," the narrator soon dedicates his time to searching out "precious anomalies" that unsettle even if they cannot entirely undo it (30, 140). "Things in the real," he admits, "have a way of not balancing"; the fount's "fine symmetry" has "artificial proportion"—it is hard to "make the cases fit" (130, 161). After all, the funds being transferred are emotional and energic. It is possible to give feeling away without loss: "[i]t doesn't cost you anything" (93). One can even give away, as May Server does, more than one has.

Thrilling whenever the pieces fit, the narrator soon begins taking stock of the system's tremendous costs. Once set in motion, artificial laws acquire a life of their own, squeezing out whatever exceptions are introduced. The novel combines *The Theory of Moral Sentiments* with *Wealth of Nations* but destabilizes Smith's harmonious balance of give and take, leaving instead a sentimental disequilibrium of surplus and deficit, too much for one but not enough to go around.[33] Indeed, the nineteenth century might be thought of as a sustained period of worry about that sympathetic economy, whether one shorts oneself by investing feeling in those who don't need or deserve it, how to ensure that one never runs out, that one's emotional deficits are made up. In Dickens, a character is likely to gain back whatever feelings are sent out of the self, growing ever happier or more miserly in proportion to funds given away. *The Sacred Fount* explores the possibility that others strip our feelings from us, leaving us to starve. Its narrator's desire to register feelings that escape our intellectual systems is for this reason both hopeful and poignant.[34] "Isn't there such a state," he asks, "as being in love by the day?" (109). Feeling "a new emotion" occasions in him the desire to "unthink every thought with which [he] had been occupied"; he grants his feelings enormous creative power even when he cannot figure them out (131). May appears on the horizon "as if . . . by the operation of [his] intelligence, or even by that—in a still happier way—by [his] feeling . . . Yet what *was* this feeling, really?" (97). He cannot say. Accused of having fallen in love with her, he admits to having "only a thin idea of the line of feeling in her·that had led her so to spare me" (79). Yet love is "as good a name as another for an interest springing up in an hour," the "odd feeling" to which he can assign no better (75). Even May and Briss "[feel] their way" to a "common fate" without being able "to name it or to phrase it"; "possibly," the narrator suggests, they "couldn't had they tried" (104).

The book is considered a turning point for James, away from the nineteenth to the twentieth century, from realism to the symbolic. Its plot, writes one critic, signals "the death of the Realist narrator" and James's "departure from Realist narrative" (Bentley 256). It "stands at the threshold of a full return to Hawthornian symbolism" says another (Halpern 57). Heath Moon says it best in writing that "two assumptions have held the field: that the narrator is unreliable, separated from author and reader with an ironic distance, and that consequently the book is ambiguous," and so modernist, "impenetrability" being modernism's "hallmark." Affirming the by now standard idea that in the transition from a Victorian to a modernist sensibility one moves from sympathy to irony, identification to distance, the novel has seemed to secure its "cachet of profundity" by refusing what the Victorian novel religiously supplied (121). Moon wryly notes that to celebrate the novel as inexplicable is to reproduce the attitude held by its early detractors, for whom it was equally, if less happily, opaque. "Saving James from Modernism" (Moon's title) involves saving the narrator of *The Sacred Fount* from long disparagement, accusations of insanity included, but, most pertinently, an insane refusal to relinquish abstract theory in the face of contravening fact. Moon concludes that James was at the time worrying about the survival of a leisured, rentier class "drifting ever further from the culture at large and managing to preserve itself by feeding on its own kind."[35] It is one law among many that critics have found in a novel whose extreme formalism distinguishes it from its predecessors. Blackmur's description of it as a "fable" (331), like Stein's "poetics of nothing" (389), emphasize James's experimentation with formulas built up so as to be undermined or surpassed. "In a significant number of James's novels and stories," says Halpern, "a system is established which must undergo substantial internal transposition (or disruption) for the text to come to an end."[36] What makes *The Sacred Fount* unique is that the narrator's system isn't destroyed but is canceled out by someone else's. In the end, "the missing link or word has not been produced" (Halpern 63).

The narrator does suffer a "smash" when, in the final pages, Grace confronts him with her "finished system," but hers is his come hauntingly back (*Sacred Fount* 218). Having given others a taste of his passion for systems, he is shocked to discover in them an appetite more ruthless than his own. The hunger to see and know all, his "effective omniscience," looks when he sees it in others like a mechanism for eating people alive (123). Once set in motion, his habit of making cases of others loses whatever sympathizing energies it might have had, for now it is a form of mental cannibalism. Indeed, the word "case" (occurring, by my count, some fifty times) seems constantly to be making an appearance: "the case of Mr. and Mrs. Brissenden . . . positively excited [him]"; Gilbert's is "an excessive case, a case that in him happens to show . . . what goes on whenever two persons are so much mixed up."[37] And so it goes. Soon every case, no matter how strange, becomes systematic, one more proof of an all-consuming logic. Once having "communicated to them a consciousness"—"the last thing," the narrator says, "I wanted to do"—that hermeneutic begins "throb[bing]" all around him "into life" (189). The narrator feels paralyzed to control the mentality he has unleashed.

Dazzled, Ford Obert declares, with apparent admiration: "I don't see the end of what may be done with it" (56).

Laced with nautical metaphors, *The Sacred Fount* comes closest to *The Nigger of the 'Narcissus'* in taking as its central problem the difficulty in striking a balance between self and other whenever people "so much mixed up" together join forces in voraciously thinking a thought that then takes on a life of its own (66).[38] A damning effect of the sacred fount's success is the paranoia it inspires about anything contrary to it. May Server's "peculiar case" is a case in point. Briss wants to be kind to her, but, he says, "she terrifies me. She has something to hide." He thinks her radiant happiness suspicious; her children are dead, "and nobody that belongs to her appears ever to have been particularly nice to her" (91). Convinced that she feigns happiness, Briss dreads an impending collapse, while the narrator, with "supernatural acuteness," tells him that May wants him to know her secret, "for sympathy, for fellowship, for the wild wonder of it" (95). Yet sympathy is nowhere near as "wild" as it needs to be, having so far resulted in a dismal conglomerate of groupthink, shared egotism, and defensive pride. Struggling to prevent his—their—totalizing formula from swallowing her up, the narrator realizes to his shame that it is in apparent sympathy with *him* that the others emulate his devouring consciousness. Together they confer an ever more solid reality to a theory he set in motion.

Hume thought of his skeptical self as being "like a man, who having struck on many shoals, and having narrowly escaped shipwreck in passing a small frith, has yet the temerity to put out to sea in the same leaky weather-beaten vessel" (*Treatise* 1.4.7: 172). James's narrator suffers under the painful impression that his sentiments have sunk someone else's ship. May is his *Narcissus*, the "weaker vessel" he tries to save from "crack[ing] . . . in pieces," "left behind . . . for ever" yet not at all: "I see her now; I shall see her always; I shall continue to feel at moments in my own facial muscles the deadly little ache of her heroic grin" (140). May seems to him what James Wait seemed to Conrad's crew, "limp and empty," evacuated by the pressure of others' thoughts, a "poor banished ghost" (103, 171). "[S]ailing all day, though scarcely able to keep afloat, under the flag of her old reputation for easy response," May becomes "the absolute wreck of her storm, but to which the pale ghost of a special sensibility still clung, waving from the mast, with a bravery that went to the heart, the last tatter of its flag" (102–3). As the narrator tells Grace, "I certainly had my reasons . . . for not indeed deserting our dear little battered, but still just sufficiently buoyant vessel, from which everyone else appears, I recognize, to *s'être sauvé*. She'll float a few minutes more!" (172). He means the sacred fount, but it is May whose very name now threatens to sink her "as if to mention her had been to get rid of her." Grace, with "no intention . . . of sinking" herself, engulfs the narrator with a mounting, hungry pride "unutterabl[y] opposite" to that other, "tragic lady"—not "the arid channel forsaken by the stream, but the full-fed river sweeping into the sea, the volume of water, the stately current, the flooded banks into which the source had swelled" (171–72).

Sympathy in *The Sacred Fount* seems a recipe for liquefaction, a device for turning many into one. As Stacy Margolis suggests, while it may seem that James's aristocratic vampires provide the other guests "with a more terrible and accurate image of their hidden selves than any mirror could reflect," external-izing the hideousness they harbor inside, the novel's characters are finally less fragmented into multiple selves than monolithically collapsed, one into the other (398). It's hard to say whose thoughts belong to whom. Though it staggers the narrator when she says it, Grace cannot recall precisely when she changed her mind on the all-consuming question of May. Likewise, the narrator and Ford Obert are uncertain who is first responsible for thinking the thoughts they share ("Yours *was* mine, wasn't it? . . . Or was it mine that was yours?") (147). Margolis calls the novel "anti-introspective" because self-knowledge appears to operate in reverse: characters "come to know what is internal to the self through what is external to it" (400). We might also call that process "sympathetic," but here it takes on a nightmarish aspect. Indeed a process reminiscent of Smithian so-cial theory is offered as evidence that that very theory has run its course, that its actuarial understanding of an externalized subjectivity, consolidated through imagined consensus, can make the self so dependent on others as to be utterly self-estranged, so defined by others as to have no interiority of its own. Jamesian psychology, for all its deep plunges, seems intent in this novel to show how easily overtaken by others the self has become. Modernism's killing-off of the narrator, whose intrusive, controlling presence is said to define the nineteenth-century realist novel, is from this view less prompted by a desire for an immersive psy-chological complexity unloosed from moral certitude than proof that that narra-tor's function has become ever more deeply engrained—so thoroughly part of the social fabric as to be alive and well, eating away at us.

Sympathy versus Empathy

The Ends of Sympathy at Century's End

I began this book by arguing that the sympathetic foundation of nineteenth-century realist form is evident in some of realism's most familiar narrative practices. I outlined how realist metonymy, for instance, once released from strict mimetic indexing, facilitates realism's historicist project by emphasizing the causal and contextual relationships ordering historical life. Yet we also saw that by comparing one's point-of-view to that of an imagined other, or scrutinizing that viewpoint from a perspective outside it, historicist thinking of this kind operated in tandem with the sympathetic process, sharing its basic assumptions and relying on its protocols. From that starting point, my argument moved on to investigate further how several nineteenth-century writers incorporated sympathetic protocols into their fictional projects: in Jeremy Bentham's sympathetic grammar, with its stress on virtual emotion, anticipated or potential rather than experienced feeling; in Charles Dickens's tongue-tied aphasics, standing in need of sympathetic semantic assistance. These examples highlighted sympathy's partiality, the imperfect approximations to be forged with others and, sometimes, with ourselves. These didn't last; they were fictive and incomplete. But they made social reality possible by making it possible to feel confidently that others were "going along" with us (Smith *TMS* 83).

As the metonymic realism of Dickens and Eliot shifted at the fin de siècle toward the modernist poetics of fiction associated with Conrad and James, another transformation was also under way. A new concept, empathy, had been gaining significance, and was being used to mark the transition from one psychological-aesthetic paradigm to another. That shift is often seen as a flat rejection of sympathetic realism. As Stephen Arata argues, the "turn away from sympathy . . .

was perceived by many as the defining feature of late-Victorian realism" (178). From this view, Heath Moon's assessment of James's *The Sacred Fount* seems more exception than rule, though one suspects empathy, not sympathy, to be his intended subject. The novel is modernist, he says, in featuring "not a contemptuous distance between author and character but close imaginative sympathy." Its primary effects are achieved through an "exploration of subjective worlds, of unusual psychological states, and the interpenetration of inner and outer worlds" (141).

Moon describes an enhanced and improved sympathy, but empathy is the term typically used to describe this more intimately psychologized and "poetical fusing of consciousness and reality."[1] The notion of "poetical fusing" is key. For just as fusion—or its lack thereof—distinguishes metaphor from metonymy, the desire to fuse with others—or lack thereof—distinguishes empathy from sympathy as we have defined it. Thus, this book's final claim: we should recognize that nineteenth-century metonymic realism entails a commitment to sympathetic, more than empathetic, relations, evidence of which can be seen in its rejection of the tropes (and ideal) of fusion. Likewise, empathy, rather than sympathy, is better affiliated with modernism's symbolic project.

The *Stanford Encyclopedia of Philosophy* credits the British psychologist Edward Bradford Titchener with translating the German word *Einfühlung* into English, introducing "empathy" into the vocabulary in 1909.[2] He was one among many prominent thinkers attempting to overhaul or replace the term "sympathy" so as to better explain how feeling-with-others gives rise to aesthetic experience.[3] These writers (Vernon Lee among them) were indebted to the German philosophers Robert Vischer and Theodor Lipps, who from the 1870s onward had given the concept of *Einfühlung,* already important to philosophical aesthetics, a much wider significance. *Einfühlung,* in Vischer's view, described the way humans projected emotion into aesthetic objects so as to animate our relationship to the phenomenal world: it was a "feeling into" of the self into aesthetic form.[4] For Lipps, *Einfühlung* was a process in which the boundary between subject and object, now called an "ego object," disappeared.[5] Aesthetic experience resulted from an empathetic fusion of forms, art object and self. Lipps considered this process so essential to human understanding that he presented it as the engine of self-consciousness. That I am able to have a self, he believed, depends on my ability to humanize objects, including the object that is myself. Moreover, my ability to "feel into" myself allows me to comprehend the feelings of others, whose bodies provide no reliable confirmation of their emotional states. One couldn't simply read the other's emotions from physiological signs; feeling into bodies and feeling into art required identical acts of projection, an activity that took place "in the mind's muscles."[6] As Lipps saw it, this muscular mentalism was both introspective and social, a way for the ego to gaze upon itself and transport itself into others.[7] For this reason, empathy involved an aesthetic experience "of another human" (Lipps, *Aesthetik* 49).[8]

As I have tried to demonstrate, sympathy in the long nineteenth century, well before "empathy" entered the lexicon, was thoroughly implicated in questions of aesthetic form. Moreover, sympathy served an important purpose for the realist novelists precisely because the fusion of self with other, empathy's most highly prized accomplishment, remained largely if not entirely impossible. If their efforts to maintain the border between self and other has seemed prudish and reactionary, a moralistic response to Romantic or sentimental excesses, the realists had powerful aesthetic and ethical reasons for creating forms of narrative that could generate experiences of sympathetic connection without requiring that others' feelings and minds be known or identically shared. Adam Smith's major insight into the figural nature of sympathetic understanding—that one need not feel what others feel in order to sympathize with them—finds parallels in a realism that proceeds by way of tropes emphasizing approximate likenesses and close proximities rather than identity and simultaneity. It was crucial for Smith, and then for the realists, that sympathy not secure the sort of intimacy associated with empathy and cast as one of empathy's major improvements. The distance they maintained between self and other need not be proof of a collective moral or aesthetic failure. Recalling Rousseau's distinction between a distanced, judging "pity" and an ostensibly superior "compassion" that is free of those qualities, Martha Nussbaum suggests that it "isn't right to suppose that approaching the predicament of another with one's own best judgment, rather than the sufferer's, need involve condescension," to which she adds an insight that would have resonated with the nineteenth-century realists: "there is condescension in suspending one's own reflection, and true compassion in trying to get things right" (310 n.24).

Nevertheless, empathy in the parlance of the day has come to seem something like "sympathy minus the attitude," sympathy bumped off its moral high ground into something more pleasingly democratic, a method for feeling *with* rather than *for* others. Sympathy belongs to the Victorians, empathy to us. This was intentional on the part of those who sought to remake sympathy for aesthetics. When Vischer emphasized the identity that obtains in empathy between a subject and its object, that more total identification was made to seem preferable in contrast to a hierarchical sympathy. As Vischer explained, when looking upon an aesthetic object, "I see . . . a sort of duplicate of myself, the photographic image of my own mood" ("Aesthetic" 691). But sympathy as the realist novelists understood it maintains an awareness that the other *is* other—not me, not my photographic image. Smith's "going along with" others has been our model for what that sympathy might look like and require, a virtual relation for generating a contentless companionship freed from duplication, not limited to a single feeling circulating unchangingly between subject and object. To re-create other people's mental movements; to reflect on the situations out of which their feelings arise; to gauge the appropriateness of their feelings and ours; to go along with others imaginatively, and imagine them going along with us—these are the mental processes such a sympathy emphasizes in forging relations even with those with whom we do not identify, and without our having to feel anything at all.

We'll end where we began, with Roman Jakobson's distinction between metaphor, the dominant trope of poetry, and metonymy, that of (realist) narrative. As we saw, Jakobson granted metaphor a level of inventiveness denied to metonymy, by highlighting poetry's power to create similitudes between unlike things. Metonymy, with far less invention, was left imputing relations that were already there. We then began to revise that thesis, focusing on metonymy's usefulness in cultivating what now seems a decidedly nonempathetic sympathetic mode. For realist metonymy emphasized the contextual embeddedness of sentiment and meaning as these came to be perceived in the nineteenth century; it was one of several techniques used to elicit in readers a sympathetic understanding of the mind as situated in time and place. By contrast, the turn in modernism toward a more highly symbolic and poetic form not only reclaimed metaphor for narrative, making for a highly poeticized fiction, but also discovered in empathy a sympathy purged of its apparent stodginess and revamped for a twentieth-century aesthetic. In short, with its fusion of subject and object, empathy more readily accommodated metaphor and so found a welcome home in a modernism seeking to distance itself from realism and the forms of sympathy embedded in it.

Empathy then and now carries the cachet of the modern. We need hardly mention the importance empathy would have for one Sigmund Freud, certainly the most influential of those writers who, at the century's cusp, heralded the birth of a concept better outfitted to modern conceptions of mind. But in letting go of sympathy—collapsing it synonymously into empathy, or replacing it entirely with an empathy that improves on its ostensible flaws—we let slip some of the most distinctive elements of the aesthetic mode that sought, by as many means possible, to embrace it. The phrase "sympathetic realism" is intended to enhance our understanding of sympathy, realism, and the relation between them: in the sympathetic features of nineteenth-century realist form and in the sympathy whose unique protocols inform its reception and design.

Notes

INTRODUCTION. THINKING OF ME THINKING OF YOU:
SYMPATHETIC REALISM

1. Accounts of sympathy are many. The following list is partial, and supplemented in this and later chapters. These texts, not mentioned elsewhere, treat sympathy as a central concept and roughly fit my historical time frame: Parrinder; Ermarth, "George Eliot's Conception"; Adams, "Gyp's Tale"; Cvetkovich; Arata, "Realism, Sympathy"; Hinton; Rai; Gottlieb; and Nieland.

2. The exploding interest in cognitive science among literary critics makes any complete list of relevant titles impractical. For an introduction to the field, one might start with Damasio, Turner, and Zunshine.

3. Lanzoni 279. In *Science,* Stephen associates sympathy with altruism. On Stephen's evolutionary metaphors for sympathy, see Richards.

4. Smith, *Theory of Moral Sentiments* (hereafter *TMS*), 10. Two useful Web sites are "Adam Smith's Lost Legacy," www.adamsmithslostlegacy.com, and the International Adam Smith Society, www.adamsmithsociety.net.

5. Sympathy is regularly linked to identification. Nancy Armstrong, discussing Mary Shelley's *Frankenstein* in *How Novels Think,* writes, "The monster's propensity for violence stems from . . . the fact that no human who sees him can sufficiently tolerate his difference to perform the leap of sympathetic identification" (74). In William A. Cohen's "Envy," sympathy "forestalls and defeats envy through its forms of identification, incorporation, and selflessness" (302).

6. Sully 471. Sully was one of several *Mind* contributors "anxious not to lose sight of the social aspect of aesthetics in an atmosphere where aesthetics was increasingly grounded in a physiology of pleasure" (Lanzoni 282).

7. Darwin, *Expression* 74. There are many accounts of Darwin's treatment of the emotions, far fewer on his treatment of sympathy. Psomiades, in an unpublished paper ("How to Make People Like You"), argues that Darwin "provided a new 'developmental narrative of biological-model sympathy' to replace Adam Smith's 'exchange narrative of economic-model sympathy'" (Kreilkamp 107).

8. Critics sometimes characterize the "emotional turn" in literary criticism as a turn away from mind and spirit, toward the body. See Carolyn Williams. "In our present time," she writes, "it seems that instead of *hoc credo*—or even *cogito*—we have 'I feel' as the most

substantive, persuasive claim of the subject" (48). On the feeling of reading, see Dames and the book from which my phrasing derives, Ablow, *Feeling of Reading*.

9. Oncken published "The Consistency of Adam Smith" in 1897. See also his 1898 essay "The Adam Smith Problem."

10. Tribe, "Das Adam Smith" 514. Tribe notes that the Germans undertook this project without easy access to German editions of *TMS:* "Most of those who wrote in Germany about *TMS* had not read the book" (518).

11. Tribe, "Das Adam Smith" 515, n. 5. See also Buckle.

12. Additional allusions to Smith appear in Robert Burns, "To a Louse" (1786); Maria Edgeworth, *Ennui* (1809); Thomas Carlyle, "Signs of the Times" (1829); John Stuart Mill, *Autobiography* (written in the 1850s but published in 1873); Mary Margaret Busk, "Machinery" (1837); and Elizabeth Gaskell, *Mary Barton* (1848) and *North and South* (1855). John Ruskin describes Smith as "that half-bred and half-witted Scotchman who had taught the deliberate blasphemy that 'thou shalt hate the Lord thy God, damn his laws, and covet thy neighbour's goods'" (91). In *Invisible Hand,* Courtemanche surveys the nineteenth-century fictional afterlife of Smith's most lasting metaphor.

13. Bagehot 17, 19–20. See also Haldane.

14. Lowe 9. Many critics have been interested in Hume's influence on late-eighteenth- and nineteenth-century literature and culture, including Pinch, *Strange Fits;* Bellamy; and Gallagher, *Nobody's Story.*

15. The two most familiar accounts, respectively, are in Watt's *Myths* and Barthes's *Rustle of Language.*

16. Duncan writes of Hogg's *Confessions,* "Gil-Martin's art collapses the system of individual differences that sympathy, in Smith's account, was meant to secure" (introduction xxxiii).

CHAPTER I. GOING ALONG WITH OTHERS: ADAM SMITH AND THE REALISTS

1. Brown 226. Brown's schema includes (1) medieval realism, which treats general, universal categories as real; (2) "formal realism," which treats particulars as real; and (3) causal realism, which locates the real in rational relationships and is hostile to arbitrary interference. On Watt's formal realism, see *Rise.*

2. Shaw 106. Two Web sites devoted to the topic of realism have compiled a fuller bibliography than is included here: www.philwebb.net and (on American realism) www .wsu.edu/~campbelld/amlit/realbib.htm. Edited volumes and essays include Levin, Becker, Krieger, and Walder. Major critical works not cited elsewhere include Lukács, *Studies* and *Essays;* I. Williams, *Realist Novel;* and Ermarth, *English Novel* and *Realism.*

3. Smith, *Theory* (*TMS*) 83. The phrase "to go along with," or "going along with," appears many times in *TMS,* where it fosters commonness as a good. "To see the emotions of [the spectators'] hearts, in every respect, beat time to his own, in the violent and disagreeable passions, constitutes [the sufferer's] sole consolation," Smith writes. "But he can only hope to obtain this by lowering his passion to that pitch, in which the spectators are capable of going along with him" (22). "All men endeavour in some measure to common themselves, and to bring down their selfish passions to something which their neighbour can go along with" (141).

4. Shaw 129. For Gross, emotions define "the contours of a dynamic social field manifest in what is imagined and forgotten, praised and blamed, sanctioned or silenced" and, for this reason, should be studied from the point of view of rhetoric, where language and real-world experience meet (15).

5. As Schneewind writes, Smith demands that "we must live with an irreducible plurality of laws and of their corresponding virtues, and be moved by many motives other than benevolence" (391).

6. Hume, *Treatise* 2.1.11:208. See also Fleischacker, "Sympathy."

7. Sensation was considered a cause for concern. See Aikin, "Enquiry" from 1773: "Much has been said in favour of [representations that] are generally thought to improve the tender and humane feelings; but this, I own, appears to me very dubious. That they exercise sensibility is true, but sensibility does not increase with exercise . . . [In] these writings our sensibility is strongly called forth without any possibility of exerting itself in virtuous action, and those emotions, which we shall never feel again with equal force, are wasted without advantage" (227).

8. Distance and nearness are, of course, relative. Hume writes that it is "not contrary to reason to prefer the destruction of the whole world to the scratching of my finger"; the welfare of distant others may stimulate our imaginations without producing a lasting effect on our passions or conduct (*Treatise* 2.3.3:267). Likewise, Smith suggests that were China "swallowed up by an earthquake," most Europeans would merely twinge before returning to their usual pursuits; meanwhile, contemplating the "most frivolous disaster"—the loss of one's pinkie—raises serious alarm (*TMS* 136).

9. Duncan describes Smithian sympathy as "a moral technique which regulates the boundaries of self and other in order to maintain individual 'propriety' as the ethical basis of civil society," a "system of individual differences" held together by sympathetic bonds (introduction xxxiii).

10. Rick suggests that for Hume inferring the agent's passion "is the sole operation of sympathy" (139). Conversely, Pinch argues that "Hume seems relatively unconcerned with the question of how we really know what other people's feelings truly are," while Smith "makes [that question] central" (*Strange* 30). Other texts dealing with sympathy in Smith and Hume, not cited elsewhere, include Bate, Sutherland, Dawson, Tweyman, and Baier and Waldow. A special issue of the *Journal of Scottish Philosophy* contains essays by Macleod, Remow, and Rick ("Hume's and Smith's").

11. Arguments presenting sympathy as a form of theater include Marshall, *Figure* and *Surprising Effects;* Litvak; Griswold, *Adam Smith;* Jaffe, *Scenes;* Harkin, "Adam Smith's"; and Goring.

12. *TMS* 48. See Ellison's *Cato's Tears* for an account of how, in the early eighteenth century, "sentiment" ceased to define transactions between social equals and began to describe unequal social relations. According to Bell, sentiment at that time shifted from "principle" to "feeling," modulating into full-blown sensibility in the literature of that name.

13. As McKenna argues in *Adam Smith,* by considering "how our interests are interrelated with the interests of others," Smithian sympathy acknowledges "the need to adapt discourse appropriately to an audience" (132).

14. In a lecture from 5 January 1762, Smith noted that "[as] newness is the only merit in a novel and curiosity the only motive which induces us to read them, the writers are

necessitated to make use of [suspense] and keep it up." Thus, "most modern historians and all the romance writers" heavily rely on "dull nonsensical stories," distracting readers from "the grand event" (*Lectures* 91).

15. Korsgaard describes the sentimental philosophers as rejecting the idea that "knowledge is what we need for normativity," putting "something more like confidence in its place"; "once we understand what is in our nature that gives rise to morality and what its consequences are, we can then raise the normative question: whether it is good to have such a nature, and to yield to its claims." The capacity of moral motives "to survive the test of reflection" is thus "not a test for something else, the existence of a normative entity. It is normativity itself" (48).

16. Korsgaard 138; Eliot, "Letter to John Blackwood (1 April 1858)," in *Selections* 187.

17. My use of the term "realism" refers to nineteenth-century realism unless otherwise noted.

18. Shaw 6. For more on this idea, see Lukács, "Realism."

19. Levine, *Realistic* 6. In "Realism," Levine claims that antirealistic elements (wish, dream) "create the form of every novel" in the realist tradition (359).

20. Shaw 130. Here, Shaw is indebted to Auerbach's *Mimesis*, particularly his notion of "historically becoming" (23).

21. Shaw 232. On the difference between novel and romance, see Girard, *Deceit*. To cite one relevant distinction, the novelistic reveals "the illusion of spontaneous desire" (29).

22. Shaw 233. Shaw's larger point is that both metaphorical and metonymic figures can coexist, since historical shifts alter their definitions. Dante's figural realism seems metaphorical because "our culture's sense of the real has itself shifted" (103). White makes a similar argument: "as Auerbach makes quite clear in a passage in which he likens his own method of textual analysis to the style of Virginia Woolf, it remains possible to be a modernist and a historicist at the same time. It requires only a different way of construing the field of historical occurrences, or, at least, the field of literary-historical events" (98).

23. *TMS* 89–90. Compare Dames's argument, in *Amnesiac Selves*, that nineteenth-century fiction privileges forms of memory which generalize so as to ameliorate the past (to make it "summarizable") (7).

24. Warner describes this as a public no longer opposed to the private because it "*was* private": as "the self-consciousness of civil society, it was opposed to the state" (47, original emphasis).

25. These features of realism contribute to its rhetorical function. See Booth, *Rhetoric of Fiction*, and Phelan, *Narrative* and *Experiencing*. Phelan describes rhetorical narratives as those which "explicitly or more often implicitly establish their own ethical standards in order to guide their audiences to particular ethical judgments." Readers "proceed from the inside out rather than the outside in" and "seek to reconstruct the ethical principles on which the narrative is built"; they "bring values to the text" but remain "open to having those values challenged and even repudiated by the experience of reading" (*Experiencing* 10).

26. See Jakobson.

27. Atkinson 51–52. See also Lodge.

28. McHale, *Constructing Postmodernism* 189. Spector is representative in claiming that the "rhetorical figures informing realism tend to be invisible, because they belong to a mode of discourse in which, by convention, tropes are overlooked" (367).

29. Many critics link metonymy to realism and to the naturalizing effect literary realism ostensibly seeks to produce. Among the most influential is Miller, "Fiction of Realism."

30. On this issue, see Booth, *Rhetoric of Rhetoric.*

31. Abercrombie 190. Griswold notes that *TMS* "focuses our attention on particulars and experience and attempts to get us to 'see' things in a certain light rather than simply to argue us into accepting a philosophical position" (*Adam Smith* 61).

32. *TMS* 135. On stylistic "plainness" and the development of "skeptical understandings of style," see Stark 323.

33. Griswold, "Rhetoric" 223. See also his "Imagination: Morals, Science, and Arts." The sympathetic actor, Griswold argues there, has "no exclusive epistemic access to his or her own emotions, none that dispenses with the [impartial] spectator—with the public, with the community, and with 'mankind.' The claim to that privileged access cannot even be stated, except through the mediating presence of the spectator or other (language itself being a public phenomenon). Our understanding and moral assessment not just of others, but of ourselves as well, depend on an exercise of the imagination" (38).

34. Ferguson, "Jane Austen" 159. For Bender, third-person narration (the "interior personification of juridical presence as character") is best understood "historically" by way of Smith (218). Duncan describes Smith's impartial spectator as "a figure within the scene [functioning] as the reader's mirror or proxy" ("Adam Smith" 46).

35. According to Keen, "most theorists agree that purely externalized narration tends not to invite readers' empathy" ("Theory" 22).

36. For an overview of approaches, see McHale, "Free Indirect Discourse," and Fludernik, *Fictions.*

37. Aczel 478. In *Unspeakable Sentences,* Banfield argues against "dual voice" theory.

38. Jahn 451; Fludernik, "Linguistic" 102. Jahn concludes that "all FID forms can be related to a hypothetical and approximate original version of some linguistic activity." It implies that one has "recourse to an 'approximately equal' version" of a character's represented thoughts and feelings, even though such recovery rarely occurs (451–52).

39. Fludernik, "Linguistic" 103. Critics often argue that FID produces one of two typical effects, ironic distance or sympathetic (Chatman) or empathetic (McHale) closeness. See Chatman, *Story,* and McHale, "Dual Voice."

40. As Ferguson explains, some Foucauldian arguments "identify a social collective, but only in such a way as to make all the individuals who are part of it look as if they ought to be relatively interchangeable" ("Jane Austen" 162). Both she and Bender link that attitude to Smith.

41. Gunn 50. Gunn's description of FID's "pervasive atmosphere" recalls Balzac's association of nineteenth-century realism with "atmospheric" effects. On realism's atmospheric "hallmark" (39), see Gallagher and Greenblatt.

42. Gunn 45. Gunn borrows from Cohn the idea of "stylistic contagion" (40). In *Realism,* Morris describes language in FID as "infected or invaded by the speech and perspective of a character" (116). On how nineteenth-century novels provided access to "silent or virtual speech" (33), see Kreilkamp, *Voice.*

43. Some critics distinguish represented thought from FID. McHale discusses the relationship between FID and stream-of-consciousness, for some (though not for Shaw) a conceptual analogue to FID. On "focalization" as a formal technique capturing physical (spatiotemporal) and psychological modes of thought, see Bal.

44. Flesch 50. Tuite describes the sympathetic *distance* of FID when she writes, of *Sense and Sensibility,* that Elinor Dashwood's "sense" involves "the narrator's controlling sympathy that subsumes and ironizes 'sensibility,' domesticating sensibility by subjecting it to the sympathetic patronage of the sensible sister's anxious concern" (*Romantic* 71).

45. Altieri 2. See Fisher on how "passions, moods, emotions and feelings are profoundly different configurations of the underlying notion of a temporary state of a person" (7).

46. Gallagher, "George Eliot" 61. Exploring these issues more fully in *Nobody's Story,* Gallagher explains why the novel's "nobodies" were sympathetic: because they were "conjectural, suppositional identities *belonging* to no one, they could be universally appropriated" (168, original emphasis).

47. As Gray notes, exceptionality is "inherently dialectical": "when the exception, or exceptionality itself, becomes the rule, what was formerly the rule becomes the exception" (647).

48. Eliot, "Worldliness" 201. The essay was first published in 1857 in the *Westminster Review.*

49. Jaffe, *Affective* 39. See Fleming for an account of how originality "replaces rules on the level of form, which in turn frees up common life as the content of high art" (28).

50. I am thinking especially of Woloch's *One vs. the Many* and Miller's *Burdens of Perfection.*

CHAPTER 2. THE ART OF KNOWING YOUR OWN NOTHINGNESS: BENTHAM, AUSTEN, AND THE REALIST CASE

1. On Bentham's school, see Ferguson, "Envy Rising."

2. Chandler, *England* 227. Some of the ensuing formulations are indebted to Chandler's interpretation of the German philosopher André Jolles's *Einfache Formen* (simple forms). See also Berlant, "Introduction" and "On the Case." The two issues of *Critical Inquiry* in which these essays appear are devoted to studies of case form.

3. Mitchell 89. Hume's historical method was criticized as overly distancing, thus lacking in sympathy.

4. Hume, "Of the Study of History" 566. On the relationship between history and experience, see Mack.

5. On this issue, see Ferguson, "Coherence."

6. Phillips, "Belletrist" 71 n. 24; *Society* 84. See also Hogan.

7. Collingwood 441, original emphasis. On Collingwood's legacy, see Collini.

8. To be clear, this stance does not entail a denial of extralinguistic reality but objects to the possibility that it can be directly known.

9. Thomas Carlyle, in "Sign of the Times," complained that Smith and Bentham privileged "external" causes. "The Philosopher of this age is not a Socrates, a Plato, a Hooker, or Taylor, who inculcates on men the necessity and infinite worth of moral goodness, the great truth that our happiness depends on the mind which is within us, and not on the circumstances which are without us; but a Smith, a De Lolme, a Bentham, who chiefly inculcates the reverse of this,—that our happiness depends entirely on external circumstances; nay, that the strength and dignity of the mind within us is itself the creature and consequence of these" (106).

10. In "How to Avoid Speaking," Derrida asks what it might mean to speak without "manner": that is, "in speaking and saying, [how] to avoid this or that discursive, logical, rhetorical mode," or prevent inaccuracies by avoiding predicates, "and even predication itself" (15).

11. Iser 120. Ankersmit argues that "*identifiable individual things* in the past" are not the historian's object, which is instead "the *aspects* thereof—and these are not identifiable individual things" (42, original emphasis). "Historical representations focus our attention on certain aspects of the past," and this "is where [one] should discern its truth claims—so not in the truth or falsity of a historical narrative's assertion."

12. The eighteenth-century linguist James Harris writes of the Stoics, "and the Grammarians with them," words "they considered (as it were) *to fall from the mind*" (278, original emphasis).

13. Bentham's discovery that replacing one word with another is ineffective in communicating word meanings can be compared to Sir Walter Scott's rejection of a word-for-word "dead metonymy." See chapter 1.

14. Locke writes that men "often suppose their Words to stand for the reality of Things" (407).

15. de Champs n.p. See also Blake. On Benthamite "deontology" as a "cost/benefit analysis of the consequences of an action" (166), see McLaughlin.

16. On this point, see Ferguson, "Canons."

17. Gallagher, *Body* 4. Gallagher describes the systematic attempt made by political economists to value "*potential*" over "*actual*" enjoyment, so as to construct "an organic totality far larger than the sum of its human participants . . . to explain where the pleasures and pains went while they were not being felt" (51, original emphasis).

18. Bentham, "Logic" n.p. On this issue, see also Schofield.

19. Bender 40. Rosen and Santesso rebut this view, placing Bentham squarely in the sentimental tradition.

20. Ogden previously published some of these materials in *The Theory of Legislation*.

21. Harrison sharpens the distinction between "non-entities" (like demons) and "fictitious entities," which are "completely different" because they "must be spoken of as existing" (83).

22. Bentham, *Chrestomathia* 85. There, the obituary is credited to the *Monthly Magazine* (April 1814); Ogden attributes it to the *Gentleman's Magazine* (February 1814).

23. Esterhammer 55. See also de Champs: "Bentham saw in Hume's distinction between ideas and impressions the sketch of his own separation of fictitious entities from real ones" but insisted that language and thought are "inseparable" (n.p.). Arguing that "the stock of a man's ideas is limited and determined by the stock of the words which he finds at his command for giving expression to his ideas," Bentham reverses "the customary link between logic and grammar: logic is not seen as a tool to make sense of grammar, but it is grammar itself that appears to be the necessary foundation of logic" ("Essay on Language," n.p.).

24. Bentham, *Theory* 71. As Esterhammer writes, when we think we are making assertions about reality, we "are actually conveying our opinion of, or persuasion about those things" (73). See also Stolzenberg.

25. This problem is explored in novels like Ann Radcliffe's *The Mysteries of Udolpho*. On Radcliffe and the legal fiction of civil death, see Clery. On the relation between sympathy and coverture, see Ablow, *Marriage*.

26. Blackstone, *Commentaries* vol. 3, n.p. Also cited in Harmon 8.

27. On "as if" in nineteenth-century scientific and novelistic discourse, see Farina.

28. Iser 124. He continues, "There is no predominance of either predication or representation; predication professes to understand the qualities of real bodies as if they were integral to them, and representation acts as if such a reality were graspable by the subject. This 'as if' indicates the difference—now minimalized but nevertheless ineradicable—between the two poles of will and reality" (126).

29. On how writers of the period emphasized "the rhetorical function of literary discourse in a modern culture" (38), see Duncan, "Adam Smith."

30. *TMS* 327–28. On this point, see Chandler, *England,* and Griswold, "Rhetoric."

31. On casuistry in the Victorian novel, see A. Miller, *Burdens.* The "power of casuistry" for authors like George Eliot, he writes, "derives not from the application of maxims or the calculation of debts but from the display it offers of other people thinking" (105). "It is best thought of as an experimental or interrogative preoccupation, one not taking either thinking or its representation for granted, as given and essential, but as testing both" (112).

32. D. A. Miller, for instance, describes disembodied neutrality—"absolute style"—as the hallmark of Austenian narration (56).

33. Robert Hopkins (opening with "a hypothetical case" about a nineteen-year-old Anne) focuses on this passage in "Moral Luck." He emphasizes the "consequentialism" of the notion that moral judgments might be good or bad based on later outcomes, an idea he borrows from Smith (150). See also Zietlow.

34. Austen, *Persuasion* 11. On the importance of this assertion, see Tave.

35. Phillips argues that Romantic-era history, stressing "the need for empathetic absorption in the materials of the past," adopted "a historical vocabulary that was soaked in metaphors of presence or proximity" ("Distance" 132). Austen scholars who note that reading *Persuasion* feels like re-reading it include Tanner, *Jane Austen;* Cottom; and Morgan.

36. Nazar argues that certain "antimodern dimensions" of Austen's work reflect the modern value of "private deliberation" (147). See Kroll for the argument that privileging "method over the mere contents of knowledge" is a feature of Restoration-era neoclassicism (56–57).

37. Favret, *War* 165, 171. On the practice of renting country houses (to returning soldiers, among others), see Spring.

38. Galperin, *Historical* 5; Favret, "Periods" 406. See also Shaw.

39. On injury and falling in Austen, see Favret, *War,* and Markovitz.

40. *Persuasion* 188. And there the pen stays; the last pen we see is in Sir Walter's hand, signing Anne's married name into "the volume of honor" (200).

41. On reading bodily gestures, see Richardson.

42. Levine claims that in *Persuasion,* Austen "moves very close to a disabling fiction" by endorsing rather than subduing the heroine's ambitions (*Realistic* 77). See also Butler.

43. Marshall, *Frame* 83. On "nothing" in *Emma,* see Duncan, *Scott's Shadow.* Lynch offers a related explanation for why "nothing happens" in "Austen."

CHAPTER 3. DICKENSIAN SYMPATHY:
TRANSLATION IN THE PROPER PITCH

1. As Bruner suggests, the idea that human minds are alike, working "'mentally' in common," is best understood as "a major prophylactic against alienation": we are not so much trapped inside our own heads as crafting common narratives with others in a "process of joint narrative accrual" (20).

2. Levine, *Realistic* 14. On Dickens's complex (not merely critical) relation to Bentham's ideas, see Gallagher, *Body*. Describing the felicific calculus of *Hard Times*, she notes that "[w]hen Dickens blames Coketown's unhappiness on its severe workfulness . . . he unwittingly adheres to Bentham's view" (66).

3. Vande Kieft notes that sympathy can fail even when communication and language do not.

4. See especially A. Miller, *Burdens*, and Puckett.

5. On mortification and petrifaction in Dickens, see Van Ghent; F. R. and Q. D. Leavis; Carey; and, more recently, Vrettos. For a Lacanian reading of intransigence in Victorian fiction, see Lougy. On "posthumous" reading, see Brooks.

6. Stewart, *Dickens* 16. On the "extra-linguistic" in Dickens, see Kincaid, *Dickens*, and Tore.

7. Quoted in Chapman 20, original emphasis. See also Kreilkamp, *Voice,* and Page.

8. Chapman 20. In *Our Mutual Friend,* Mr. Podsnap more viciously treats a "foreign gentleman" who mispronounces various words ("rich" as "retch," "horse" as "orse"): "Our English adverbs do Not terminate in Mong and We Pronounce the 'ch' as if there were a "t" before it. We Say Ritch . . . In England, Angleterre, England, We Aspirate the 'H,' and We say 'Horse.' Only our Lower Classes say 'Orse'!" "Pardon," the foreigner responds; "I am alwiz wrong!" (132–33).

9. Ginsburg 228. Critics like Ginsburg have tried to account for the fact that only some of Dickens's characters speak in the accents and with the slang of their economic and social peers, while others (like Oliver Twist) do not. Nancy Sikes, for instance, moves in and out of the "marked" language of her class and/or moral station (224).

10. Dickens's writings were often illustrated, of course. But the illustrations sometimes depict scenes and characters in ways inconsistent with the texts. For a discussion of this phenomenon, see John Jordan, "The Ghost in *Bleak House*." On how much access Dickens's illustrators had to the finished product, and other issues pertaining to the novels' illustration, see Patten, Steig, and J. Cohen.

11. For this reason, as de Man understands it, Benjamin's translation undoes Bentham's formula, wherein syntax provides the grounds for linguistic meaning. A literal translation that preserved all the elements of grammar would still be meaningless, he argues; translation proves grammar and meaning incompatible (41).

12. *Our Mutual Friend* 739, 742. Eugene's use of the third-person pronoun is another symptom of aphasia, as discussed below.

13. Jakobson 78–79. Bateman provides case studies and an overview of French and English diagnostics. For a contemporary account, see Code. See also Aaltonen for an account of "shared narration" between aphasics and their translator-interlocutors (56).

14. "Aphasia" 44. "[If] we remember rightly," the authors say, "somebody" in *Dombey*

and Son recites the "Mahometen formula in the very lucid form, 'There's no what's his name but Thingumy, and what you may call him is his prophet'" (ibid.).

15. Deleuze 110. On stuttering, trauma, and war, see Gubar.

16. Kucich, *Repression* 1. Kucich characterizes the midcentury as retreating from the forms of public life dominant in the eighteenth century into the realm of personal and emotional values. For a response, see N. Armstrong, "Review." On the period's turn to cultural rather than personal values, see Gallagher, *Industrial*. On the post-Reform decline in utopian sentiments, see Brantlinger, *Spirit*.

17. Kucich, *Repression* 24, 121, 27. On the issue of anti-individualism, see Kucich, *Excess*.

18. Lewes 60; James, "Limitation" 50. On child narrators in Dickens, see Andrews and Sadrin. See also Fisher, who argues that, while "rare," the use of child narrators requires readers to compensate with their own for passions absent because children cannot properly feel them. In his view, passion places a "stronger demand" on the reader than sympathy because the latter copies preexisting emotion: "I feel what the other is [already] feeling" (142).

19. Or of the static moral order of melodrama. See Hadley.

20. On this last point, see Nord. Citing Steven Marcus's conclusion that Dickens "could not imagine his own history in terms separable from 'his imagination of society,'" she suggests that Dickens's early critics, accusing his novels of lacking philosophical (adult) ideas, failed to appreciate that a "correspondence between mind and social structures" orders his fiction (284).

21. In the Marseilles prison, "echoes were the weaker for imprisonment, and seemed to lag" (*Dorrit* 22).

22. *Dorrit* 298. Dickens makes the verbal "arrear" an explicit joke in the case of "the noble Refrigerator," Lord Lancaster Stiltstalking, who delivers "solemn political oracles" that are "about five centuries in arrear," and so "appropriate to that epoch" (334). Miss Rugg "mak[es] up some of her arrears" with a healthy appetite for mutton (320).

23. *Dorrit* 158. According to Yeazell, "more than most Dickens novels . . . *Little Dorrit* frustrates any attempt to trace human acts—or failures to act—to single determining origins" (39). "Nobody's Fault" was the name Dickens gave the novel in manuscript. Several critics seek to explain the change, including Welsh.

24. *Dorrit* 55, original emphasis. Convinced that Arthur only pretends not to know why the two should be at odds, John Chivery resorts to the language of nothing when describing Little Dorrit. "What is the matter between us?" asks Arthur. John replies, "I decline to name it, sir. . . . Nothing's the matter" (755).

25. Stewart, "Tempo" 125. Buzard describes a similarly "self-interrupting" tendency as an antidote to English universalization.

26. Stainer and Barrett 24. In phrases like *nè l'uno nè l'altro*, "altro" functions as shorthand for "neither" or "nothing."

27. All from the *Oxford English Dictionary*, 2nd ed.

28. Nunokawa claims that by the end of the novel, Little Dorrit is "safe property for the man who marries her because this elegiac state is as distant from the circuit of exchange as an echo is from its origin or a sign is from its referent" (14).

CHAPTER 4. NOT GETTING TO KNOW YOU: SYMPATHETIC DETACHMENT

1. Stephen 229–30.

2. In *Burdens*, Andrew H. Miller discusses the danger to one's will of taking on third-person perspectives. "For all of its powers," he writes, "adopting an external, third-person point of view—to see situations in *that* distinctive way—seems to invite those disabilities of will that were so robustly feared by Victorians" (62–63, original emphasis). On the bad things that can happen when third-person abilities are "housed within" characters, see Anderson, "Trollope's Modernity" 517.

3. Culler and Sternberg debate (among other things) the equation of omniscience and (divine) omnipotence.

4. Galvan 172. On narrative media both human and technological, see Argyros, Royle, Picker, and Menke. On "powerless absorption" and sympathy in Eliot, see Ablow, *Marriage*.

5. Galvan 171. See also Ashby.

6. *Lifted Veil* 9. Law argues that in this scene we see the "abrupt eviction of one state of consciousness and categorical replacement by another," which is, as he notes, "chiefly an effect of its *narrative enunciation*." While we learn from Latimer that in fact the change comes on gradually, this prevision and others like it are represented by the narrative as simultaneous (90, emphasis added).

7. Hertz 43. See also Swann, who writes, "It is significant that Eliot interrupted her work on *The Mill on the Floss* . . . to write 'The Lifted Veil': she interrupted her biography in the form of fiction to write a fiction in the form of autobiography" (43).

8. Albrecht 439. Albrecht echoes Swann and Beer, for whom Latimer is analogous to novelist and reader.

9. *Impressions* 4, 7. According to Henry, Theophrastus's criticism is a "double-sided mirror held up to those around him, but ruthlessly reflecting his own image back to him, scourging him to fashion himself according to the standards he would apply to others and bringing—writing him [*sic*]—into a community" (xviii).

10. *Impressions* 3–4. In a similar vein, Latimer considers what "a dreary thing" it is to "to live on doing the same things year after year, without knowing why we do them" (*Lifted Veil* 28).

11. Picker 83. On this issue, see also Stewart, *Reading Voices*, and Beer, *George Eliot*.

12. Eliot, "Letter to the Brays and Sara Hennell 27 June 1859," in *Selections* 215–16.

13. James, "Novels" 104, original emphasis. James's review essay, originally published in the *Atlantic Monthly*, October 1866, preceded the publication of *Middlemarch*.

14. Donald C. Watts 25.

15. Anderson, *Powers* 89. In *Little Dorrit*, for instance, Anderson finds that "once one has achieved a systemic or global perspective, one is dangerously estranged and one's moral temperament is implicated; yet if one fails to achieve it, one runs the risk of 'sicken-ing.'" A way beyond that impasse is suggested in Amy Dorrit's personal history, which "becomes the basis, not the limit, for a larger understanding that remains open to cultural and historical alterity" (ibid.).

16. Conrad, preface xlvii. One complication is Conrad's claim, in "To my Readers in America," that the advice he gave in the preface (or, the act of giving it) was "wrong" (xlvi). In 1897, Conrad published a version of the preface as an "Author's Note" in the *New*

Review's serial run of the novel, and again in 1905 as an essay, "The Art of Fiction," in *Harper's Weekly*.

17. Conrad, preface xlviii–xlix. Compare this to Eliot's 1868 "Notes on Form in Art." According to Eliot, the proper understanding of aesthetic form involves an appreciation of parts in relation to wholes, for parts *are* wholes, held together by feeling. The "prerogative" of poetry is to choose "images and ideas," then order them into a sequence "determined by emotion and intended to express it." Poetic form, shaped by feeling, gives feeling shape: structured by "a set of relations selected and combined in accordance with the sequence of mental states in the constructor," it orders the "mental states" of those who experience it (233). Art provides an experience of the emotional ordering of form. A grouping of "a less spontaneous and more conscious order," form begins "in the choice of rhythms and images as signs of a mental state" (234–35).

18. Conrad, preface xlviii. J. Hillis Miller glosses the preface in saying that for Conrad "true art" shifts the reader's gaze "from the unreal dream of the future to the immediate moment of sensation" (*Poets* 39).

19. Conrad, *Narcissus* 110. All citations are from the 2007 Penguin edition.

20. Conrad, "Stephen Crane" 95. W. L. Courtney's 1897 *Daily Telegraph* review is reprinted in Sherry.

21. *Narcissus* 110. Cedric Watts describes as "the main psycho-political thesis of the novel" the idea that "apparent solidarity based on 'sympathy' may frequently be a false solidarity based on vicarious egotism" (xxvi). Many critics discuss sympathy in relation to Conrad's (conservative) politics, including Fleishman, Hay, Panichas, and Wollaeger. Jameson discusses Conrad at length in *Political Unconscious*.

22. Henricksen 786. Ambrosini describes this as an "impersonal" narration (70).

23. Watt, *Essays*, 71, 83. Watt attributes this to Conrad's "Romantic and Victorian" sensibility (83).

24. Watt, *Conrad* 106. See also Guerard.

25. Lane, *Hatred* 162. As Lane argues, Conrad alters the terms of eighteenth-century discourse, which had it that misanthropes "hate only for want of love" (166). Ousted from the hermitage, the Romantic misanthrope turns from eccentric but justified recluse to petulant naysayer, perversely refusing sociability. Lane attributes the change to a shift away from Smithian society, as the site of happy commerce in moral sentiments, to an evangelical model whose goal is to reintegrate everyone, from malcontent to wet blanket, into the communal fold. On fellow-feeling as a source of suffering, see Noble. On sympathy in Henry and William James, see Boudreau.

26. Lane, *Hatred* 182, in reference to *Caxtoniana*. Even this imperative, Lane notes, "is at bottom selfish" in Bulwer-Lytton's view. We "avoid morbid introspection by tolerating company as a forced choice, and so become better able to cope with alienation and enmity" (39).

27. Conrad, *Narcissus* 113. Conrad's financial situation in the early years of his literary career contributed to his feeling an outcast: "I am sitting on my bare ass in the lee scuppers," he wrote to Garnett (*Letters* 52).

28. Conrad, "To My Readers" xlv. Conrad published the note to American readers alongside the preface in pamphlet form in the 1905 *Joseph Conrad on the Art of Writing* (C. Watts xxxv).

29. Watt, *Conrad* 205. He goes on to say, "Conrad goes much further than James both in the abandonment of authorial omniscience, and in the related transition from a closed to an open fictional form" (207). *The Nigger of the 'Narcissus,'* I am arguing, dramatizes that abandonment from the perspective of a believer in, and usurper of, its powers.

30. Polloczek 208. As Polloczek defines it, "resentful solidarity entails the hope that structures of participation in social bonding may be distributed sentimentally" (209).

31. Blackmur 330. See also Follett. In a similar vein, Stein describes the novel as "a rhetorical psychograph," a word portrait of the narrator's mind (373).

32. Blackmur, calling the narrator "James," inserts the author into the plot (as in "Mrs. Brissenden comes running to James at midnight and with all the eloquence of guilt protests that she is at one with her husband") (349). Against this view, see Klein.

33. Economic and sentimental language are endlessly combined in this novel's representation of sympathy, as in the narrator's comment that his "appearance of intellectual sympathy" buys him "credit" in others (125). There may even be a veiled reference to *TMS* in the narrator's comment that he keeps Grace Brissenden "for some seconds on the rack" in persuading her to reveal her conclusions first (103).

34. As Kent Puckett remarks, the narrator is "the outsider, the uncoupled, the excluded, the exiled, the sensitive single gentleman," one who tries to be both inside and outside the novel's social and formal system; this effort renders him "crazy" even as it exposes the ideology "behind the sociable" as crazily incoherent (*Bad Form* 128).

35. Moon 125. That discovery makes the novel more *Belinda* than Beckett, in Moon's estimation, since the narrator's views are confirmed by several other characters, and by James.

36. Halpern 59. See also Wilson, Rowe, and Paul B. Armstrong, *Challenge*.

37. *Sacred Fount* 66. On the "mixing up" of persons, see Furbank.

38. *Sacred Fount* 91–92. The narrator comments, for instance, that he has "burnt his ships," and says of Obert, "I saw him, my approval, safely into port" (92, 157). He also compares May Server to a "sponge wrung dry," with a "shell [that] was merely crushable" (101).

CODA. SYMPATHY VERSUS EMPATHY:
THE ENDS OF SYMPATHY AT CENTURY'S END

1. Moon 141. Nussbaum distinguishes similarly between the two, except that for her, sympathy (unlike empathy) always entails an ethical stance: "a malevolent person who imagines the situation of the other and takes pleasure in her distress may be empathetic, but will surely not be judged sympathetic. Sympathy, like compassion, includes a judgment that the other person's distress is bad" (302).

2. See Titchener.

3. See, especially, Lee and Anstruther-Thomson. Depew claims "empathy" was coined to replace "sympathy" and emphasizes empathy's expressive (rather than imitative) force. The shift, he says, marks the "deflation" and "descent" of sympathy, "from the sense of universal attunement and resonance in romanticism to the smarmy sense of pity and superiority that the term now connotes" (104–5).

4. Vischer, *Optical* 104. Lipps writes, "I project my own life into the lifeless form, just as I quite justifiably do with another living person" (*Aesthetik* 104).

5. Lipps, "Empathy" 188. See also Jahoda.

6. Titchener 181. See also Vischer, for whom such "muscular movement[s]" are not passive but imply "a stronger act of the will" ("Optical" 95).

7. Scholars continue to debate the extent to which such "muscular" empathy differed from, or was continuous with, sympathy, especially as sympathy began acquiring a host of new meanings in the post-Darwinian era, when an emphasis on biological instincts and drives began replacing older, Enlightenment explanations privileging rational choice and efforts of will. Conceptions of sympathy from the 1860s onward reflect an evolutionary theory that left many emotional expressions automatic, possibly the "vestigial remnants of movements . . . that originated in animal and prehumen ancestors" (Winter 138).

8. For a longer treatment of these issues, see Mallgrave and Ikonomou, Burdett, and Greiner.

Bibliography

PRIMARY SOURCES

Abercrombie, John. *The Philosophy of the Moral Feelings.* Edited by Jacob Abbott. New York: Collins & Brother, 1859.

Aikin, Anna Laetitia (Barbauld). "An Enquiry into Those Kinds of Distress Which Excite Agreeable Sensations." In I. Williams, *Novel and Romance,* 215.

"Aphasia." *The London Spectator.* 14 July 1866. Reprinted in *Every Saturday: A Journal of Choice Reading, Selected from Foreign Current Literature,* 2:44–46. Boston: Ticknor & Fields, 1866.

Austen, Jane. *Persuasion.* New ed. Edited by James Kinsley. Introduction by Deidre Shauna Lynch. Oxford: Oxford University Press, 2004.

Bagehot, Walter. "Adam Smith as a Person." *Fortnightly Review* 20 (1876): 17–42.

Bateman, Frederic. *On Aphasia, or Loss of Speech, and the Localisation of the Faculty of Articulate Language.* London: John Churchill & Sons, 1870.

Bentham, Jeremy. *Bentham's Theory of Fictions.* Edited by C. K. Ogden. London: Routledge & Kegan Paul, 1932.

———. *Chrestomathia: Being a Collection of Papers, Explanatory of the Design of an Institution, Proposed to Be Set on Foot, under the Name of, the Chrestomathic Day School, or Chrestomathic School, for the Extension of the New System of Instruction to the Higher Branches of Learning, for the Use of the Middling and the Higher Ranks of Life.* London: Payne & Foss, 1815. http://books.google.com/books?id=zlcXAAAAYAAJ.

———. "Chrestomathic Instruction Tables: Table 1." In *Works of Jeremy Bentham,* vol. 8.

———. "Constitutional Code." In *Works of Jeremy Bentham,* vol. 9.

———. "Essay on Language." In *Works of Jeremy Bentham,* vol. 8.

———. "Essay on Logic." In *Works of Jeremy Bentham,* vol. 8.

———. "Exposition." In *Jeremy Bentham's Political Thought,* edited by Bhikhu C. Parekh. London: Trinity Press, 1973.

———. "A Fragment on Government." In *Works of Jeremy Bentham,* vol. 1.

———. "Fragments on Universal Grammar." In *Works of Jeremy Bentham,* vol. 8.

———. *Memoirs of Bentham.* In *Works of Jeremy Bentham,* vol. 10.

———. "Scotch Reform." In *Works of Jeremy Bentham,* vol. 5.

———. *A Table of the Springs of Action.* London: R. Hunter, 1817.

———. *The Works of Jeremy Bentham, Published under the Superintendence of His Execu-*

tor, John Bowring. New York: Russell, 1962. http://oll.libertyfund.org/?option=com _staticxt&staticfile=show.php%3Fperson=172&Itemid=28.

Blackstone, Sir William. *Commentaries on the Laws of England.* 4 vols. http://www.lonang .com/exlibris/blackstone/.

Blaze de Bury, Marie, Baroness. "The Decadence of Thought in France." *Fortnightly Review* 51 (1889): 395–412.

Bowring, John. "Introduction to the Study of the Works of Jeremy Bentham," in Bentham, *Works of Jeremy Bentham,* 1–154.

Brontë, Anne. *The Professor.* Edited by Heather Glen. New York: Penguin, 1989.

Buckle, Henry Thomas. *History of Civilization in England.* Vol. 2. London: Parker, Son & Bourn, 1861.

Bulwer-Lytton, Edward. *Caxtoniana: A Series of Essays on Life, Literature, and Manners.* New York: Harper & Brothers, 1868.

Burns, Robert. *Selected Poems.* Edited by Carol McGuirk. New York: Penguin, 1994.

Carlyle, Thomas. "Signs of the Times." In *Critical and Miscellaneous Essays,* 187–96. New York: Appleton, 1870.

Conrad, Joseph. *Letters from Conrad, 1895 to 1924.* Edited by Edward Garnett. London: Nonesuch Press, 1928.

———. *The Nigger of the 'Narcissus' and Other Stories.* Edited by J. H. Stape and Allan H. Simmons. New York: Penguin, 2007.

———. Preface. In *The Nigger of the 'Narcissus,'* edited by Cedric Watts, xlvii–li. New York: Penguin, 1988.

———. *The Secret Sharer.* Edited by Daniel R. Schwarz. New York: Bedford–St. Martin's, 1997.

———. "Stephen Crane." In *Last Essays,* edited by Richard Curle, 93–118. 1926; reprint, Freeport, NY: Books for Libraries, 1970.

———. "To My Readers in America." In *The Nigger of the 'Narcissus,'* ed. Watts, xlv–xlvi.

Darwin, Charles. *The Descent of Man.* Vol. 1. New York: Appleton, 1871.

———. *The Expression of the Emotions in Man and Animals.* Introduction by Paul Ekman. Oxford: Oxford University Press, 1998.

———. *Origin of Species.* Edited by Gillian Beer. Oxford: Oxford University Press, 1996.

Dickens, Charles. *Bleak House.* Edited by Nicola Bradbury. New York: Penguin, 2003.

———. *David Copperfield.* Edited by Jeremy Tambling. New York: Penguin, 1996.

———. *Dombey and Son.* Edited by Peter Fairclough. New York: Penguin, 1984.

———. *Great Expectations.* Edited by Margaret Cardwell. Oxford: Oxford University Press, 2008.

———. *Hard Times.* Edited by Kate Flint. New York: Penguin, 2003.

———. *Little Dorrit.* Edited by Stephen Wall and Helen Small. New York: Penguin, 2003.

———. *Nicholas Nickleby.* Edited by Mark Ford. New York: Penguin, 1999.

———. *The Old Curiosity Shop.* Edited by Elizabeth M. Brennan. Oxford: Oxford University Press, 1998.

———. *Oliver Twist.* Edited by Philip Horne. New York: Penguin, 2002.

———. *Our Mutual Friend.* Edited by Michael Cotsell. Oxford: Oxford University Press, 1998.

———. *The Posthumous Papers of the Pickwick Club.* Edited by Mark Wormald. New York: Penguin, 2003.

————. *Sketches by Boz*. Edited by Dennis Walder. New York: Penguin, 1995.

Edgeworth, Maria. *Castle Rackrent* and *Ennui*. Edited by Marilyn Butler. New York: Penguin, 1992.

Eliot, George. *Adam Bede*. Edited by Carol A. Martin. Oxford: Oxford University Press, 2008.

————. *Daniel Deronda*. Edited by Graham Handley. Oxford: Clarendon Press, 1980.

————. *The George Eliot Letters*. Edited by Gordon S. Haight. 9 vols. New Haven: Yale University Press, 1954–78.

————. *Impressions of Theophrastus Such*. Edited by Nancy Henry. Iowa City: University of Iowa Press, 1984.

————. *The Lifted Veil* and *Brother Jacob*. Edited by Helen Small. Oxford: Oxford University Press, 1999.

————. *Middlemarch*. Edited by David Carroll. Oxford: Oxford University Press, 1998.

————. *The Mill on the Floss*. Edited by A. S. Byatt. London: Penguin, 2003.

————. "The Natural History of German Life." In *George Eliot: Selected Essays, Poems, and Other Writings*, edited by A. S. Byatt and Nicholas Warren, 107–39. New York: Penguin, 1990.

————. "Notes on Form in Art." In *George Eliot: Selected Essays*, 231–36.

————. *Scenes of Clerical Life*. Edited by Thomas A. Noble. Oxford: Oxford University Press, 1985.

————. *Selections from George Eliot's Letters*. Edited by Gordon S. Haight. New Haven: Yale University Press, 1985.

————. "Translations and Translators." In *George Eliot: Selected Essays*, 339–42.

————. "Worldliness and Other-Worldlinesss: The Poet Young." *George Eliot: Selected Essays*, 164–213.

Engels, Friedrich. *The Condition of the Working Class in England in 1844*. New York: Penguin, 1987.

Forster, John. *The Life of Charles Dickens*. Edited by A. J. Hoppé. Vol. 2. London: Dent; New York: Dutton, 1969.

Froude, James Anthony. *The Life and Times of Thomas Carlyle: A History of the First Forty Years of His Life, 1795–1835*. Vol. 1. New York: Harper & Brothers, 1882.

Gaskell, Elizabeth. *Mary Barton*. Edited by Shirley Foster. Oxford: Oxford University Press, 2006.

————. *North and South*. Edited by Sally Shuttleworth. Oxford: Oxford University Press, 2008.

Haldane, R. B. *Life of Adam Smith*. London: Walter Scott, 1887.

Harris, James. *Hermes, or a Philosophical Inquiry Concerning Universal Grammar*. 6th ed. London: Wright, 1806.

Hume, David. "Of the Study of History." In *Essays: Moral, Political, and Literary*, edited by Eugene F. Miller, 563–68. Indianapolis: Liberty Fund, 1985.

————. *A Treatise of Human Nature*. Edited by David Fate Norton and Mary J. Norton. Oxford: Oxford University Press, 2000.

James, Henry. "The Future of the Novel." In *The Art of Criticism: Henry James on the Theory and Practice of Fiction*. Edited by William Veeder and Susan M. Griffin. Chicago: University of Chicago Press, 1986.

————. "The Limitation of Dickens." In Ford and Lane, *Dickens Critics*, 48–53.

————. "The Novels of George Eliot." In *Views and Reviews by Henry James,* introduction by Le Roy Phillips, 1–37. New York: Ball Publishing, 1968.

————. *The Sacred Fount.* Introduction by Leon Edel. New York: New Directions, 1995.

————. *Selected Letters.* Edited by Leon Edel. Cambridge, MA: Belknap Press of Harvard University Press, 1974.

Lee, Vernon, and Clementina Anstruther-Thomson. *Beauty & Ugliness and Other Studies in Psychological Aesthetics.* London: Ballantyne Press, 1912.

Lewes, George Henry. "Dickens in Relation to Criticism." In Ford and Lane, *Dickens Critics,* 54–76.

Lipps, Theodor. Aesthetik. Vol. 2. Hamburg: Voss Verlag, 1905. http://plato.stanford.edu/entries/empathy.

————. "Empathy, Inner Imitation, and Sense Feelings." Translated by Melvin Rader and Max Schertel. In *A Modern Book of Aesthetics,* 5th ed., edited by Melvin Rader, 371–78. New York: Holt, Rinehart & Winston, 1979.

Locke, John. *An Essay Concerning Human Understanding.* Edited by Peter H. Nidditch. Oxford: Oxford University Press, 1975.

Mill, John Stuart. *Autobiography.* Edited by John Robson. New York: Penguin, 1989.

Oncken, August. "The Adam Smith Problem." In *Adam Smith: Critical Responses,* edited by Hiroshi Mizuta, 1:84–105. London: Routledge, 2000.

————. "The Consistency of Adam Smith." *Economic Journal of London* 7.3 (1897): 443–50.

Price, L. L. "Adam Smith and His Relation to Recent Economics." *Economic Journal* 3 (1893): 239–54.

Quincey, Thomas de. "The Casuistry of Duelling." In *The Uncollected Writings of Thomas de Quincey,* vol. 2. London: BiblioBazaar, 2007.

Ruskin, John. *The Complete Works of John Ruskin.* Edited by E. T. Cook and Alexander Wedderburn. Vol. 27. London: George Allen, 1907.

————. *"Unto This Last": Four Essays on the First Principles of Political Economy.* 2nd ed. Kent, UK: George Allen, 1877.

Scott, Sir Walter. *"Emma; a Novel." Quarterly Review* 4 (1816): 188–201.

————. *The Heart of Mid-Lothian.* Edited by Tony Inglis. New York: Penguin Books, 1994.

————. *Minstrelsy of the Scottish Border.* Edited by T. F. Henderson. Vol. 2. Edinburgh: Blackwood, 1902.

Smith, Adam. *Lectures on Rhetoric and Belles Lettres.* Edited by John M. Lothian. Edinburgh: Thomas Nelson & Sons, 1963.

————. *Lectures on Rhetoric and Belles Lettres, Works and Correspondence.* Glasgow ed. Edited by J. C. Bryce and A. S. Skinner. Vol. 4. Indianapolis: Liberty Fund, 1985.

————. *The Theory of Moral Sentiments.* Glasgow ed. Edited by D. D. Raphael and A. L. Macfie. Indianapolis: Liberty Fund, 1982.

Stephen, Leslie. *The Science of Ethics.* New York: G. P. Putnam's Sons, 1882.

Sully, James. "Art and Psychology." *Mind* 1.4 (1876): 467–78.

Titchener, Edward. *Lectures on the Experimental Psychology of Thought-Processes.* New York: Macmillan, 1909.

Trollope, Anthony. *The Way We Live Now.* Edited by John Sutherland. Oxford: Oxford University Press, 2008.

Vischer, Robert. "The Aesthetic Act and Pure Form." In *Art in Theory, 1815–1900: An An-*

thology of Changing Ideas, edited by Charles Harrison, Paul Wood, and Jason Gaiger, 690–704. New York: Blackwell, 1998.

———. *On the Optical Sense of Form: A Contribution to Aesthetics.* Translated by Nicholas Walker. In *Empathy, Form, and Space: Problems in German Aesthetics, 1873–1893,* edited by Harry Francis Mallgrave and Eleftherios Ikonomou, 90–123. Santa Monica, CA: Getty Publications, 1994.

SECONDARY SOURCES

Aaltonen, Tarja. "'Mind-Reading': A Method for Understanding the Broken Narrative of an Aphasic Man." In *Beyond Narrative Coherence,* edited by Matti Hyvärinen, Lars-Christer Hydén, Marja Saarenheimo, and Maria Tamboukou, 49–66. Amsterdam: John Benjamins, 2010.

Ablow, Rachel. *The Marriage of Minds: Reading Sympathy in the Victorian Marriage Plot.* Stanford: Stanford University Press, 2007.

———, ed. *The Feeling of Reading: Affective Experience and Victorian Literature.* Ann Arbor: University of Michigan Press, 2010.

Abrams, M. H. *A Glossary of Literary Terms.* 4th ed. New York: Holt, Rinehart & Winston, 1981.

Aczel, Richard. "Hearing Voices in Narrative Texts." *New Literary History* 29.3 (1998): 467–500.

Adam, Ian, ed. *This Particular Web: Essays on "Middlemarch."* Toronto: University of Toronto Press, 1975.

Adams, James Eli. "Gyp's Tale: On Sympathy, Silence, and Realism in *Adam Bede.*" *Dickens Studies Annual* 20 (1991): 227–42.

———. *A History of Victorian Literature.* Oxford: Blackwell, 2009.

Albrecht, Thomas. "Sympathy and Telepathy: The Problem of Ethics in George Eliot's *The Lifted Veil.*" *English Literary History (ELH)* 73 (2006): 437–63.

Altieri, Charles. *The Particulars of Rapture: An Aesthetics of the Affects.* Ithaca: Cornell University Press, 2003.

Ambrosini, Richard. *Conrad's Fiction as Critical Discourse.* New York: Cambridge University Press, 1991.

Anderson, Amanda. *The Powers of Distance: Cosmopolitanism and the Cultivation of Detachment.* Princeton: Princeton University Press, 2001.

———. "Trollope's Modernity." *ELH* 74 (2007): 509–34.

Andrews, Malcolm. *Dickens and the Grown-Up Child.* Iowa City: University of Iowa Press, 1994.

Anger, Suzy. *Victorian Interpretation.* Ithaca: Cornell University Press, 2005.

Ankersmit, Frank. "Truth in History and Literature." *Narrative* 18.1 (2010): 29–50.

Anonymous. Review. *Saturday Review* 91 (4 May 1901): 574. Reprinted in *Henry James: the Contemporary Reviews,* edited by Kevin J. Hayes, 355–56. New York: Cambridge University Press, 1996.

Arata, Stephen D. "Realism." In *The Cambridge Companion to the Fin de Siècle,* edited by Gail Marshall, 169–87. New York: Cambridge University Press, 2007.

———. "Realism, Sympathy, and Gissing's Fictions of Failure." *Victorians Institute Journal* 23 (1995): 27–49.

Argyros, Ellen. *"Without Any Check of Proud Reserve": Sympathy and Its Limits in George Eliot's Novels*. New York: Peter Lang, 1999.

Armstrong, Isobel. *Victorian Poetry: Poetry, Poetics, and Politics*. New York: Routledge, 1996.

Armstrong, Nancy. *How Novels Think: The Limits of Individualism from 1719–1900*. New York: Columbia University Press, 2005.

———. "Review: Repression in Victorian Fiction: Charlotte Brontë, George Eliot, and Charles Dickens." *Nineteenth-Century Literature* 44.4 (1990): 556–59.

Armstrong, Paul B. *The Challenge of Bewilderment: Understanding and Representation and James, Conrad, and Ford*. Ithaca: Cornell University Press, 1987.

———. "Form and History: Reading as an Aesthetic Experience and Historical Act." *Modern Language Quarterly (MLQ)* 69.2 (2008): 195–219.

Ashby, Kevin. "The Centre and the Margins in 'The Lifted Veil' and Blackwood's *Edinburgh Magazine*." *George Eliot–George Henry Lewes Studies* 24.5 (1993): 132–46.

Atkinson, Paul. *The Ethnographic Imagination: Textual Constructions of Reality*. New York: Routledge, 1990.

Auerbach, Erich. *Mimesis: The Representation of Reality in Western Literature*. Edited by Edward Said. Princeton: Princeton University Press, 2003.

Baier, Annette C., and Anik Waldow. "A Conversation between Annette Baier and Anik Waldow about Hume's Account of Sympathy." *Hume Studies* 34.1 (2008): 61–87.

Bal, Mieke. *Narratology: Introduction to the Theory of Narrative*. 3rd ed. Toronto: University of Toronto Press, 1997.

Banfield, Ann. *Unspeakable Sentences: Narration and Representation in the Language of Fiction*. New York: Routledge, 1982.

Barthes, Roland. *The Rustle of Language*. Translated by Richard Howard. Berkeley: University of California Press, 1989.

Bate, Walter Jackson. "The Sympathetic Imagination in Eighteenth-Century English Criticism," *ELH* 12.2 (1945): 144–64.

Becker, George J., ed. *Documents of Modern Literary Realism*. Princeton: Princeton University Press, 1963.

Beer, Gillian. *Darwin's Plots: Evolutionary Narrative in Darwin, George Eliot, and Nineteenth-Century Fiction*. New York: Cambridge University Press, 2000.

———. "Myth and the Single Consciousness: *Middlemarch* and *The Lifted Veil*." In Adam, *This Particular Web*, 94–101.

Bell, Michael. *Sentimentalism, Ethics, and the Culture of Feeling*. New York: Palgrave, 2000.

Bellamy, Liz. *Commerce, Morality, and the Eighteenth-Century Novel*. New York: Cambridge University Press, 1998.

Bender, John. *Imagining the Penitentiary: Fiction and the Architecture of Mind in Eighteenth-Century England*. Chicago: University of Chicago Press, 1987.

Benjamin, Walter. "The Task of the Translator." In *Illuminations*, translated by Harry Zhon, 69–82. New York: Schocken Books, 1969.

Bentley, Nancy. "Adams, James, du Bois, and Social Thought." In *The Cambridge History of American Literature*, edited by Sacvan Berkovitch, vol. 3: *Prose Writing, 1860–1920*, 247–86. Cambridge, UK: Cambridge University Press, 2005.

Berlant, Lauren. "Introduction: What Does It Matter Who One Is?" *Critical Inquiry* 34.1 (2007): 1–4.

———. "On the Case." *Critical Inquiry* 33.4 (2007): 663–72.

Blackmur, R. P. "The Sacred Fount." *Kenyon Review* 4.3 (1942): 328–52.

Blake, Kathleen. *Pleasures of Benthamism: Victorian Literature, Utility, Political Economy.* Oxford: Oxford University Press, 2009.

Blanchot, Maurice. *Friendship.* Translated by Elizabeth Rottenberg. Stanford: Stanford University Press, 1997.

Booth, Wayne C. *The Rhetoric of Fiction.* 2nd ed. Chicago: University of Chicago Press, 1983.

———. *The Rhetoric of Rhetoric: The Quest for Effective Communication.* Malden, MA: Blackwell, 2004.

Boudreau, Kristin. "Henry James's Inward Aches." *Henry James Review* 20.1 (1999): 69–80.

Bowen, John. *Other Dickens: Pickwick to Chuzzlewit.* New York: Oxford University Press, 2000.

———. "Performing Business, Training Ghosts: Transcoding *Nickleby*." *ELH* 63.1 (1996): 153–75.

Brantlinger, Patrick. *The Spirit of Reform: British Literature and Politics, 1832–1867.* Cambridge, MA: Harvard University Press, 1977.

———. "What Is 'Sensational' about the 'Sensation Novel'?" *Nineteenth-Century Fiction* 37.1 (1982): 1–28.

Brooks, Peter. *Reading for the Plot: Design and Intention in Narrative.* New York: Knopf, 1984.

Brown, Marshall. "The Logic of Realism: A Hegelian Approach." *Proceedings of the Modern Language Association (PMLA)* 96.2 (1981): 224–41.

Bruner, Jerome. "Narrative Constructions of Reality." *Critical Inquiry* 18.1 (1991): 1–21.

Burdett, Carolyn. " 'The Subjective Inside Us Can Turn into the Objective Outside': Vernon Lee's Psychological Aesthetics." *19: Interdisciplinary Studies in the Long Nineteenth Century* 12 (2011): 1–31.

Burke, Kenneth. *A Rhetoric of Motives.* Berkeley: University of California Press, 1969.

Butler, Marilyn. *Jane Austen and the War of Ideas.* Oxford: Clarendon, 1975.

Buzard, James. *Disorienting Fiction: The Autoethnographic Work of Nineteenth-Century British Novels.* Princeton: Princeton University Press, 2005.

Cameron, Sharon. *Thinking in Henry James.* Chicago: University of Chicago Press, 1989.

Carey, John. *The Violent Effigy: A Study of Dickens' Imagination.* London: Faber, 1973.

Carroll, David. "*Middlemarch* and the Externality of Fact." In Adam, *This Particular Web,* 73–90.

Cavell, Stanley. *Disowning Knowledge in Seven Plays of Shakespeare.* Cambridge, UK: Cambridge University Press, 1987.

Champs, Emmanuelle de. "The Place of Jeremy Bentham's Theory of Fictions in Eighteenth-Century Linguistic Thought." *Journal of Bentham Studies* 2 (1999): 1–28. http://discovery.ucl.ac.uk/647/.

Chandler, James. *England in 1819: The Politics of Literary Culture and the Case of Romantic Historicism.* Chicago: University of Chicago Press, 1998.

———. "The Languages of Sentiment." *Textual Practice* 22.1 (2008): 21–39.

———. "On the Face of the Case: Conrad, *Lord Jim*, and the Sentimental Novel." *Critical Inquiry* 33.4 (2007): 837–64.

———. "The Theory of Sentiment and the History of Casuistry: Adam Smith and the Case of the Other." Lecture, 12 Dec. 2003. http://mingching.sinica.edu.tw/english/activi ties/activities_records_03.html.

Chapman, Raymond. *Forms of Speech in Victorian Fiction*. New York: Longman, 1994.

Chatman, Seymour. *The Later Style of Henry James*. Oxford: Blackwell, 1972.

———. *Story and Discourse: Narrative Structure in Fiction and Film*. Ithaca: Cornell University Press, 1978.

Childers, Joseph. "*Nicholas Nickleby*'s Problem of *Doux Commerce*." *Dickens Studies Annual* 25 (1996): 49–65.

Clery, E. J. *The Rise of Supernatural Fiction, 1762–1800*. Cambridge, UK: Cambridge University Press, 1999.

Code, Chris, ed. *The Characteristics of Aphasia*. London: Taylor & Francis, 1989.

Cohen, Jane R. *Charles Dickens and His Original Illustrators*. Columbus: Ohio State University Press, 1980.

Cohen, William A. "Envy and Victorian Fiction." NOVEL: *A Forum on Fiction* 42.2 (2009): 297–303.

Cohn, Dorrit. *Transparent Minds: Narrative Modes for Presenting Consciousness in Fiction*. Princeton: Princeton University Press, 1978.

Collingwood, R. G. *The Idea of History*. Revised ed. Edited by Jan van der Dussen. New York: Oxford University Press, 1994.

Collini, Stefan. *Absent Minds: Intellectuals in Britain*. Oxford: Oxford University Press, 2006.

Cottom, Daniel. *The Civilized Imagination: A Study of Anne Radcliffe, Jane Austen, and Sir Walter Scott*. Cambridge, UK: Cambridge University Press, 1985.

Courtemanche, Eleanor. *The "Invisible Hand" and British Fiction, 1818–1860*. New York: Palgrave, 2011.

Courtney, W. L. Review. *Daily Telegraph*, 8 Dec. 1897. Reprinted in Sherry, *Conrad: The Critical Heritage*, 85–88.

Culler, Jonathan. "Omniscience." *Narrative* 12.1 (2004): 22–34.

Cvetkovich, Anne. *Mixed Feelings: Feminism, Mass Culture, and Victorian Sensationalism*. New Brunswick: Rutgers University Press, 1992.

Damasio, Antonio. *The Feeling of What Happens: Body and Emotion in the Making of Consciousness*. New York: Harcourt Brace, 1999.

Dames, Nicholas. *Amnesiac Selves: Nostalgia, Forgetting, and British Fiction, 1810–1870*. Oxford: Oxford University Press, 2001.

———. *The Physiology of the Novel: Reading, Neural Science, and the Form of Victorian Fiction*. Oxford: Oxford University Press, 2007.

Darwall, Stephen. "Sympathetic Liberalism: Recent Work on Adam Smith." *Philosophy and Public Affairs* 28.2 (1999): 139–64.

———. *Welfare and Rational Care*. Princeton: Princeton University Press, 2002.

Davis, Lennard. *Resisting Novels: Ideology and Fiction*. New York: Methuen, 1987.

Dawson, Deidre. "Is Sympathy So Surprising? Adam Smith and French Fictions of Sympathy." *Eighteenth-Century Life* 15.1–2 (1991): 147–62.

Deleuze, Gilles. *Essays Critical and Clinical*. Translated by David W. Smith and Michael A. Greco. Minneapolis: University of Minnesota Press, 1997.

De Man, Paul. "'Conclusions' on Walter Benjamin's 'The Task of the Translator.'" *Yale French Studies* 97 (2000): 10–35.

Depew, David. "Empathy, Psychology, and Aesthetics: Reflections on a Repair Concept." *Poroi* 4.1 (2005): 99–107.

Deresiewicz, William. "Conrad's Impasse: *The Nigger of the 'Narcissus'* and the Invention of Marlow." *Conradiana* 38.3 (2006): 205–27.

Derrida, Jacques. "How to Avoid Speaking: Denials." In *Languages of the Unsayable: The Play of Negativity and Literature and Literary Theory*, edited by Wolfgang Iser and Sanford Budick, 3–70. Stanford: Stanford University Press, 1987.

Dever, Carolyn. "The Gamut of Emotions from A to B: *Nickleby*'s 'Histrionic Expedition.'" *Dickens Studies Annual* 39 (2008): 1–16.

Dixon, Thomas. *The Invention of Altruism: Making Moral Meaning in Victorian Britain*. Oxford: Oxford University Press, 2008.

Duncan, Ian. "Adam Smith, Samuel Johnson and the Institutions of English." In *The Scottish Invention of English Literature*, edited by Robert Crawford, 37–54. Cambridge, UK: Cambridge University Press, 1998.

———. Introduction to *The Private Memoirs and Confessions of a Justified Sinner*, by James Hogg, ix–xxxiv. Oxford: Oxford University Press, 2010.

———. *Scott's Shadow: The Novel in Romantic Edinburgh*. Princeton: Princeton University Press, 2007.

Dwyer, John. *The Age of the Passions: An Interpretation of Adam Smith and Scottish Enlightenment Culture*. East Linton, UK: Tuckwell Press, 1998.

Eagleton, Terry. "Power and Knowledge in 'The Lifted Veil.'" *Literature and History* 9.1 (1983): 52–61.

Edel, Leon. Introduction to *The Sacred Fount*, by Henry James, 3–15. New York: New Directions, 1995.

Edgecombe, Rodney Stenning. "Dickens, Hood, and the Comedy of Language Learning." *English Studies: A Journal of English Language and Literature* 90.3 (2009): 274–83.

Ellison, Julie. *Cato's Tears and the Making of Anglo-American Emotion*. Chicago: University of Chicago Press, 1999.

Ermarth, Elizabeth Deeds. *The English Novel in History, 1840–1895*. New York: Routledge, 1997.

———. "George Eliot's Conception of Sympathy." *Nineteenth-Century Fiction* 40.1 (1985): 23–42.

———. *Realism and Consensus in the English Novel: Time, Space, and Narrative*. Edinburgh: Edinburgh University Press, 1998.

Esterhammer, Angela. "Of Promises, Contracts, and Constitutions: Thomas Reid and Jeremy Bentham on Language as Social Action." *Romanticism: The Journal of Romantic Culture and Criticism* 6.1 (2000): 55–77.

Farina, Jonathan. "'As Separate as If We Were in Two Worlds': Analogy and Victorian Virtual Reality." *Victorian Studies* 53.3 (2011): 427–36.

Favret, Mary. "Austen's Periods." In *A Companion to Jane Austen*, edited by Claudia L. Johnson and Clara Tuite, 402–12. Malden, UK: Wiley-Blackwell, 2009.

———. *War at a Distance: Romanticism and the Making of Modern Wartime*. Princeton: Princeton University Press, 2010.

Ferguson, Frances. "Beliefs and Emotions (From Stanley Fish to Jeremy Bentham and John Stuart Mill)." In *Politics and the Passions, 1500–1850*, edited by Victoria Kahn, Neil Saccamano, and Daniela Coli, 231–50. Princeton: Princeton University Press, 2006.

————. "Canons, Poetics, and Social Value: Jeremy Bentham and How to Do Things with People." *MLN* 110.5 (1995): 1148–64.

————. "Coherence and Changes in the Unknown World." *New Literary History* 35 (2004): 303–19.

————. "Envy Rising." In *Romantic Metropolis: The Urban Scene of British Culture, 1780–1840*, edited by James Chandler and Kevin Gilmartin, 132–48. Cambridge, UK: Cambridge University Press, 2005.

————. "Jane Austen, *Emma*, and the Impact of Form." *MLQ* 61.1 (2000): 157–80.

Festa, Lynn. *Sentimental Figures of Empire in Eighteenth-Century Britain and France*. Baltimore: Johns Hopkins University Press, 2006.

Fisher, Philip. *The Vehement Passions*. Princeton: Princeton University Press, 2002.

Fleischacker, Samuel. *On Adam Smith's "Wealth of Nations": A Philosophical Companion*. Princeton: Princeton University Press, 2004.

————. "Sympathy in Hume and Smith: A Comparison, Contrast, and Reconstruction." Conference paper presented at "Reclaiming Adam Smith," Columbia University, New York, Sept. 2006. http://www.columbia.edu/cu/seminars/seminar-sites/political-and -social-thought/index.html.

Fleishman, Avrom. *Conrad's Politics: Community and Anarchy in the Fiction of Joseph Conrad*. Baltimore: Johns Hopkins University Press, 1967.

Fleissner, Jennifer. "Henry James's Art of Eating." *ELH* 75.1 (2008): 27–62.

Fleming, Paul. *Exemplarity and Mediocrity: The Art of the Average from Bourgeois Tragedy to Realism*. Stanford: Stanford University Press, 2009.

Flesch, William. *Comeuppance: Costly Signaling, Altruistic Punishment, and Other Biological Components of Fiction*. Cambridge, MA: Harvard University Press, 2007.

Fludernik, Monika. *The Fictions of Language and the Languages of Fictions*. New York: Routledge 1993.

————. "Linguistic Signals and Interpretive Strategies: Linguistic Models in Performance, with Special Reference to Free Indirect Discourse." *Language and Literature* 5.2 (1996): 93–113.

Follett, Wilson. "Henry James's Portrait of Henry James." *New York Times Book Review*, 23 August 1936.

Ford, George H., and Lauriat Lane Jr., eds. *The Dickens Critics*. Ithaca: Cornell University Press, 1961.

Furbank, P. N. "The Story in *The Sacred Fount*." *Essays in Criticism* 56.4 (2006): 370–84.

Gallagher, Catherine. *The Body Economic: Life, Death, and Sensation in Political Economy and the Victorian Novel*. Princeton: Princeton University Press, 2006.

————. "George Eliot: Immanent Victorian." *Representations* 90 (2005): 61–74.

————. *The Industrial Reformation of English Fiction, 1832–1867*. Chicago: University of Chicago Press, 1985.

————. *Nobody's Story: The Vanishing Acts of Women Writers in the Marketplace, 1670–1920*. Berkeley: University of California Press, 1994.

Galperin, William. "'Describing What Never Happened': Jane Austen and the History of Missed Opportunities." *ELH* 73.2 (2006): 355–82.

————. *The Historical Austen*. Philadelphia: University of Pennsylvania Press, 2003.

Galvan, Jill. *The Sympathetic Medium: Feminine Channeling, the Occult, and Communication Technologies, 1859–1919*. Ithaca: Cornell University Press, 2010.

Garcha, Amanpal. *From Sketch to Novel: The Development of Victorian Fiction.* Cambridge, UK: Cambridge University Press, 2009.

Gates, Henry Louis. *The Signifying Monkey: A Theory of African-American Literary Criticism.* New York: Oxford University Press, 1989.

Gelley, Alexander. "Idle Talk: Scarcity and Excess in Literary Language." In *Talk, Talk, Talk: The Cultural Life of Everyday Conversation,* edited by S. I. Salamensky, 49–61. New York: Routledge, 2001.

Gilmour, Robin. "Memory in *David Copperfield.*" *The Dickensian* 71 (1975): 30–42.

Ginsburg, Marcus Peled. "Truth and Persuasion: The Language of Realism and of Ideology in *Oliver Twist.*" NOVEL: *A Forum on Fiction* 20.3 (1987): 220–36.

Girard, René. *Deceit, Desire, and the Novel: Self and Other in Literary Structure.* Translated by Yvonne Freccero. Baltimore: Johns Hopkins University Press, 1965.

Goring, Paul. *The Rhetoric of Sensibility in Eighteenth-Century Culture.* Cambridge, UK: Cambridge University Press, 2005.

Gottlieb, Evan. *Feeling British: Sympathy and National Identity in Scottish and English Writing, 1707–1832.* Lewisburg, PA: Bucknell University Press, 2007.

Gray, Erik. " 'Save Where . . .': The Trope of Exceptionality." *ELH* 77.3 (2010): 645–63.

Greenblatt, Steven, and Catherine Gallagher. *Practicing New Historicism.* Chicago: University of Chicago Press, 2000.

Greiner, Rae. "1909: The Introduction of the Word 'Empathy' into English." *BRANCH: Britain, Representation, and Nineteenth-Century History* (2012). http://www.branchcollective .org/?ps_articles=rae-greiner-1909-the-introduction-of-the-word-empathy-into-english.

Griswold, Charles L. *Adam Smith and the Virtues of Enlightenment.* Cambridge, UK: Cambridge University Press, 1998.

———. "Imagination: Morals, Science, and Arts." In *The Cambridge Companion to Adam Smith,* edited by Knud Haakonssen, 22–25. Cambridge, UK: Cambridge University Press, 2006. 22–56.

———. "Rhetoric and Ethics: Adam Smith on Theorizing about the Moral Sentiments." *Philosophy and Rhetoric* 24.3 (1991): 213–37.

Gross, Daniel M. *The Secret History of Emotion: From Aristotle's "Rhetoric" to Modern Brain Science.* Chicago: University of Chicago Press, 2006.

Gubar, Susan. "The Long and the Short of Holocaust Verse." *New Literary History* 35.3 (2004): 443–68.

Guerard, Albert J. *Conrad the Novelist.* Cambridge, MA: Harvard University Press, 1958.

Gunn, Daniel P. "Free Indirect Discourse and Narrative Authority in *Emma.*" *Narrative* 12.1 (2004): 35–54.

Hadley, Elaine. *Melodramatic Tactics: Theatricalized Dissent in the English Marketplace, 1800–1855.* Stanford: Stanford University Press, 1995.

Halpern, Joseph. "Changing Partners in Henry James." *Southern Humanities Review* 15.1 (1981): 53–65.

Harkin, Maureen. "Adam Smith's Missing History: Primitives, Progress, and Problems of Genre." *ELH* 72.2 (2005): 429–51.

———. "Smith's *The Theory of Moral Sentiments:* Sympathy, Women, and Emulation." *Studies in Eighteenth-Century Culture* 24 (1995): 175–90.

Harmon, Louise. "Falling Off the Vine: Legal Fictions and the Doctrine of Substituted Judgment." *Yale Law Journal* 100.1 (1990): 1–71.

Harrison, Ross. *Bentham.* London: Routledge & Kegan Paul, 1983.

Hay, Eloise Knapp. *The Political Novels of Joseph Conrad.* Chicago: University of Chicago Press, 1981.

Henricksen, Bruce. "The Construction of the Narrator in *The Nigger of the 'Narcissus.'* *PMLA* 103.5 (1988): 783–95.

Henry, Nancy. Introduction to *Impressions of Theophrastus Such,* by George Eliot, edited by Nancy Henry, vii–xxxvii. Iowa City: University of Iowa Press, 1994.

Hertz, Neil. *George Eliot's Pulse.* Stanford: Stanford University Press, 2003.

Hinton, Laura. *The Perverse Gaze of Sympathy: Sadomasochistic Sentiments from "Clarissa" to "Rescue 911."* Albany: SUNY Press, 1999.

Hogan, J. Michael. "Historiography and Ethics in Adam Smith's Lectures on Rhetoric, 1762–1763." *Rhetorica* 2.1 (1984): 75–91.

Hopkins, Robert. "Moral Luck and Judgment in Jane Austen's *Persuasion.*" *Nineteenth-Century Literature* 42.2 (1987): 143–58.

Houghton, Walter E. *The Victorian Frame of Mind, 1830–1870.* New Haven, CT: Yale University Press, 1957.

Iser, Wolfgang. *The Fictive and the Imaginary: Charting Literary Anthropology.* Baltimore: Johns Hopkins University Press, 1993.

Jaffe, Audrey. *The Affective Life of the Average Man: The Victorian Novel and the Stock-Market Graph.* Columbus: Ohio State University Press, 2010.

———. *Scenes of Sympathy: Identity and Representation in Victorian Fiction.* Ithaca: Cornell University Press, 2000.

———. *Vanishing Points: Dickens, Narrative, and the Subject of Omniscience.* Berkeley: University of California Press, 1991.

Jahn, Manfred. "Frames, Preferences, and the Reading of Third-Person Narratives: Toward a Cognitive Narratology." *Poetics Today* 18.4 (1997): 441–68.

Jahoda, Gustav. "Theodor Lipps and the Shift from 'Sympathy' to 'Empathy.'" *Journal of the History of the Behavioral Sciences* 41.2 (2005): 151–63.

Jakobson, Roman, and Morris Halle. "Two Aspects of Language and Two Types of Aphasic Disturbances." In *Fundamentals of Language,* 2nd ed., 69–96. The Hague: Mouton, 1971.

Jameson, Frederick. *The Political Unconscious: Narrative as a Socially Symbolic Act.* Ithaca: Cornell University Press, 1981.

Johnson, Barbara. *Persons and Things.* Cambridge, MA: Harvard University Press, 2008.

Jordan, John. "The Ghost in *Bleak House.*" *Dickens Quarterly* 27.1 (2010): 23–37.

Keen, Suzanne. *Empathy and the Novel.* Oxford: Oxford University Press, 2007.

———. "A Theory of Narrative Empathy." *Narrative* 14.3 (2006): 207–36.

Kettle, Arnold. *An Introduction to the English Novel.* Vol. 1. London: Hutchinson, 1977.

Kincaid, James R. "Blessings for the Worthy: Dickens's *Little Dorrit* and the Nature of Rants." *Dickens Studies Annual* 37 (2006): 17–30.

———. *Dickens and the Rhetoric of Laughter.* Oxford: Clarendon, 1971.

Klein, Marcus. "Henry James's *Sacred Fount:* The Theory, the Theorists, and the Lady." *Arizona Quarterly* 62.3 (2006): 83–104.

Korsgaard, Christine. *The Sources of Normativity.* Cambridge, UK: Cambridge University Press, 1996.

Kreilkamp, Ivan. "Petted Things: *Wuthering Heights* and the Animal." *Yale Journal of Criticism* 18.1 (2005): 87–110.

———. *Voice and the Victorian Storyteller.* Cambridge, UK: Cambridge University Press, 2005.

Krieger, Murray, ed. *The Aims of Representation: Subject/ Text/ History.* New York: Columbia University Press, 1987.

Kroll, Richard. *The Material World: Literate Culture in the Restoration and Early Eighteenth Century.* Baltimore: Johns Hopkins University Press, 1991.

Kucich, John. *Excess and Restraint in the Novels of Charles Dickens.* Athens: University of Georgia Press, 1981.

———. *Repression in Victorian Fiction: Charlotte Brontë, George Eliot, and Charles Dickens.* Berkeley: University of California Press, 1987.

Lane, Christopher. *The Burdens of Intimacy: Psychoanalysis and Victorian Masculinity.* Chicago: University of Chicago Press, 1999.

———. *Hatred and Civility: The Antisocial Life in Victorian England.* New York: Columbia University Press, 2004.

Lanser, Susan Sniader. *Fictions of Authority: Woman Writers and Narrative Voice.* Ithaca: Cornell University Press, 1992.

Lanzoni, Susan. "Sympathy in *Mind* (1876–1900)." *Journal of the History of Ideas* 70.2 (2009): 265–87.

Law, Jules. *The Social Life of Fluids: Blood, Milk, and Water in the Victorian Novel.* Ithaca: Cornell University Press, 2010.

Leavis, F. R. *The Great Tradition.* London: Chatto & Windus, 1960.

Leavis, F. R., and Q. D. Leavis. *Dickens the Novelist.* 2nd ed. London: Chatto & Windus, 1970.

Levin, Harry. "A Symposium on Realism." *Comparative Literature* 3 (1951).

Levine, Caroline. *The Serious Pleasures of Suspense: Victorian Realism and Narrative Doubt.* Charlottesville: University of Virginia Press, 2003.

Levine, George. "Literary Realism Reconsidered: 'The World in Its Length and Breadth.'" In *Adventures in Realism,* edited by Matthew Beaumont, 13–32. Malden, MA: Blackwell, 2007.

———. "Realism; or, In Praise of Lying: Some Nineteenth-Century Novels." *College English* 31.4 (1970): 355–65.

———. *The Realistic Imagination: English Fiction from "Frankenstein" to "Lady Chatterley."* Chicago: University of Chicago Press, 1981.

Litvak, Joseph. *Caught in the Act: Theatricality in the Nineteenth-Century English Novel.* Berkeley: University of California Press, 1992.

Lodge, David. *The Modes of Modern Writing: Metaphor, Metonymy, and the Typology of Modern Literature.* Chicago: University of Chicago Press, 1977.

Lougy, Robert. *Inaugural Wounds: The Shaping of Desire in Five Nineteenth-Century English Narratives.* Athens: Ohio University Press, 2004.

Lowe, Brigid. *Victorian Fiction and the Insights of Sympathy: An Alternative to the Hermeneutics of Suspicion.* London: Anthem Press, 2007.

Lukács, Georg. *Essays on Realism.* Translated by David Fernbach. London: Lawrence & Wishart, 1980.

———. "Realism in the Balance." Translated by Rodney Livingstone. In *The Norton Anthology of Theory and Criticism,* edited by Vincent B. Leitch, 1033–58. New York: Norton, 2001.

———. *Studies in European Realism.* Translated by Edith Bone. New York: Grosset & Dunlap, 1964.

Lynch, Deidre Shauna. "Austen Extended / Austen for Everyday Use." In *Imagining Selves: Essays in Honor of Patricia Meyer Spacks,* edited by Elise Lauterbach and Rivka Swenson, 235–65. Newark: University of Delaware Press, 2009.

———. *The Economy of Character: Novels, Market Culture, and the Business of Inner Meaning.* Chicago: University of Chicago Press, 1998.

Mack, Ruth. *Literary Historicity: Literature and Historical Experience in Eighteenth-Century Britain.* Stanford: Stanford University Press, 2009.

Macleod, Alistair M. "Invisible Hand Arguments: Milton Friedman and Adam Smith." *Journal of Scottish Philosophy* 5.2 (2007): 103–17.

Macpherson, Sandra. *Harm's Way: Tragic Responsibility and the Novel Form.* Baltimore: Johns Hopkins University Press, 2010.

Mallgrave, Harry Francis, and Eleftherios Ikonomou. Introduction to *Empathy, Form, and Space: Problems in German Aesthetics, 1873–1893.* Santa Monica, CA: Getty Publications, 1994.

Marcus, Steven. *Dickens, from "Pickwick" to "Dombey."* New York: Basic Books, 1965.

Margolis, Stacy. "Homo-Formalism: Analogy in 'The Sacred Fount.'" NOVEL: *A Forum on Fiction* 34.3 (2001): 391–410.

Markovitz, Stephanie. "Jane Austen and the Happy Fall." *Studies in English Literature* 47.4 (2007): 779–97.

Marshall, David. *The Figure of Theater: Shaftesbury, Defoe, Adam Smith, and George Eliot.* New York: Columbia University Press, 1986.

———. *The Frame of Art: Fictions of Aesthetic Experience, 1750–1815.* Baltimore: Johns Hopkins University Press, 2005.

———. *The Surprising Effects of Sympathy: Marivaux, Diderot, Rousseau, and Mary Shelley.* Chicago: University of Chicago Press, 1988.

McHale, Brian. *Constructing Postmodernism.* New York: Routledge, 1992.

———. "Dual Voice Hypothesis." In *The Routledge Encyclopedia of Narrative Theory,* edited by D. Herman, M. Jahn, and M. Ryan, 188–89. London: Routledge, 2005.

———. "Free Indirect Discourse: A Survey of Recent Accounts." In *Narrative Theory: Critical Concepts in Literary and Cultural Studies,* edited by Mieke Bal, 249–87. New York: Routledge, 2004.

McKenna, Stephen J. *Adam Smith: The Rhetoric of Propriety.* Albany: SUNY Press, 2005.

McKeon, Michael. *The Secret History of Domesticity: Public, Private, and the Division of Knowledge.* Baltimore: Johns Hopkins University Press, 2005.

McLaughlin, Kevin. "The Financial Imp: Ethics and Finance in Nineteenth-Century Fiction." NOVEL: *A Forum on Fiction* 29.2 (1996): 165–83.

Menke, Richard. *Telegraphic Realism: Victorian Fiction and Other Information Systems.* Ithaca: Cornell University Press, 2008.

Michie, Helena. "Victorian(ist) 'Whiles' and the Tenses of Historicism." *Narrative* 17.3 (2009): 274–90.

Miller, Andrew H. *The Burdens of Perfection: On Ethics and Reading in Nineteenth-Century British Literature.* Ithaca: Cornell University Press, 2009.

———. "Lives Unled in Realist Fiction," *Representations* 98.1 (2007): 118–34.

Miller, D. A. *Jane Austen, or, The Secret of Style.* Princeton: Princeton University Press, 2004.

Miller, J. Hillis. "The Fiction of Realism: *Sketches by Boz, Oliver Twist,* and Cruikshank's Illustrations." In *Victorian Subjects,* 119–77. New York: Harvester/Wheatsheaf, 1990.

———. *Poets of Reality: Six Twentieth-Century Writers.* Cambridge, MA: Belknap Press of the Harvard University Press, 1965.

———. *Reading Narrative.* Norman: University of Oklahoma Press, 1998.

Mitchell, Robert. *Sympathy and the State in the Romantic Era: Systems, State Finance, and the Shadows of Futurity.* New York: Routledge, 2007.

Moon, Heath. "Saving James from Modernism: How to Read *The Sacred Fount.*" *MLQ* 49.2 (1998): 120–41.

Morgan, Susan. *In the Meantime: Character and Perception in Jane Austen's Fiction.* Chicago: University of Chicago Press, 1988.

Morris, Pam. *Realism: The New Critical Idiom.* New York: Routledge, 2003.

Mudrick, Marvin. "The Artist's Conscience and *The Nigger of the 'Narcissus.'* In *Twentieth Century Interpretations of "The Nigger of the 'Narcissus,'"* edited by John A. Palmer, 69–77. Englewood Cliffs: Prentice-Hall, 1969.

Nazar, Hina. "The Imagination Goes Visiting: Jane Austen, Judgment, and the Social." *Nineteenth-Century Literature* 59.2 (2004): 145–78.

Nelles, William. "Omniscience for Atheists: Or, Jane Austen's Infallible Narrator." *Narrative* 14.2 (2006): 118–31.

Nieland, Justus. *Feeling Modern: The Eccentricities of Public Life.* Urbana: University of Illinois Press, 2008.

Noble, Marianne. *The Masochistic Pleasures of Sentimental Literature.* Princeton: Princeton University Press, 2000.

Nord, Deborah Epstein. "The Making of Dickens Criticism." In *Contemporary Dickens,* edited by Eileen Gillooly and Deirdre David, 264–87. Columbus: Ohio State University Press, 2009.

Nunokawa, Jeff. *The Afterlife of Property: Domestic Security and the Victorian Novel.* Princeton: Princeton University Press, 1994.

Nussbaum, Martha. *Upheavals of Thought: The Intelligence of Emotions.* Cambridge, UK: Cambridge University Press, 2003.

Ogden, C. K. Introduction to *Bentham's Theory of Fictions.* London: Routledge & Kegan Paul, 1932.

———. *The Theory of Legislation.* London: Paul, Trench, Trubner, 1931.

Page, Norman. *Speech in the English Novel.* London: Macmillan, 1998.

Palmer, Alan. *Fictional Minds.* Lincoln: University of Nebraska Press, 2004.

Panichas, George A. *Joseph Conrad: His Moral Vision.* Macon, GA: Mercer University Press, 2005.

Parrinder, Patrick. "The Look of Sympathy: Communication and Moral Purpose in the Realistic Novel." NOVEL: *A Forum on Fiction* 5.2 (1972): 135–47.

Patten, Robert. *George Cruikshank's Life, Times, and Art.* 2 vols. New Brunswick: Rutgers University Press, 1996.

Peck, Harry Thurston. "A Budget of Books." *The Bookman* 13. New York: Dodd, Mead, 1901. 441–48.

Phelan, James. *Experiencing Fiction: Judgments, Progressions, and the Rhetorical Theory of Narrative.* Columbus: Ohio State University Press, 2007.

———. *Living to Tell about It: A Rhetoric and Ethics of Character Narration.* Ithaca: Cornell University Press, 2005.

———. *Narrative as Rhetoric: Techniques, Audiences, Ethics, Ideology.* Columbus: Ohio State University Press, 1996.

Phillips, Mark Salber. "Adam Smith, Belletrist." In *The Cambridge Companion to Adam Smith,* edited by Knud Haakonssen, 57–78. Cambridge, UK: Cambridge University Press, 2006.

———. "Distance and Historical Representation." *History Workshop Journal* 57 (2004): 123–41.

———. *Sentiment and Society: Genres of Historical Writing in Britain, 1740–1820.* Princeton: Princeton University Press, 2000.

Picker, John. *Victorian Soundscapes.* Oxford: Oxford University Press, 2003.

Pinch, Adela. *Strange Fits of Passion: Epistemologies of Emotion, Hume to Austen.* Stanford: Stanford University Press, 1996.

———. *Thinking about Other People in Nineteenth-Century British Writing.* Cambridge, UK: Cambridge University Press, 2010.

Polloczek, Dieter Pail. *Literature and Legal Discourse: Equity and Ethics from Sterne to Conrad.* Cambridge, UK: Cambridge University Press, 1999.

Poovey, Mary. "Mediums, Media, Mediation: Response." *Victorian Studies* 48.2 (2006): 249–55.

Psomiades, Kathy. "How to Make People Like You: Victorian Evolutionary Narratives of Sympathy and Nation." Unpublished paper cited in Ivan Kreilkamp, "Petted Things: *Wuthering Heights* and the Animal." *Yale Journal of Criticism* 18.1 (2005): 87–110.

Puckett, Kent. *Bad Form: Social Mistakes and the Nineteenth-Century Novel.* Oxford: Oxford University Press, 2008.

Rai, Amit S. *Rule of Sympathy: Sentiment, Race, and Power, 1750–1850.* Basingstoke, UK: Palgrave, 2002.

Remow, Gabriela. "General Rules in the Moral Theories of Smith and Hume." *Journal of Scottish Philosophy* 5.2 (2007): 119–34.

Richards, Robert J. *Darwin and the Emergence of Evolutionary Theories of Mind and Behavior.* Chicago: University of Chicago Press, 1987.

Richardson, Alan. *The Neural Sublime: Cognitive Theories and Romantic Texts.* Baltimore: Johns Hopkins University Press, 2010.

Rick, Jon. "Hume's and Smith's Partial Sympathies and Impartial Stances." *Journal of Scottish Philosophy* 5.2 (2007): 135–58.

"Robin George Collingwood." *Stanford Encyclopedia of Philosophy.* http://plato.stanford.edu/entries/collingwood/.

Rosen, David, and Aaron Santesso. "The Panopticon Reviewed: Sentimentalism and Eighteenth-Century Interiority." *ELH* 77.4 (2010): 1041–59.

Rowe, John Carlos. *The Theoretical Dimensions of Henry James.* Madison: University of Wisconsin Press, 1984.

Royle, Nicholas. "The 'Telepathy Effect': Notes toward a Reconsideration of Narrative Fiction." In *Acts of Narrative,* edited by Carol Jacobs and Henry Sussman, 93–109. Stanford: Stanford University Press, 2003.

Sadrin, Anny. *Parentage and Inheritance in the Novels of Charles Dickens.* Cambridge, UK: Cambridge University Press, 1994.

Schneewind, J. B. *The Invention of Autonomy: A History of Modern Moral Philosophy.* Cambridge, UK: Cambridge University Press, 1998.

Schofield, Philip. *Utility and Democracy: The Political Thought of Jeremy Bentham.* Oxford: Oxford University Press, 2006.

Schor, Hilary. *Dickens and the Daughter of the House.* Cambridge, UK: Cambridge University Press, 1999.

Sedgwick, Eve Kosofsky. *Touching Feeling: Affect, Pedagogy, Performativity.* Durham: Duke University Press, 2003.

Shaw, Harry E. *Narrating Reality: Austen, Scott, Eliot.* Ithaca: Cornell University Press, 1999.

Sher, Richard. "Early Editions of Adam Smith's Books in Britain and Ireland, 1759–1804." In *A Critical Bibliography of Adam Smith,* edited by Keith Tribe, 13–26. London: Pickering & Chatto, 2002.

Sherry, Norman, ed. *Conrad: The Critical Heritage.* London: Routledge & Kegan Paul, 1973.

Slater, Michael. *An Intelligent Person's Guide to Dickens.* London: Gerald Duckworth, 1999.

Small, Helen. Introduction to *The Lifted Veil* and *Brother Jacob,* by George Eliot, ix–xxxviii. Oxford: Oxford University Press, 2009.

Smith, David R. *Conrad's Manifesto: Preface to a Career.* Philadelphia: Philip H. & A. S. W. Rosenbach Foundation, 1966.

Solomon, Robert C. Introduction to *Thinking about Feeling: Contemporary Philosophers on Emotions,* edited by Robert C. Solomon, 3–8. Oxford: Oxford University Press, 2004.

Spector, Stephen J. "Monsters of Metonymy: *Hard Times* and Knowing the Working Class." *ELH* 51.2 (1984): 365–84.

Spring, David. "Interpreters of Jane Austen's Social World: Literary Critics and Historians." In *Jane Austen: New Perspectives,* edited by Janet Todd, 53–72. Women and Literature 3. New York: Holmes & Meier, 1983.

Stark, Ryan J. "From Mysticism to Skepticism: Stylistic Reform in Seventeenth-Century British Philosophy and Rhetoric." *Philosophy and Rhetoric* 34. 4 (2001): 322–34.

Steig, Michael. *Dickens and Phiz.* Bloomington: Indiana University Press, 1978.

Stein, William Bysshe. " 'The Sacred Fount': The Poetics of Nothing." *Criticism* 14 (1972): 373–89.

Sternberg, Meir. "Omniscience in Narrative Construction: Old Challenges and New." *Poetics Today* 28.4 (2007): 683–794.

Stewart, Garrett. "Dickens and Language." In *The Cambridge Companion to Charles Dickens,* edited by John O. Jordan, 136–51. Cambridge, UK: Cambridge University Press, 2001.

———. *Dickens and the Trials of Imagination.* Cambridge, MA: Harvard University Press, 1974.

———. "Ethical Tempo of Narrative Syntax: Sylleptic Recognitions in *Our Mutual Friend.*" *Partial Answers: Journal of Literature and the History of Ideas* 8.1 (2010): 119–45.

———. *Reading Voices: Literature and the Phonotext.* Berkeley: University of California Press, 1990.

Stoehr, Taylor. "Realism and Verisimilitude." *Texas Studies in Language and Literature* 11.3 (1969): 1269–88.

Stolzenberg, Nomi Maya. "Bentham's Theory of Fictions—a 'Curious Double Language.'" *Cardozo Studies in Law and Literature* 11.2 (1999): 223–61.

Stone, Marjorie. "Dickens, Bentham, and the Fictions of the Law: A Victorian Controversy and Its Consequences." *Victorian Studies* 29.1 (1985): 125–54.

Strang, Richard. "The Literary Criticism of George Eliot." *PMLA* 72.5 (1957): 952–61.

Sutherland, Kathryn. "Fictional Economies: Adam Smith, Sir Walter Scott, and the Nineteenth-Century Novel." *ELH* 54.1 (1987): 97–127.

Swann, Charles. "Déjà Vu; Déjà Lu: 'The Lifted Veil' as an Experiment in Art." *Literature and History* 5.1 (1979): 40–57.

Symons, Arthur. Review. *Saturday Review,* 29 Jan. 1898. Reprinted in Sherry, *Conrad: The Critical Heritage,* 97–98.

Tanner, Tony. "In Between: *Persuasion.*" In *Persuasion,* by Jane Austen, Norton Critical Edition, edited by Patricia Meyer Spacks, 231–64. New York: Norton, 1995.

———. *Jane Austen.* Cambridge, MA: Harvard University Press, 1986.

Tave, Stuart. *Some Words of Jane Austen.* Chicago: University of Chicago Press, 1973.

Terada, Rei. *Feeling in Theory: Emotion after the "Death of the Subject."* Cambridge, MA: Harvard University Press, 2003.

Thrailkill, Jane. *Affecting Fictions: Mind, Body, and Emotion in American Literary Realism.* Cambridge, MA: Harvard University Press, 2007.

Toker, Leona. *Towards the Ethics of Form in Fiction: Narratives of Cultural Remission.* Columbus: Ohio State University Press, 2010.

Tore, Rem. *Dickens, Melodrama, and the Parodic Imagination.* New York: AMS Press, 2002.

Tracy, Robert. "W. C. Macready in *The Life and Adventures of Nicholas Nickleby.*" *Dickens Quarterly* 24.3 (2007): 159–66.

Tribe, Keith. "Adam Smith in English: From Playfair to Cannan." In *A Critical Bibliography of Adam Smith,* edited by Keith Tribe, 27–49. London: Pickering & Chatto, 2002.

———. "Das Adam Smith Problem and the Origins of Modern Scholarship." *History of European Ideas* 34.4 (2008): 514–25.

Trilling, Lionel. "*Little Dorrit.*" In Ford and Lane, *Dickens Critics,* 279–93.

Tuite, Clara. *Romantic Austen: Sexual Politics and the Literary Canon.* Cambridge, UK: Cambridge University Press, 2002.

Turner, Mark. *Reading Minds: The Study of English in the Age of Cognitive Science.* Princeton: Princeton University Press, 1993.

Tweyman, Stanley. "Hume on Sympathy and the Indirect Passions." *Studies on Voltaire and the Eighteenth Century* 303 (1992): 377–81.

Vande Kieft, Ruth M. "Patterns of Communication in *Great Expectations.*" *Nineteenth-Century Fiction* 15.4 (1961): 325–34.

Van Ghent, Dorothy. "The Dickens World: A View from Todger's Window." *Sewanee Review* 58 (1950): 419–48.

Vermeule, Blakey. *Why Do We Care about Literary Characters?* Baltimore: Johns Hopkins University Press, 2010.

Vrettos, Athena. "Defining Habits: Dickens and the Psychology of Repetition." *Victorian Studies* 42.3 (2000): 399–426.

Walder, Dennis, ed. *The Realist Novel.* London: Routledge, 1995.

Warner, Michael. *Publics and Counterpublics.* New York: Zone Books, 2002.

Watt, Ian. *Conrad in the Nineteenth Century.* Berkeley: University of California Press, 1979.

———. *Essays on Conrad.* Cambridge: Cambridge University Press, 2000.

———. *Myths of Modern Individualism.* Cambridge, UK: Cambridge University Press, 1996.

———. *The Rise of the Novel: Studies in Defoe, Richardson, and Fielding.* Berkeley: University of California Press, 1959.

Watts, Cedric. Introduction to *The Nigger of the 'Narcissus,'* by Joseph Conrad, edited by Cedric Watts, xi–xxx. New York: Penguin, 1988.

Watts, Donald C. *Elsevier's Dictionary of Plant Lore.* London: Elsevier, 2007.

Welsh, Alexander. *The City of Dickens.* Oxford: Clarendon, 1971.

White, Hayden. *Figural Realism: Studies in the Mimesis Effect.* Baltimore: Johns Hopkins University Press, 2000.

Williams, Carolyn. "Response: Vehicular Traffic." *Textual Practice* 22.1 (2008): 47–54.

Williams, Ioan, ed. *Novel and Romance, 1700–1800: A Documentary Record.* London: Routledge & Kegan Paul, 1970.

———. *The Realist Novel in England: A Study in Development.* Pittsburgh: University of Pittsburgh Press, 1975.

Williams, Raymond. *The Country and the City.* Oxford: Oxford University Press, 1973.

———. "The English Novel." In Walder, *Realist Novel,* 241–48.

———. *The English Novel from Dickens to Lawrence.* Oxford: Oxford University Press, 1970.

Wilson, Edmund. *The Triple Thinkers: Twelve Essays on Literary Subjects.* London: John Lehmann, 1952.

Winter, Sarah. "Darwin's Saussure: Biosemiotics and Race in *Expression.*" *Representations* 107 (2009): 128–61.

Wollaeger, Mark A. *Joseph Conrad and the Fictions of Skepticism.* Stanford: Stanford University Press, 1990.

Woloch, Alex. *The One vs. the Many: Minor Characters and the Space of the Protagonist in the Novel.* Princeton: Princeton University Press, 2003.

Woodfield, Malcolm. "The Endless Memorial: Dickens and Memory/Writing/History." *Dickens Studies Annual* 20 (1991): 75–102.

Yeazell, Ruth Bernard. "Do It or Dorrit." *NOVEL: A Forum on Fiction* 25.1 (1991): 33–49.

Yntema, Hessel E. Review of *Bentham's Theory of Fictions,* by C. K. Ogden. *Columbia Law Review* 33.6 (1933): 1082–84.

Zangwill, I. Unsigned review. *Academy,* 1 Jan. 1898. Reprinted in Sherry, *Conrad: The Critical Heritage,* 94–96.

Zietlow, Paul N. "Luck and Fortuitous Circumstance in *Persuasion:* Two Interpretations." *ELH* 32 (1965): 179–95.

Zunshine, Lisa. *Why We Read Fiction: Theory of Mind and the Novel.* Columbus: Ohio State University Press, 2006.

Index